Advance Praise for
Fallout: Recovering from Abuse in Tibetan Buddhism.

'*Fallout* is a very personal, emotionally literate, and thoroughly researched and documented account of Tahlia Newland's journey in regards to leaving a religious group. It's an excellent account of the immensely heart-rending difficulty of honouring and following your spiritual longing while at the same time sensing that there is something 'not quite right' with the reality of the spiritual teacher. Newland includes the heart-breaking, mind-tangling and spirit-breaking dilemmas involved in her journey as she explores the issue of trying to reconcile and discern the reality of Rigpa with the wisdom she gained from being part of Rigpa.

'Down to earth yet passionately heartfelt at the same time, what stands out in Newland's book is her profound common sense. It's a very real account that includes following the most powerful human longing to join with a religious teacher who speaks to your longing, the intense sense of betrayal when the teacher emerges as abusive, and subsequently the healing journey required to move on with one's life.

'*Fallout* is about being with a Tibetan Buddhist teacher, but the journey she underwent is applicable far beyond Buddhist groups. It's a sensible guide to any person who is thinking to become involved, is currently involved in, or who is leaving or has left a religious group or spiritual teacher.

'The material on healing trauma is an up-to-date, well considered and highly readable summary of the therapeutic journey for people healing from involvement in a religious group. Newland's book is ultimately full of hope.' **Geoffrey Beatson, psychotherapist.**

'Written with passion and clarity, this shocking exposé is a must-read for anyone who has ever been involved with Rigpa and a compelling account of what can go wrong in religious groups for everyone else. Though she pulls no punches, Newland writes with compassion for the victims and makes an attempt at understanding the flawed human beings behind the guru masks. Tibetan Buddhism has always seemed like the 'good guy' of religions; to discover corruption of the message at the heart of some groups is painful, even for one who has only ever been an outsider.' **Barbara Scott Emmett, author.**

'In recent years the long-standing problem of physical, sexual and psychological abuse of students by their spiritual teachers has been revealed and highlighted. Tahlia Newland takes the classic case of Sogyal Lakar and the Rigpa organisation to explore and try to understand the dynamics behind this painful issue. Her report lays bare the harm and anguish left behind in the wake of such appalling behaviour and the subsequent efforts, by those who seek to maintain their power and control, to condone such conduct and meanwhile denigrate the victims. In this feudal outlook, both physical violence and sexual predatory behaviour towards dependents are viewed as acceptable. In certain cases this power-based attitude has sought to be imported into Western Dharma circles. This is a complete distortion of the impeccable Vajrayana path and creates much confusion, disenchantment and pain. So we are grateful to Ms Newland for bravely looking into this controversial issue with such compassion and insight.' **Jetsumna Tenzin Palmo.**

'I am personally moved by and deeply grateful to the author for this fine work. It reveals the excruciating pain, resistance and fear of those within the organisation as they grapple with a 180 degree shift in perspective of the teacher they loved and admired—the insightful, brilliant and yet deeply flawed author of *The Tibetan Book of Living and Dying*—and shows how people can come together in the age of the internet to find truth and express love and caring for one another. The author captures this painful moment in Buddhism's history where cruelty—that most harmful of human flaws and the polar opposite of loving-kindness—has crept into and corrupted the Buddhadharma. She brings both compassion for survivors and deeply penetrating wisdom, dispelling the myth of crazy wisdom and enlightenment-by-abuse with a clear-headed vision.

The End does not justify The Means, and we cannot yearn for a world free from cruelty if we do not strive to address it within our organisations and our own personal conduct. It is not the role of one person to 'help' another with their karma by harming them: this is a wrong view that Sogyal and the organisation he created fell into. Buddhism as a whole would do well to acknowledge that to justify wrong-doing or an unwillingness to help another or do the right thing when it's uncomfortable or difficult, using arguments based on the 'people get what they deserve' view of karma, is to confuse the heart of the Buddha's teachings.' **Dr. Jack Wicks**

'*Fallout* has been to me an unexpected gift of clarity and compassion. As a survivor of spiritual abuse in Tibetan Buddhism myself, I want to deeply thank Tahlia Newland for making this work available to everyone. It's based on the Rigpa experience but it applies to all Tibetan Buddhism. To me it's more than a book, it's a manual for recovering from this kind of trauma. ... If you've been in a cult, or have been a victim of spiritual abuse and institutional betrayal, reading *Fallout* could literally be even better than going to a psychologist, because it will go straight to the point, it will take you step by step through a process of recognizing what you've been through, in order to deal with it. ... Even though I've built a new life for myself, this book allowed me to look back without the feeling of being alone, blamed or misunderstood. Finally all this makes sense and I can put a name on all the past experiences and situations! I can now freely say without any regret, "This indeed happened, and it was not my fault, I was right to speak up, and it's ok not to forgive."' **Dr J Perez**

FALLOUT

RECOVERING FROM
ABUSE
IN TIBETAN
BUDDHISM

Tahlia Newland

AIA PUBLISHING

Fallout: Recovering from Abuse in Tibetan Buddhism
Copyright © 2019 Tahlia Newland
Published by Escarpment Publishing, an imprint of AIA Publishing,
Australia

Ebook ISBN: 978-0-6485130-3-2
Paperback: ISBN: 978-0-6485130-4-9

Cover design by Velvet Wings Media

DEDICATION

I dedicate this book to the survivors of abuse by Tibetan Buddhist gurus, in particular to those who broke the seal of silence to reveal the truth to others. May your suffering not have been in vain; may it be a cause for the removal of corruption from all Buddhadharma, and may you fully heal from your trauma.

CONTENTS

INTRODUCTION

In July 2017 eight formerly close students of Tibetan Buddhist teacher Sogyal Rinpoche sent a letter to him and his students detailing the emotional, physical and sexual abuse they'd experienced at his hands, and the decades-long cover up by management of Rigpa—the organisation that manages his network of study and practice centres. For the majority of students, reading the attestations of abuse came as a great shock and had a huge impact on their lives. This book, written twenty months after the release of the letter, is the story of the process I and a group of dharma friends went through as we came to terms with the repercussions of the revelations.

Sogyal Rinpoche was my spiritual teacher for twenty years, from 1997 to 2017, during which I had an idealised and inaccurate view of the culture of Tibetan Buddhism. I set up and ran the Rigpa Australia distance education centre (known as the Bush Telegraph), working long hours without pay, which I was happy to do, dedicated, as were all who worked for Rigpa, to the cause of spreading Buddhadharma in the Western world. I trained as an instructor in 2000 and remained an instructor until I left.

I became Sogyal's student after my first retreat when he gave an introduction to the nature of mind and then said, 'If you got it, you're now my student. We have samaya. You're

1

stuck with me.' I didn't know what samaya was back then, but I accepted that he was my teacher because I'd glimpsed what I'd assumed was the nature of my mind. I had no idea at the time that if I wished to get the highest teachings, I would be required to profess unquestioning devotion to Sogyal. After several years, I was so immersed in the pervading Rigpa culture that I fostered the required devotion without question.

I only saw Sogyal in the flesh once a year at retreats, and I had no idea until June 2017 how he behaved in private. As an ordinary student, I only saw what everyone saw of him at retreats, and I interacted personally with Sogyal Rinpoche on only a few occasions. At those times I found him kind and attentive, and our interactions were either beneficial or puzzling, but never harmful. I trusted that he would never hurt anyone.

This book is a memoir telling the story of my awakening, not into any vision of enlightenment, but into a more educated and accurate view of the religion into which I'd enthusiastically thrown myself. In my role as facilitator for the *What Now?* Facebook group for abuse survivors and their supporters, I communicated deeply with many students from all levels of the Rigpa organisation, and I include many of their voices here along with my own.

I've written this book from the perspective of a bystander because that's how I and many of my friends experienced these events. Abuse in a spiritual context does not just affect those directly abused; it affects every single member of a community, and if this is nothing more than the story of how one of those ordinary members found closure, then so be it. I share my story in the hope that it will help others like me to find closure for themselves.

Few are aware of the psychological effects of spiritual abuse in a Tibetan Buddhist context, especially on the general sangha, or the complexity of the issues at play, and I hope this book will contribute to a greater understanding of both.

The book begins with my personal experience when I first heard testimonies of Sogyal's abuse, and then it becomes a description of a group healing, investigation, and learning process. It's divided into three sections: Part One, Processing the Revelations of Abuse; Part Two, An Examination of Abuse-Enabling Beliefs; and Part Three, Lessons for the Future.

DISCLAIMER, SOURCES AND CONVENTIONS

My sources are my own experiences plus direct, unembellished testimonies given to me by victims or witnesses via phone calls, emails, messages or social media comments. However, memories are not perfect, and the testimonies are unproven in a court of law, and so, legally speaking, should be considered allegations rather than statements of fact. This book is a record of the honest opinions of myself and my sources, however, the opinions expressed in the social media comments I've included are the personal opinions of the commenter and do not necessarily reflect my own.

I recognise that the experiences, memories, perceptions, and interpretations others have of the events described in this book are different to my own, and that many Rigpa members and Tibetan Buddhist teachers are decent, good-hearted people who genuinely believe they are doing the right thing. This book is not intended to hurt anyone, only to assist in closure for survivors and to provide education on an area of public and moral interest—the form and results of abuse in a Tibetan Buddhist context. I regret any unintentional harm resulting from its publishing and marketing.

I write here about true events and real people. However, some names have been changed, and I avoid using names at all where possible because those involved didn't want the kind of exposure and possible retribution that using their names might bring. Direct comments are mostly unattributed for the same reason, but they are all genuine comments from real people.

Though written messages with 'Jane' are, apart from light editing to retain anonymity, actual communications I received, Jane is a hybrid of several people with whom I conversed. For the sake of pacing, thematic flow, and clarity of ideas, my phone conversation with her, and with others, are a combination of conversations that may have taken place days or weeks apart. These and other conversations as written are truthful to the content and meaning of the conversations but are not the exact words.

I've tried to contact everyone I've quoted, but failed in a couple of instances, so if you find something here that you recognise as your words, feel they can be attributed to you and don't want them included, please contact me and I will remove them. I have not included anything posted in Facebook groups without the express permission of the author.

Please also note that though this book is written using Australian (UK) punctuation and spelling conventions, for the sake of authenticity, written quotes retain their original spelling and punctuation, and these are quite often US conventions. Social media and other personal comments are italicised. Substantial quotes along with those from books, articles, papers and emails are indented. References for the books and articles mentioned are listed alphabetically at the end of the book.

ACKNOWLEDGEMENTS

Thanks to the eight students who wrote the July 2017 letter to Sogyal Lakar. I am extremely grateful for your courage in exposing the truth, your support of my writing, and your ongoing integrity. Your courage in speaking out freed me from a fog of lies, projections, and ignorance, and gave me the kind of stimulus I needed to reclaim responsibility for my own spiritual path.

Thanks also to all those who participated in the *What Now?* Facebook group for their ongoing encouragement, kindness, openness, and willingness to deeply examine themselves and the issues raised by abuse in Buddhism. The deep love and respect we have developed for each other through our shared journey are quite remarkable for an online group and is a tribute to the integrity, compassion and wisdom of all of you who remain active in the group to this day. Without you, this book would never have been written. Together we did the research and together we learned all that I report here. Though we haven't all come to the same conclusions in response to this debacle, the support the group showed for each member's personal journey never wavered. For that support, I thank you all from the bottom of my heart.

A particular thank you to those who permitted me to include their comments and those who provided links to references when I couldn't locate them.

A big thank you to those who assisted by beta reading the book and giving valuable feedback—Jack, Dot, Gwenda, Sangye, Drolma, and Joanne—and to those who encouraged me to write this book, either through verbal or written encouragement or by helping fund the project by being a patron on Patreon—an online membership platform for supporting artists, writers, and other creatives. In particular I want to thank the patrons who continued their financial support even after I told them I no longer needed it. Your faith in me encouraged me to have faith in myself. You get the lion's share of any merit created by the publication of this book.

Thank you to those who helped me understand the issues by writing great books or articles or giving clear teachings—see the list in the reference section.

And finally, thank you to those in my family who never once told me I should just 'let it go'.

PART ONE: PROCESSING THE REVELATIONS OF ABUSE

'Remembering and telling the truth about terrible events are prerequisites both for the restoration of the social order and for the healing of individual victims. ... Creating a protected space where survivors can speak their truth is an act of liberation. They remind us that bearing witness, even within the confines of that sanctuary, is an act of solidarity. They remind us also that moral neutrality in the conflict between victim and perpetrator is not an option.' Trauma and Recovery: *The Aftermath of Violence - From Domestic Abuse to Political Terror* by Judith Herman.

1
THE SHOCK OF DISCOVERY

I looked at the Facebook post and frowned. My ex-monk friend had written a post insinuating that my spiritual teacher, my lama Sogyal Rinpoche, had abused him. My friend's recent posts had made it clear that he'd had major problems with Rigpa, the Buddhist organisation of Sogyal Rinpoche's students I'd been part of for twenty years, but this latest post took it a step further. Was he really saying what I thought he was saying?

I had to know the truth.

I typed a comment on the post: *Are you saying he actually hit you?*

Another comment appeared in reply to mine, from a Facebook friend I'd never met but friended because of our shared guru. We'd started interacting recently because she'd made a lot of supportive, caring, and sensible comments on my ex-monk friend's recent posts. I'd come to trust her because she seemed like an honest and honourable person. She wrote: *He did a lot of things you'd be surprised about.*

Like what?

I waited for a moment, but no more words appeared. Clearly, she knew something more, but it appeared that she wasn't going to say it publicly.

I contacted my ex-monk friend through Messenger: *Did our lama hit you?*

The answer came back immediately: *Yes*

I blinked, shocked, then typed the vital question: *Was it only once?*

Again the reply came without a moment's delay: *No, he hit me many times.*

Many times? I shook my head, staring at those words in disbelief. Why would a spiritual teacher, a Tibetan lama who was supposed to be a model of wisdom and compassion, hit someone, not once but many times? Maybe it was a playful thing misinterpreted.

Hard? I typed.

Yes. It hurt. A lot. Left bruises.

It hurt? A lot? My frown deepened and my heart dropped. My world shifted.

My friend added three more shocking words: *Every day one or more of us was getting hit.*

My world shattered. A veil fell from my eyes. The ground fell away beneath me.

Almost everyone who worked in Rigpa with him got hit at some point, my friend added.

In one instant I was liberated from dependency on my lama, my guru. I realised that the central focus of my spiritual path was based on a lie—my lama was not who I'd thought him to be.

The traditional stories of students of great masters attaining realisation when their master slapped them with a sandal or threw stones at them flashed through my mind. I could see that if such a thing happened once, or at least rarely, it could be a powerful way to make someone pay attention, and this was the idea behind the term 'crazy wisdom' which referred to a realised master using 'unconventional' actions to awaken a student. Such actions were supposed to be only for the rare student who was so spiritually advanced that they would respond positively to such behaviour, not regularly and for every student close to the master. And the actions resulted in awakening, not injury. Injuries caused by a genuine crazy wisdom master's actions supposedly healed spontaneously and immediately, yet my ex-monk friend, Sangye, said he was left with bruises.

Our senior Rigpa instructors had regularly told us, with great pride, that Sogyal Rinpoche was a great crazy wisdom master, one who has such love and compassion for his students that he's willing to wake them up by any means necessary, even if it means that what he says or does appears a bit harsh. And I'd believed them. Now it seemed that the crazy wisdom story had been nothing more than a convenient explanation for behaviour that otherwise would be seen as abusive.

Though shocked, I didn't doubt what my friend said for a moment. I knew him to be a sensitive soul with a good heart and earnest in his endeavours to lead a spiritual life. He had no reason to lie. And speaking out publicly on Facebook about his lama—the Tibetan word for guru—wasn't something he (or any Tibetan Buddhist) would do without good reason. I recognised that it took enormous courage to expose unsavoury details of a lama. I also knew Sogyal was capable of such behaviour because it wasn't out of character. It was just a matter of degree, worse than, but entirely in accord with, what I'd seen.

I'd seen Sogyal publicly humiliating people many times, but they'd said afterwards that they'd experienced it as love and learned from it so they didn't see it as harmful, rather they'd experienced it as helpful. I'd figured that if they didn't experience it as harmful, then for them it wasn't, so why should I be bothered? Sogyal had called it 'activity training'. It was supposed to make us more efficient workers, better team players, that kind of thing, and since I'd even learned myself from some of the things he'd pointed out to people, it all seemed quite reasonable—until I learned the extent of this so-called 'kindness'.

I'd thought that, no matter how grumpy he might appear, he would never actually hurt anyone. After all, he'd taught that the basic vow when you took refuge to formally enter the Buddhist path was to do no harm, and the bodhichitta vow, taken to enter the Mahayana Buddhist path, was to always help all beings. I'd heard those words from his lips countless times. I knew off by heart what he'd called the essence of the Buddhist teachings: Do no harm; do good; and transform your mind; these are the teachings of the Buddha.

Clearly Sogyal wasn't walking his talk. Apart from being, quite simply, wrong, hitting everyone he worked closely with didn't show the compassion or wisdom in which we were all supposed to be training. Hitting always hurt, no matter how you tried to rationalise it away. And hitting was assault, even if you thought it was kindness.

A spiritual teacher shouldn't be hurting anyone, I figured. Not one single person. And it was clear from the Facebook post that my ex-monk friends Sangye's treatment at the hands of my lama had only brought him pain. The emotional pain was clear to see. My heart ached when I read the post. When I'd seen him, I tried to be appreciative of the huge amount of work he did—work that was largely responsible for the success of the organisation as a teaching service. I thought of him as a brother in a big spiritual family—a family I was later to learn was highly dysfunctional. That Sogyal had allegedly repeatedly hit and hurt this man who had done so much to further Sogyal's vision blew my respect for my guru out of the water. I realised right then that, despite the benefit I had personally received from being Sogyal's student, the crazy wisdom label was a lie. He had hurt people, and so, regardless of his place in my heart, I could no longer take him as my teacher.

It wasn't a decision I had to agonise over. It was quite clear to me then that, no matter what our relationship had been in the past, now I knew what he was really like, this was not a person I could take as my spiritual teacher.

Another message came in. This time from the woman who'd left the tantalising comment suggesting there was more to know. I clicked to open it and read:

> *I didn't want to respond on FB because I don't want to further inflame the people who are finding it challenging, but you bring up many important points that deserve a fuller reply.*

> *I don't think anyone is interested in losing the dharma because of a teacher who has lost his way. I would never deny Sogyal's deep understanding and gift of being able to transmit the dharma to the west. But there's some seriously disturbing baggage, and I've had to face it due to circumstances I could no longer avoid.*

15

Once I faced that, it dissolved my sense of having to see everything Sogyal did as a blessing. Which made some very troubling behaviour incredibly problematic ...

In my time in Rigpa I was physically abused more times than I can count, sexually harassed and assaulted, subjected to extreme humiliation and emotional abuse. I'm quite resilient so I was able to look for the lesson each time our lama groped me, exposed himself, hit me with anything at hand including hurling a cell phone he didn't like directly at my face from four feet away. His favourite 'weapon' is his back scratcher. I hate to say how many times I walked around retreat with lumps on my head and sore hands from being beaten with it, but he was resourceful, he once hurled a bowl of hot soup at me, tore a phone off the wall and broke it over my head, tore my ear to the point of not being able to stop the bleeding for hours due to grabbing me and dragging me around by it. I was told to strip, show him my pussy, give him a photo of it, give him a blow job - none of which I ever did, which is why some of the beatings happened.

Unfortunately, I couldn't always dodge the gut punches, being punched in the breasts or being groped. I often had bruised arms where he'd grab me so hard it left marks. Yes, EVERYTHING you've ever read about him is absolutely true. The emotional abuse came in the form of constantly being told I was a complete failure that I couldn't do anything right, balanced with being told I was incredibly special, I had amazing insight, I was one of the best organizers he's ever worked with. One minute physical

16

abuse, the next minute having high tea with him or out to dinner at hundreds of dollars a plate. I've since realized that this is a tried and true technique called trauma bonding, one that sex traffickers use.

I felt so physically ill at reading those words that I almost gagged.

OMG, OMG, OMG! I typed back with shaking fingers, then I put my phone down, walked onto the veranda, slumped into a chair, and stared at the bush that surrounds my house, my mind blank with shock. I'd thought hitting was bad, but this … this was … depraved.

The ache in my heart intensified, but the love at its core spread across the world to embrace both my friends, and then to everyone who had experienced anything like this, and then to all those who had never experienced it either. Why leave anyone out? Thinking this way, trained into me from two decades of Tibetan Buddhist practice, was so much a part of me that it was automatic—no thought required.

I sat and stared at nothing, aware that my world had changed irrevocably, and then the emotions came, rolling up and battering me like waves in the ocean. Anger, betrayal, disappointment, grief. I let them wash over me, but still tears fell.

'How could you?' I screamed into the rainforest. 'I trusted you!' I imagined Sogyal before me, let loose a stream of expletives, and told him exactly what damage he'd done, not just to individuals but also to the tradition of which he was a part. 'You're a fricken idiot,' I shouted. 'How could you ever think any of that was okay?'

Then I let out a big sigh. Images of all the good times flittered through my mind: the love I'd felt in his presence; the kindness with which he'd treated me; the hugs; the personal thank you; the blessing for my *Diamond Peak* fantasy series, which was an analogy of the path to enlightenment; and the practices I'd done at his direction. The times he'd rejected me followed: the gift I worked on for months that he threw away; the time he called me stupid; the questions he'd dismissed or ignored or mocked. And then all those little things I'd pushed aside rushed in: how he left us sitting for hours in the middle of the day in a tent in the searing heat of an Australian summer; how his sessions went so late that lunch was two or three hours late; how he shouted at people and threw things at them; kept changing things that needn't have been changed; demanded perfection; did his practice for hours—or made phone calls— while we sat there watching him with no idea what he was saying as he rushed through countless prayers and practices in Tibetan. I shook my head. What now?

When your spiritual path is based on your trust in a person and that person shatters your trust, what happens to your spiritual path? This question would plague me for months and take me and others on a journey of discovery that took me places I'd never expected to go.

What, I wondered, was trauma bonding? I'd have to do some research. Another part of the message popped into my mind. *'EVERYTHING you've ever read about him is absolutely true.'* I snorted at myself because I'd never read any of it. Suddenly I felt a little naive, even stupid.

When 'allegations' of abuse had surfaced on the internet a few years ago, senior Rigpa instructors gave a special

18

'Representing Rigpa' session to teach instructors how to deal with students who asked questions about the abuse allegations. I'd not heard of it before then. They told us not to look online because every search would increase the hits on the site hosting the allegations and make it come up when people searched for Sogyal's name. They disparaged those who revealed the abuse and led me to believe Sogyal was the victim of cyber-bullying.

I hadn't looked online, not only because they'd told me not to and I'd assumed it was a bullying campaign but also because I hadn't wanted my devotion tested. I'd told myself my devotion was unshakable, so nothing I read would change it. What a good little student I'd been—compliant and uncomplaining. I'd been proud of my unshakable faith in my lama. Proud! Wow. What a realisation! I hadn't noticed the pride before, but now I realised it had stopped me from even wanting to see the truth, and it was important that people did see the website listing the testimonies of abuse. The action required here wasn't to stop cyber bullies who were 'out to get' Sogyal; it was to stop the real bully—Sogyal.

Shattered trust on a spiritual level is devastating. And if it was hard for me, how much harder it must be for those directly abused. But the betrayal, I realised, extended to every one of my vajra brothers and sisters; even if they didn't know the truth, they believed in a lie.

At retreats when faced with Sogyal's grumpy and demanding behaviour, we were told that for those who were the focus of his apparent aggression, this was the enlightened action of a crazy wisdom master speeding up the student's spiritual progress. We were told not to look at it with our ordinary judgemental mind, because that mind was unreliable; it obscured the truth. The truth was supposed to be that what appeared to us as public humiliation was actually an act of great kindness. We were told to let whatever rose in our mind fall away and not get caught up in our risings, to see it as just a rising, something to let go of.

Unfortunately our innate wisdom of discernment was lumped in with the term 'judgemental mind' and we were taught not to trust it. Reacting to our gut feeling that something wasn't right in Sogyal's behaviour was seen as a mark of a lack of spiritual accomplishment, so we all tried very hard not to react. They trained us to not trust our own perception, to see something we intuitively saw as harmful as kindness. They trained us to watch abuse without complaint. Oh, how I'd been manipulated!

At that 'Representing Rigpa' session, I'd done what the senior instructors had told me to do—evaluate based on my own experience of my guru, not on what others say they'd experienced. Hearing allegations directly from two people I trusted, however, had brought the matter right into my experience. Back then, I'd asked one of the instructors, someone very close to Sogyal, if any of it was true. She'd said, 'We don't believe he has harmed anyone.'

I'd taken those words to mean that he hadn't harmed anyone. Now I noticed the key word—*believe*. What we believe happened and what really happened are not always the same thing. Someone who was part of the inner circle told me later:

Many of the instructors and "older" students saying they didn't believe people were harmed all knew and experienced the beatings themselves; they just didn't believe that the beatings were harmful on the absolute level. They think it's okay for a vajra master to kill a student "if it's for their own good", so of course blood, bruises, what's the problem? That added twist doesn't come through, that saying someone wasn't harmed is in no way saying they don't think they were ever physically, mentally, emotionally or sexually abused.'

Another friend who'd also been in the inner circle later revealed to me that this instructor had once told her about *'the severe beatings that she'd received at the hand of Sogyal.'* A different friend told me that a close friend of hers had seen the same instructor in the garden at Lerab Ling cowering behind a bush with her arms over her head in a protective fashion, crying and saying, *'Please don't hit me,'* while Sogyal yelled at her. Despite being beaten herself, this instructor *believed* Sogyal hadn't harmed her or anyone else, but a belief is not reality. Belief filters reality and makes us see what we want to see. I wanted to drop all beliefs, all filters, so I could see reality directly. After all, wasn't that the whole point of the spiritual path?

The enormity of my ignorance of the truth was yet to reveal itself.

2
A Plan for Truth Telling

I looked up into the sky, so blue and endless and spacious. I felt as if I floated there, groundless, then out of that groundlessness came a knowing so strong that it sent me back inside to collect my phone. My vajra brothers and sisters had to know this terrible truth. I strode inside, grabbed my phone, and sent a message to Jane, the woman who'd dropped the bombshell in her message:

People need to know this.

I waited. The three little dots on Messenger did their someone-is-typing dance, and then the answer appeared:

Can I call you?

Sure.

Then she rang me. I pressed the button to accept the call and found myself talking to a calm American. After a general chat to get to know each other, the conversation moved onto the abuse. It went something like this:

'This has been going on for decades,' she said, 'and it's not healthy, not for Rinpoche, not for the students around him, and certainly not for the sangha, but some students are going to try to stop it.'

Relief washed through me at the knowledge that someone was doing something about it. 'What are they doing?'

'You can't tell anyone this,' she said, 'not yet, but a group of eight students are writing a letter detailing what they've seen and experienced—things they know can be verified by someone else. They're going to send it to Sogyal, all Rigpa management teams, some Tibetan lamas, and international senior instructtors.'

'What about ordinary students like me? I'm an instructor, but I'm not on that list, and I want to read it. If they only send it to those people, then people like me will never see it. Management will suppress it.'

'Yeah, others have said the same thing. But some of the letter writers are very queasy about broadening the audience.'

'It should at least go to the Dzogchen Mandala. People who're deeply committed to Sogyal need to know the truth about who they've committed themselves to.'

'I'll pass that on, but they won't do or say anything they don't all support one-hundred percent.'

'Fair enough, but I hope they decide to send it to the students as well as management. We deserve to know.'

'They want to keep it in the sangha, so the sangha can deal with it.'

'That's good.'

'He needs help,' she continued. 'His behaviour's out of control.' Warmth came through her voice. Clearly, despite what she'd experienced at his hands, she cared for Sogyal still. I respected her for that.

The ache in my heart intensified. 'I'm sorry you had to go through that. It must have been very difficult.'

She snorted. 'I tried to work with it. For years, I tried to see it as enlightened action. I even convinced myself it was in the beginning, but eventually I realised I wasn't getting enlightened, only bruised and crushed. I was exhausted from being on call 24/7, from often, during retreat time, getting only a few hours' sleep, being rung up in the middle of the night, and being terrified that he might lash out at me. It could happen at any time, even if you'd done nothing wrong. His face would change. You could see the rage coming.'

I gulped, imagining myself in that situation.

'He's a very scary man when he's in a rage,' she added.

I nodded, forgetting she couldn't see me. 'I never worked closely with him,' I told her. 'My personal interactions with him weren't like that, but I don't doubt you for a moment, because I saw enough of him to know he's capable of those things. I saw the way he worked people relentlessly. I saw his petty demands for getting the shrine just right and his water in just the right place on his table, and I saw how he growled at people who got things just a tiny bit out of place, and how he thought it perfectly okay to give people a dressing down in front of everyone. It's only a matter of degree, isn't it?'

'Public humiliation,' Jane said. 'That's the correct word for it; it's a form of emotional abuse, and behind the scenes it was even worse. Shouting at you one moment and being all sweet and kind the next—love bombing—and the two things together are a method of control; they keep you looking to please him, always terrified he'll be displeased, and then being so happy when he's nice to you. Look up domestic abuse and you'll get the idea. That's how it was in the inner circle, just like

25

an abusive family. That's what Rigpa is, just a big abusive family, right down to the silence.'

Criticising one's lama is not acceptable in Tibetan Buddhism. It means you're a poor student who lacks pure perception. Anyone who criticised Sogyal for being two hours late would be considered not to have enough devotion. It might adversely affect you getting into the 'old-students club', the Dzogchen Mandala group that got the highest teachings, the Dzogchen teachings, the ones we all wanted.

But then, I reminded myself, it wasn't about being a good little student. I smiled to myself, remembering Ian Maxwell, the now-deceased Rigpa senior instructor who'd often said that. He'd inspired me into a religion when I'd never wanted a religion at all. He'd helped me make sense of the deities and the chanting. I heard later that he'd tried to moderate Sogyal's behaviour with no success, and after his death his insightful teachings unfortunately disappeared from the Rigpa curriculum.

'Who's writing the letter?' I asked.

'I only know one name—the friend who told me,' she replied. 'But they're all people who were close to him. Whoever they are, I admire their courage. I wouldn't want the kind of attention they'll get for doing it. I couldn't open myself up to that sort of exposure.'

I understood that. People would not be happy. Fingers would point. They would be accused of seeing things wrongly. I saw it all in a glance. Saw how everyone had been gagged by the belief that we mustn't criticise or we'd go to hell. Luckily, I didn't believe in hell, at least not in the way it was portrayed in Tibetan Buddhism. Besides, on this matter, my intelligence overrode any injunction laid on me by a religious belief. Silence was what allowed abuse to continue. And I had no doubt that what Jane had described was abuse.

'I'll send you a link to a document and some videos of His Holiness the Dalai Lama speaking in Dharamsala in 1993 at a conference for Western Buddhist teachers,' Jane continued. 'It's advice he gave about handling abuse by gurus back when the Janice Doe case happened.'

'What case?'

'A woman tried to sue Sogyal for sexual, emotional, and physical abuse. Rigpa paid her off and the case was dropped.'

I gulped. It'd been going on that long? How did I not know this? Tibetan Buddhist students were supposed to check out a teacher before taking one as their vajra guru, but I hadn't even searched his name online. Mind you, the internet was only starting out when I went to my first retreat with Sogyal, and I hadn't even hooked up to it then. Later I only had very slow dial-up for many years, followed by slow broadband, so googling things wasn't a part of my mindset until the last decade, and by then it was too late.

Sogyal had hooked me in my first retreat. I'd missed the examination part completely. And now I find he's the kind of teacher I wouldn't have followed had I known. Never in a million years. Too late now.

And yet I don't regret a thing. *Even this is a teaching.* I saw how I'd depended far too much on my lama. Sogyal told us, again and again, to turn our minds into the nature of our own mind, and what had I been doing? Turning it out, towards my lama, waiting for his instruction, always looking to the next teaching as if it would give me some answer I didn't already have. Twenty years along, shouldn't I be learning to trust the very nature of my mind to which my lama had introduced me? Wasn't that the whole point? To learn to rely on the truth inside us? I snorted to myself; perhaps this was his greatest teaching; a way to set us all free of our dependency on him. I doubted it, though, figuring that idea was giving him far too much credit. He could have set us free without abusing anyone!

'His Holiness says such behaviour must be exposed,' Jane continued, 'and that's why they're writing the letter, for the sake of the dharma and to stop people getting hurt, and honestly it's ripping the sangha apart. People only manage to leave after they have emotional and physical breakdowns, and some have been in therapy for years. Lots of people have raised the issue with him privately, but nothing changed, so they figure it's time to do something.'

I ran my free hand though my hair. 'It'll be like a bomb's dropped, you know.'

'I know. They're going to make a website where people can talk about it. They'll need care.'

'I'm glad they thought of that,' I said, not knowing how big a role I'd end up playing in that care.

3
INITIAL THOUGHTS

I had to go out, and I found myself driving south, singing the mani mantra at the top of my lungs with tears streaming down my face while an avalanche of emotions washed through me— *Om Mani Peme Hung. Om Mani Peme Hung. Om Mani Peme Hung.* Shock. Anger. And a bitter sense of personal betrayal. Sogyal had broken samaya with me, with all of us.

While allowing my thoughts and feelings to come and go unhindered, I saw the breadth of the betrayal, and I understood just how hard having the truth revealed would be for my vajra brothers and sisters.

Does he know what harm he's caused?

He'd behaved in a way that made him not worthy of our devotion, acted in a way that showed a lack of care for those who served him the most, and made a mockery of his teachings on love, compassion and wisdom. Where was the wisdom and compassion in someone who injured others, leaving them bleeding and bruised, and with scars both physical and emotional? A true crazy wisdom master would never act 'unconventionally' unless they knew their actions would bring awakening in that particular person at that particular time. The very fact that these actions had brought trauma, rather than awakening—and despite the students' efforts to 'work with' what they experienced in order to learn from it—proved Sogyal wasn't what he claimed himself to be.

'How could you jeopardise everything we all worked for like this?' I yelled at him.

My mind struggled with cognitive dissonance—a situation involving conflicting attitudes, beliefs or behaviours. He'd brought so much benefit to so many—given me and many others the greatest gift of an introduction to the true nature of our minds. How does one reconcile this with the fact that he'd harmed many others? And how can one believe anything such a person says? His debauchery threw everything into question.

I pulled into the parking lot of the Treat Factory in Berry. My daughter was having a birthday soon, and I planned on picking up some fancy chocolate for her. I wandered into the shop and looked about, but nothing seemed real to me. All I could think of was the students Sogyal had hurt. I imagined what it must have been like to have been punched, groped, pulled by the ear so hard that it bled, had a bowl of soup thrown at you. Asked to give him a blow job! The thought made me nauseous. Sangye had mentioned in one of his posts that he was suffering from complex post-traumatic stress syndrome. Considering that I'd seen him working almost 24/7 for a boss who was never satisfied and had no respect for time, and then add the beating and the putting down, it wasn't surprising.

How, I wondered, could you heal from that level of betrayal? The trust we put in our lama was total, unreserved, like a child with their father, and the betrayal would cut every bit as deep.

30

I thought of all those people who had worked in high levels of Rigpa for years and then left, usually after some kind of breakdown, physical or mental or both. It happened to rather a lot of people, I realised. They just disappeared; no one spoke of them afterwards, and you never saw or heard from them again. Why had I never questioned that? Never seen it as weird?

I knew why, if they had been abused, they didn't speak out, though. If you took on board the full belief system, then saying bad things against your lama, especially in public, would be considered a breakage of samaya, which meant you'd supposedly end up in a hell that made the Christian version of hell look mild.

I saw immediately how Sogyal was a result of his upbringing—just like all of us—and how many factors had contributed to his being able to behave as he did, and though I felt anger at his actions, for him as a person, I felt only sadness because he'd stuffed up so badly; he'd fallen into a great delusion. The teacher in him, the part of him that had taught me something of value, still had a place in my heart. The abusive man, not at all. Besides, if anyone had broken samaya, it was him, not me. I had a sense that he had no idea how harmful his behaviour had been.

As I wandered the aisles of the shop looking at the treats, I had an overwhelming sense that everything had changed, that nothing would be the same again, and that despite my unwavering conviction in the truth of the Buddhist teachings, the path I'd been following for twenty years had been indelibly stained by Sogyal's actions.

By the time I'd selected my chocolate-covered crunch and some liqueur chocolates in a pretty package, I'd reached a state of acceptance and equanimity. I had no idea what would happen next in this saga; all I could do was take each moment as it came and trust my own wisdom—just as the Dzogchen teachings instructed.

I returned home after finishing my shopping tasks and placed my mail on my desk. My gaze fell on a small card propped beneath my computer monitor. The photo on it showed Sogyal praying to his masters. My stomach turned—his image now associated with what I knew of his behaviour. I grabbed the card and shoved it in the bottom drawer of my desk, then I walked to my shrine and removed his photo, leaving a space, a suitable representation of the yawning chasm in my heart. I followed up with removing every photo of him from my walls and stuffing them in the cabinet beneath my shrine. I could no longer bear to look at him.

I wished I could remove him from my inner world as easily, but I knew that would not only be impossible but perhaps also not advisable—not because I feared hell, but because at that point I still gave some importance to maintaining the samaya bond. I figured if I rejected him completely, I'd be in danger of rejecting the true nature of my mind to which he'd introduced me, and rejecting that would be a tragedy. Though my disgust for his behaviour felt all-encompassing at that point, I also felt it important to have a balanced view of him, one acknowledging both the good and the bad. I had long walked the path of the middle way, and this was just another situation in which to apply the dharma. Truth is not found in extremes, in rejection or attachment. A balanced perspective seemed to me to be the key to navigating the fallout from these revelations with equanimity.

We're all capable of both love and hate, helpful actions and harmful ones, and clearly Sogyal was no different to anyone else in that respect. I attributed his ability to teach inspiringly and 'introduce' people to the nature of their mind to the Buddha in him—his Buddha nature—and the abusive behaviour to the devil in him—the driving force of attachment, aversion, and ignorance. I'd always distinguished between him as a teacher and him as a man, anyway. Anyone who managed their workers with as little skill as he did clearly wasn't enlightened, and yet his ability to introduce people to the nature of their minds couldn't be questioned—at least not by me, not at that point; later, I questioned everything, including my own realisation.

4
SUPPORT FROM THE DALAI LAMA

Jane sent me a link to a document titled *Ethics in the Teacher-Student Relationship: The Responsibilities of Teachers and Students: Interview with HH the 14th Dalai Lama, Tenzin Gyatso*. His Holiness's words brought me great relief, giving me a different voice—a common sense one from someone I respected—to counteract the voice of Sogyal whose teachings on samaya, crazy wisdom, devotion, and pure perception acted as an injunction against exposing his behaviour.

I also watched the whole eight videos from the conference and took notes.

'The real authority of a lama is given by the student. No one else,' His Holiness said early in the videos. 'Nobody gives the authority except the student. They decide: this will be my teacher.'

Why did Sogyal's first students remain with him when his abusive behaviour became evident to them? Why did they empower a teacher exhibiting such behaviour and then enable the abuse to continue by covering it up for decades and drawing more and more students into the web of deception? Perhaps some of them came from abusive family backgrounds and so the dynamics of abuse were to some extent normal for them. And

35

the lamas who encourage students to remain devoted to such a person or remain silent—does this kind of violence seem normal to them or somehow acceptable because of their own beliefs, experiences or proclivities?

When the discussion at the conference came to the issue of abusive behaviour by lamas, His Holiness mentioned that the Buddha said, 'Someone who has fallen cannot help someone up.' And that's the point, isn't it? Regardless of how profound a spiritual experience we might have in their presence, if someone cannot even abide by the accepted rules of basic decency, they cannot help us to behave any better. People we take as our spiritual teachers presumably are people we want to emulate, but why would anyone want to emulate someone who emotionally, physically, and sexually abuses their students?

His Holiness made it quite clear in these videos that it was necessary to publicly expose unethical behaviour when other avenues for moderating it failed. Jane had told me that several students had already raised the issue with Sogyal personally, but nothing had changed. His Holiness said:

> 'What is in the best interest of the Buddhadharma is much more important than anything concerning an individual guru. Therefore, if it is necessary to criticize a guru to save the Buddhadharma or to benefit several hundred of their disciples, do not hesitate.'

He also said if we criticize a teacher's abusive actions, so long as we respect them as a person at the same time, recognise any beneficial aspects, and speak with a good motivation, not out of hatred or wanting revenge, it didn't constitute a breakage of samaya. That confirmed my gut feeling on the matter. At that stage the idea of not breaking my spiritual connection with my lama was still important to me. Later I would come to question the nature of that 'connection'. Was it something real or something manufactured to suit an expectation?

I knew the Rigpa 'party line' and saw immediately how it had been used to justify Sogyal's behaviour. I figured it would also make those who covered up the abuse all those years feel they were doing the right thing. They'd think they were acting from a 'higher' perspective, a spiritual one above society and its laws. The Rigpa organisation's unwritten code was that Sogyal was a crazy wisdom master and so everything he did was enlightened action even if it didn't look like that to us 'lesser' beings. This, I saw, was the core belief that enabled the abuse.

But it was clear to me now that Sogyal's behaviour wasn't crazy wisdom. What did His Holiness say about that? He said though there were some Buddhist teachers who acted with 'strange modes of ethical conduct, they were fully realised beings and knew what was of long-term benefit to others'. However, he made it clear that nowadays such behaviour was harmful and a guru's behaviour had to conform to convention. I felt relieved to read that, 'The practice of tantra is never an excuse for unethical behaviour.' Something I figured should be obvious to everyone when the Buddha's basic teaching on ethics was to do no harm. Thank goodness His Holiness was clear on the matter.

Vajrayana practice is supposed to purify our perception such that we see our teacher, ourselves, and everyone else as a Buddha and see everything our teacher does as enlightened action. This was the doctrine behind the idea that Sogyal's public humiliation of students was enlightened action on his part, and in Rigpa, if you saw his outbursts as anything other than enlightened action, you were considered not to have much realisation and not be worthy of the highest teachings we all sought. There was no point saying anything to anyone in charge; you'd just be given a lecture on the Rigpa 'party line' that justified Sogyal's actions.

In this interview, His Holiness said:

'In tantric practice, we try to see all beings as Buddhas and the environment as a pure land, so it would be absurd not to see our teacher as a Buddha. However, this view should not be taught to beginners. If it is misunderstood, and thus gives the guru free license, it is like poison, destroying the teachings, the guru, and the disciple. … On the level of our personal spiritual practice, it is important to have faith in and reverence for our guru and to see that person in a positive light in order to make spiritual progress. But on the level of general Buddhism in society, seeing all actions of our teacher as perfect is like poison and can be misused. This attitude spoils our entire teachings by giving teachers a free hand to take undue advantage. …

'I have had many teachers, and I cannot accept seeing all their actions as pure. My two regents, who were among my sixteen teachers, fought one another in a power struggle that even involved the Tibetan army. When I sit on my meditation seat, I feel both were kind to me, and I have profound respect for both of them. Their fights do not matter. But when I had to deal with what was going on in the society, I said to them, "What you're doing is wrong!" We should not feel a conflict in loyalties by acting in this way. In our practice, we can view the guru's behaviour as that of a mahasiddha, and in dealings with society, follow the general Buddhist approach and say that that behaviour is wrong.'

I'd already separated Sogyal the man from Sogyal the lama/teacher principle in my mind—I'd been too aware of his human failings to do otherwise—and that made it relatively easy for me to understand that the little shining lama I sensed in my heart during practice didn't mean Sogyal the man who abused people was also a shining light deserving of a place in my heart. Compassion? Yes, I could have compassion for him, just as I did for anyone under the sway of such dark delusion. Devotion and respect? No; that was gone—apart from the basic respect I gave to every sentient being.

The lama in my heart was a meditation aid, a symbolic representation of an inner truth, but Sogyal, himself, was just a human being. The only link between them was that the outer teacher introduced me to the inner one, and in this case it seemed it might be due entirely to the power of the Vajrayana 'system' rather than some special attribute of Sogyal himself.

These words of His Holiness, I thought, would be enormously helpful for Rigpa students as they processed the soon-to-be-revealed abuse. It turned out I was only partially right. Some found it helpful; others fell into Tibetan Buddhist sectarianism, deciding that since His Holiness was from the Gelugpa School his ideas didn't apply to Rigpa students because their lineage was of the Nyingma School.

When you hold tight to a core belief, you'll find all kinds of ways to negate anything that conflicts with that belief, and the core belief I would come up against time and time again over the next eight months—until I stopped talking to stalwart Sogyal supporters—was the belief that Sogyal Rinpoche was truly an enlightened master.

5
TALKING WITH DHARMA FRIENDS

I wasted no time in contacting my dharma friends. They had a right to know what I knew, and I wanted to prepare them and the students I instructed for the shock these revelations bring. I felt I had to care for them as best I could before I ceased being their instructor.

I knew in an instant I couldn't remain a Rigpa instructor. I couldn't represent someone who abused people. So I resigned, but I didn't give up my Rigpa membership—not then. I had too many friends in the sangha, and I wanted to wait and see how management would handle the fallout. I never imagined then how few of these so-called friends would keep acting like friends once I made my abhorrence of the abuse known, nor did I think Rigpa management would act with anything other than compassion and integrity. Oh, how wrong I was!

I contacted my closest friends and set up a Skype group, telling them I had something important we needed to discuss. Eleven of us met that first time, some from a group I'd been instructing since 2006 when the Rigpa Three Year Retreat began and others I'd known for nearly two decades though our work on the Bush Telegraph, the distance education centre I'd set up back in 1999.

41

After we'd shared greetings and caught up on anything major that had happened in our lives, I told them about my conversations with Sangye and Jane—though as instructed, I mentioned nothing about the forthcoming letter.

One of my friends told us she'd figured the stories of abuse were likely true. She'd looked on the internet and 'worked through the issues' when a woman called Mimi had spoken on a Canadian documentary about being sexually abused by Sogyal. This friend was the only one of us who'd delved into everything written on the internet, and yet she'd decided to remain with Sogyal, primarily because she'd never had a problem with him personally. We'd all agreed back then that his grumpiness and pettiness were just part of the package—you had to take the bad with the good—and at that stage, the good had outweighed the bad, but only because we hadn't known the extent of it.

Now my friends voiced their concern. We all knew Sangye, and we owed him for setting up the internet system that delivered teachings to us every week, allowing us to follow the three-year retreat from home. We'd always been grateful to him for that. We knew how hard he'd worked to set up something that would've cost Rigpa hundreds of thousands of dollars had they had to pay for it. That he'd been hit regularly struck a chord with them as it had with me.

I mentioned Drolma, an Australian woman some of us had known before she became a nun and had taken up residence in Lerab Ling, Rigpa's main retreat centre in France. That this woman most of us knew as a sweet girl with a pure heart and earnest desire to lead a truly spiritual life should have been beaten and emotionally abused was horrifying to my friends. She'd left Rigpa and disrobed perhaps a year before this time, but none of us had known why. The reason seemed obvious now.

None of us imagined Sogyal could possibly have *meant* to hurt anyone, but hitting *everyone* didn't fit what we understood as true crazy wisdom—the kind referred to in the famous Tibetan Buddhist story of Milarepa's teacher Marpa who made Milarepa build towers, and then pull them down, and then build new ones in order to purify his karma to speed him on his progress to enlightenment.

Someone raised the idea that we couldn't know whether or not they might receive some benefit from the abuse in their next life, or the one after that, since their suffering would be purifying their negative karma.

That kind of idea, however, only made me want to scream. Even if it were true, I wasn't buying it as an excuse.

Though perturbed and concerned, my friends seemed far too calm to me. Perhaps they simply had more equanimity than I, but I wondered if perhaps I hadn't made the seriousness of the abuse clear, so I read them what Jane had sent in written form via Messenger. My hands shook as I scrolled back through the conversation to find it, and then I began to read.

At first my voice remained calm, but by the time I got to the end I'd become so upset I could barely speak, and I had to pause before finishing.

For a moment, no one said a thing, but I knew it had struck home. Hearing it in Jane's own words had made it personal.

The reason my heart bled, my stomach churned and my tears fell at these words was not only because of the depravity of the behaviour, and the compassion it invoked for Jane, but also because the thought of someone doing those things aroused all my abhorrence for anyone who tortured, bullied or abused anyone. I'd always been sensitive to abuse and injustice. I'd fought bullies off their victims as a child, and simply could not watch torture in movies or read it in books. It made me feel nauseous. And here was someone I'd looked up to as a person dedicated to benefitting beings, and now I knew him to be the kind of person I'd always thought of as the scum of the earth.

I left my friends with Jane's words, and we agreed to meet again in a couple of weeks.

Meanwhile I had to break the news to my daughter who had accompanied me every year, bar two, from the age of three to twenty-three, to retreat at a beachside caravan park near Forster. Sogyal Rinpoche had been like a spiritual grandfather to her.

She returned home from where she lived in Sydney a couple of days after I'd spoken to Jane.

'Notice anything different about the house?' I asked once she'd settled and eaten.

She looked around. 'Well, the demolition has progressed.'

I chuckled. It certainly had, in more ways than one. We were involved in major renovations, and had moved into the studio attached to our house. Our partially demolished house looked how I felt inside—abandoned and destroyed.

'Not the building. Inside,' I said.

'Try the shrine,' my husband suggested.

She wandered over to where the shrine stood against the wall. I followed her and waited behind her.

She turned with a frown. 'You've taken down the picture of Rinpoche.'

I nodded. 'There's not one left showing anywhere.'

'Why?'

I explained the reason, and as she listened, her eyes grew wider.

'Do you want to see what Jane sent me?' I asked when she said nothing.

She shook her head. 'No. I get the picture. It doesn't surprise me. He always was creepy. We all knew it.'

I snorted. 'You better than me.'

'He talked to us about sex, even when the little kids were there. That was so inappropriate.'

I nodded. She was referring to the sessions he gave for the children. I'd watched some of them. Why hadn't I seen what was so clear to the kids? Because I was blinded by belief he could do no harm. Well, he'd blown that belief out of the water.

'How do you feel about it?' I asked, thinking she might be as devastated as me.

She shrugged. 'Are the teachings true?'

'Sure,' I said without hesitation, knowing that was true at the level she'd received them.

'Then he's an asshole, but the teachings are okay. End of story.'

And it was. For her that was the end of it. She rejected him, but not the teachings.

Phew. I felt relieved it wasn't going to be an issue for her and admired her for the simplicity with which she dealt with the situation. Unfortunately for me, it wasn't so simple. I'd taken him as my lama. She had not.

6
WAITING FOR THE LETTER

The time between the moment I learned about Sogyal's behaviour behind the scenes and when the rest of the Rigpa community learned about it had a strangely spacious quality to it. Awareness of this newly revealed truth suffused my every moment and changed everything for me. The pillar of my spiritual life for twenty years had crumbled. I no longer had a teacher, and the religion I'd previously thought near perfect had revealed itself as flawed as any other.

How, I wondered, could such a thing be allowed to happen? Did the other Tibetan lamas know nothing of Sogyal's behaviour? And if they knew, how could they have allowed it to continue?

'I never wanted a religion, anyway,' I muttered to myself as I settled into my meditation seat and stared at my shrine, now devoid of any human face.

Only images of deities remained on my shrine, and I was both surprised and not surprised to discover they bore no taint. On one level, I would have expected all the practice to be associated with Sogyal and so forever stained by his behaviour, but on a deeper level, the practice of Vajrayana itself not only went far beyond any single teacher but also the deities

47

represented various aspects of enlightened mind that was, by its very nature, primordially pure and unstainable.

I found myself doing the Vajrasattva healing and purification practice, saying the hundred-syllable mantra, just as I'd done for the last several years. We'd been told to practice it for Sogyal's health after one of the masters indicated he would face some obstacles in the coming years. I snorted bleakly, guessing that the soon-to-be-revealed truth would be considered such an obstacle. To me, however, it looked like a great opportunity to heal a toxic situation.

I still visualised the liquid light from the pure-white deity above my head pouring down into Sogyal as well as me and all the beings in the world, but now I also visualised those he'd abused and sent the light to heal their trauma. The light flowing through Sogyal I now directed to purify the negative karma he'd accumulated by his actions.

Part of me wanted to eject him from this practice, but spiritual practice brought out the best in me, the part that loved everyone equally, both victim and perpetrator. People who hurt other people only did so because they were deluded. They, like everyone, wanted happiness, they were just unskilful in how they went about getting it. Sogyal should have known better, so I considered that perhaps he had psychological issues. Either way, though the thought of him and what he'd done made me feel ill, he deserved the same respect as any person anywhere, no matter how reprehensible and misguided their actions. So he remained there, right alongside the politicians I disliked.

I enjoyed the sense of stability brought about by continuing my practice, and once again I felt the enormous power of Vajrayana practice. Such power, I realised, could be alluring, intoxicating, and dangerous if one became attached to it. Sogyal I sensed had fallen into such a trap.

Sangye's posts on Facebook continued to expose the less savoury aspects of Sogyal's behaviour and Rigpa culture at the inner-circle level. His posts gained a lot of comments and a lot of resistance from some quarters. Some people blatantly tried to discredit him for speaking out, even to the extent of calling him a samaya breaker and suggesting he would go to hell for doing so.

I saw people I knew defending Sogyal, but for me his actions were indefensible. Though others seemed unsure of what was right and what was wrong, I honoured my Christian upbringing for making the difference very clear, and it was entirely in accord with the Buddha's teachings: whatever harmed people was wrong; whatever helped them was right. It's quite simple really. But beliefs can obscure our perception, as I saw in those who used their beliefs to defend Sogyal and try to justify his behaviour.

In the discussions, people tended to skip over the central issue of Sogyal's behaviour, like ignoring the elephant in the room. Even I, programmed by my years of Tibetan Buddhism not to criticise my guru, used passive-voice constructions to avoid actually saying he'd harmed anyone. For example, I'd say, 'People have been harmed,' not 'Sogyal has harmed people.' Others went a step further by referring to people who 'felt' harmed' rather than people who 'had been harmed', as if it was a fault of their perception rather than Sogyal's behaviour.

The distinction I'd made between Sogyal as a teacher teaching from his Buddha nature and him as a person exhibiting disgusting behaviour wasn't easy to communicate. It's much easier to hate someone for their bad behaviour than to see that even someone who behaves badly still has Buddha nature at their core, or even, on a more mundane level that, like everyone, they have the potential for both good and bad behaviour, and most likely aren't all good or all bad.

I came to understand, however, that my ability to see this way was partially because I hadn't experienced abuse at the hands of my guru myself, and the more the depth of the abuse was revealed to me, the harder it became to maintain the idea that everyone had basic goodness at their core. Some felt that everything Sogyal had done that seemed beneficial was nothing other than a performance and that he had no redeeming features. Given that their experience was like experiencing a demon wearing a righteous mask of compassion, it was a perfectly reasonable assumption for them to make, and led me to question my own perspective.

I could have rejected the idea of everyone having Buddha nature as nothing more than philosophy had I not, in my meditation practice, sensed this 'inner goodness' for myself, but when the behaviour of your guru is leading you to question everything he taught you, it's easy to lose touch with the ground of practice and the surety it brings. In the end I decided that even if people weren't basically good at their core, it was a helpful belief for me to hold for interacting with others in the best possible way.

It seemed logical to me that when sitting in the nature of their mind, someone like Sogyal could still, despite his ethical failings and even if only momentarily, introduce a student to the nature of their mind. His problem, I decided, wasn't that he had no recognition of the nature of his mind—many of us had that—but that he couldn't integrate it into his everyday life, and he hadn't done the work required to rid himself of whatever emotional baggage he carried that lead him to behave in the way he did. On one hand he had enough recognition of the nature of mind to evoke it in others, but on the other hand, he was emotionally stunted and possibly suffering from some form of mental disorder.

I joined the online conversation in a way that was always supportive of Sangye, and I received an unexpected email because of it. A Rigpa student I'd interacted with over a project we'd undertaken together emailed me and asked me what was going on. Why, he wanted to know, was I supporting someone who was saying these things about our lama?

Because it's true, I replied. *And it has to stop.*

A day or so after sending my reply, my landline rang.

'What's this all about,' he asked.

I explained how shocked I was when I'd discovered Sogyal had hit Sangye. 'Is it true?' I asked him, knowing he'd been close to Sogyal. 'Did you see him hit people?'

Not only had he seen it, he'd been hit himself and saw no problem in it. In fact, he felt honoured that Sogyal felt he was 'ready' to be 'taught' that way. He spouted the Rigpa 'party line', saying the beatings were wisdom love in action, and he turned the problem onto the students Sogyal had used as punching bags. 'Some people just aren't right for Vajrayana,' he told me—a refrain I would hear often in the coming months. 'If they can't hack it, they should go join the theravadens.'

He said it as if the Theravada, the tradition that came from the first teachings of the Buddha, were somehow lesser than those of the Vajrayana, the third wave of the Buddha's teachings. I didn't like the arrogance of that attitude or the suggestion that if you were a good Vajrayana student you would take the abuse. He proved himself completely taken in by the 'party line' that whatever Sogyal did was okay because he was a crazy wisdom master.

I'd figured most students would recognise abusive behaviour for what it was once they knew the extent of it. This conversation was my first indication that for some people it would prove impossible, especially those who'd been in Sogyal's inner circle for decades.

Only after years of struggling had Jane, Sangye, and others like them, faced the evidence of their senses and decided that what they were experiencing was not love, but abuse; yet the friend who rang me still thought his beating had been an expression of love. Was abuse still abuse even if we didn't think it was? A bruise, I figured, was always a bruise, always painful, even if we thought it a result of love. Hitting was easy to recognise and evaluate as harmful as it was much less dependent on our subjective perception than emotional and sexual abuse. The evidence of harm in the form of a physical injury is clear for all to see.

I became almost obsessed with working out what had gone wrong. I had to know: what hadn't we—Sogyal and his students—understood correctly? Or was the belief system itself at fault? I had faith in the truth of the Buddhadharma, but the abhorrent behaviour my lama had exhibited threw aspects of it—at least as it was expressed in Tibetan Buddhism—into question. I returned to my extensive library of Buddhist books, and I searched for articles online to see if anyone shared His Holiness's point of view, a view that matched my own.

With great relief I discovered many articles, mostly by Westerners with long experience of Tibetan Buddhism who had already walked this path of disenchantment: Is the Guru Really a Buddha?; Dealing with Problematic Teachers; Breaking the Silence on Sexual Misconduct; Abuse in the Name of Guru Devotion; Why I Quit Guru Yoga; Devotion with Discernment; Teachers are not Gods; The Teacher Student Relationship: Liberating or a Trap?

I found *Wise Teacher, Wise Student: Tibetan Approaches to a Healthy Relationship* by Alexander Birzin (Ithaca: Snow Lion, 2010) a great help, and I copied quotes from that work as well as other sources into a document examining the problematic beliefs—devotion, pure perception, samaya, and crazy wisdom. In those few weeks between my learning of the abuse and the rest of the sangha learning about it, I wrote over 10,000 words. This meant I'd processed the essential issues to some degree before the rest of the sangha learned the truth, which put me in a good position to guide others through the same process.

Jane told me they were looking for someone to run a blog where students could discuss the issues and support each other. When I heard this, I sat staring out my window as a realisation dawned, a knowing and a resistance together. 'No,' I said to myself. 'No way. I am not doing it.'

I could make the kind of blog needed in less than an hour. A Facebook group would be good, too, a secret one, nice and private. Both would cost nothing to set up. I had the skills, but I also knew whoever set it up would have the ultimate responsibility of caring for the abused and disillusioned, and I didn't want that kind of responsibility.

Nevertheless, a path opened up before me and drew me along it with a sense of inescapable destiny. I was in the wrong place at the wrong time and with the right skills and a vow to help all beings that made it impossible for me to turn away. So I offered, through Jane, to create a student support blog and Facebook group.

My offer was accepted, and I felt the weight of responsibility settle on my shoulders. I wished she'd said they'd found someone else. But they hadn't.

'What should I call it?' I asked her.

'Gee. I don't know.'

I couldn't think of anything. My usually creative mind didn't seem to be functioning, and I had no time to mull over elegant and meaningful names. I just knew shit was about to hit the fan big time, and I'd put my hand up for something I wasn't ready for, and probably never would be. I wondered what sangha members would do now. What would come next for our sangha? I rested with that question for a moment and received only a big empty space as my answer.

'How about *What Now?*' I said.

'That's perfect.'

7
THE LETTER

When I read the 'letter by the eight', I recoiled in disgust at the contents. The stories shared were personal, a testimony of what eight people had seen and experienced, and it affected me deeply. As I read the letter, I felt betrayal, anger and disgust all over again.

I had no doubt that this letter would be a game changer for the Rigpa community, and it was a game that sorely needed changing. I greatly admired the courage of those eight students. This wouldn't be easy for them.

Later one of the letter writers left a comment on the blog saying:

'We are all actually quite amazed at the way we were magnetized to each other across many times zones. There was no apparent reason for why now; it was all completely organic. It started out as simply listening to each other and offering support; there are even people in the group that historically didn't get along. I think that the turning point was when someone who didn't sign the letter said, "How are we going to feel when the next person has a physical or emotional breakdown requiring hospitalization?" That left us all feeling very uncomfortable. The letter was co-written over the space of over one month; it was very therapeutic for us. We

didn't experience the abuse in the same place or time, but we found the commonality of our experience quite startling. And there's a lot more information we could have shared that we didn't.'

Here's the letter unedited from the original:

July 14, 2017
Sogyal Lakar,

The Rigpa sangha is in crisis. Long-simmering issues with your behaviour can no longer be ignored or denied. As long-time committed and devoted students we feel compelled to share our deep concern regarding your violent and abusive behaviour. Your actions have hurt us individually, harmed our fellow sisters and brothers within Rigpa the organization, and by extension Buddhism in the West. We write to you following the advice of the Dalai Lama, in which he has said that students of Tibetan Buddhist lamas are obliged to communicate their concerns about their teacher:

> *If one presents the teachings clearly, others benefit. But if someone is supposed to propagate the dharma and their behaviour is harmful, it is our responsibility to criticize this with a good motivation. This is constructive criticism, and you do not need to feel uncomfortable doing it. In "The Twenty Verses on the Bodhisattvas' Vows," it says that there is no fault in whatever action you engage in with pure motivation. Buddhist teachers who abuse sex, power, money, alcohol, or drugs, and who, when faced with legitimate complaints from their own students, do not correct their behaviour, should be criticized openly and by name. This*

may embarrass them and cause them to regret and stop their abusive behaviour. Exposing the negative allows space for the positive side to increase. When publicizing such misconduct, it should be made clear that such teachers have disregarded the Buddha's advice. However, when making public the ethical misconduct of a Buddhist teacher, it is only fair to mention their good qualities as well." The Dalai Lama, Dharamsala, India March 1993.

This letter is our request to you to stop your unethical and immoral behaviour. Your public face is one of wisdom, kindness, humor, warmth and compassion, but your private behaviour, the way you conduct yourself behind the scenes, is deeply disturbing and unsettling. A number of us have raised with you privately, our concerns about your behaviour in recent years, but you have not changed.

Those of us who write to you today have firsthand experience of your abusive behaviours, as well as the massive efforts not to allow others to know about them. Our concerns are deepened with the organizational culture you have created around you that maintains absolute secrecy of your actions, which is in sharp contrast with your stated directive of openness and transparency within the sangha. Our wish is to break this veil of secrecy, deception, and deceit. We can no longer remain silent.

Our deep and heartfelt hope is that this collective note might yield a more tangible result than any of our individual discussions with you have. We hope that long lasting and sincere changes may come about rather than short-lived pledges.

Our primary concerns are:

1. Your physical, emotional and psychological abuse of students.
2. Your sexual abuse of students.
3. Your lavish, gluttonous, and sybaritic lifestyle.
4. Your actions have tainted our appreciation for the practice of the dharma.

1. Physical, emotional and psychological abuse

We have received directly from you, and witnessed others receiving, many different forms of physical abuse. You have punched and kicked us, pulled hair, torn ears, as well as hit us and others with various objects such as your back-scratcher, wooden hangers, phones, cups, and any other objects that happened to be close at hand. We trusted for many years that this physical and emotional treatment of students—what you assert to be your "skillful means" of "wrathful compassion" in the tradition of "crazy wisdom"—was done with our best interest at heart in order to free us from our "habitual patterns". We no longer believe this to be so. We feel that we and others have been harmed because your actions were not compassionate; rather they demonstrated your lack of discipline and your own frustration. Your physical abuse – which constitutes a crime under the laws of the lands where you have done these acts—have left monks, nuns, and lay students of yours with bloody injuries and permanent scars. This is not second hand information; we have experienced and witnessed your behaviour for years.

Why did you inflict violence upon us and our fellow dharma brothers and sisters? Why did you punch, slap, kick, and pull our hair? Your food was not hot enough; you were awakened from your nap a half hour late; the phone list was missing a name or the font was the wrong size; the internet connection was slow; the television movie guide was confusing; technology failed to work; your assistant wasn't attentive enough;[1] we failed to "tune into your mind" and predict what you wanted; or you were moody because you were upset with one of your girlfriends. There are hundreds of examples of trivial incidents that have set you off and your response has been to strike us violently.

Your emotional and psychological abuse has been perhaps more damaging than the physical scars you have left on us. When we have worked for you while organizing and setting up the infrastructure for you to teach at different places around the world (Europe, North America, Australia, and India and Nepal), your shaming and threatening have led some of your closest students and attendants to emotional breakdowns. You have always told us to be appreciative of the personal attention that you give, that you were "pointing out our hidden faults" in our character, and freeing us from "our self-cherishing ego." We no longer believe this to be so. It was done in such a way that was harmful to us rather than helpful, a method of control, a blatant means of subjugation and undue influence that removed our liberty. You have threatened us and others saying, if we do not follow you absolutely, we will die "spitting up blood like Ian Maxwell."[2] You have told us that our loved ones are at risk of ill-health, or have died, because we displeased you in some way."[3] At public teachings, you have regularly criticized, manipulated and shamed us and those working to run your retreats. You have told us for years that this is part of your unique style of "training" students and that this shaming is part of the guru-disciple relationship. We no longer believe this to be so.

As more students verged close to emotional breakdowns because of your "trainings", you introduced "Rigpa Therapy" for your closest students. Trained, practising therapists (who are also your students) were given the task of dealing with the pain that was being stirred up in the minds of those who you were abusing physically, emotionally and psychologically. During one-to-one sessions, the therapist heard from the student of your "crazy wisdom" methods and the trauma that it caused the individual. One such "Rigpa Therapy" method for processing the trauma was to negate the validity of seeing you, the teacher *and* instigator, as the source of the trauma. Instead, we were instructed to see old family relationship histories as the issue. In effect, our very tangible and clear discernment of seeing you as an abuser was blocked and instead we were blamed and made to feel inadequate. On the occasions when the "therapy" did not result in a student changing their view of you, you shamed the therapist into feeling that they weren't doing their job properly and were not skilled.

2. Sexual Abuse

You use your role as a teacher to gain access to young women, and to coerce, intimidate and manipulate them into giving you sexual favors.[4] The ongoing controversies of your sexual abuse that we can read and watch on the Internet are only a small window into your decades of this behaviour. Some of us have been subjected to sexual harassment in the form of being told to strip, to show you our genitals (both men and women), to give you oral sex, being groped, asked to give you photos of our genitals, to have sex in your bed with our partners, and to describe to you our sexual relations with our partners. You've ordered your students to photograph your attendants and girlfriends naked, and then forced other students to make photographic collages for you, which you have shown to others. You have offered one of your female attendants to another lama (who is well known in Rigpa) for sex. You have had for decades, and continue to have, sexual relationships with a number of your student attendants, some who are married. You have told us to lie on your behalf, to hide your sexual relationships from your other girlfriends. Publicly you claim that your relationships are ordinary, consensual, and proper because you are not a monk. You deny any wrongdoing and have even claimed on occasion that you were seduced.[5] You and others in your organization claim this is how a Buddhist master of "crazy wisdom" behaves, just

61

like the tantric adepts of the past. We do not believe this to be so and see such claims as attempts to explain away egregious behaviours.

3. Gluttonous lifestyle

Your lavish lifestyle is kept hidden from your thousands of students. It is one thing for you to accept an offering of the best of everything (that we may have) as an acknowledgement of our gratitude for spiritual teachings. It is quite another to demand it from us. Much of the money that is used to fund your luxurious appetites comes from the donations of your students who believe their offering is being used to further wisdom and compassion in the world.

As attendants, drivers, and organizers for you, most of our time and energy is taken up providing a steady supply of sensual pleasures. You demand all kinds of food be prepared for you—at all hours of the night and day—by your personal chefs and attendants (who Rigpa pays for) who travel the world with you. You demand all forms of entertainment; this includes having detailed TV guide schedules for the shows that you often watch for hours on end each day; elaborate movie lists so you know what's playing in theaters near you at all times; continual supply of take-out restaurant food; drivers and masseuses on call 24-hours a day to serve you and deliver you and your companions to theaters, expensive restaurants, venues to shop and secretive places where you can smoke your expensive cigars.

With impatience, you have made demands for this entertainment and decadent sensory indulgences. When these are not made available at the snap of a finger, or exactly as you wished, we were insulted, humiliated, made to feel worthless, stupid and incompetent, and often hit or slapped. Your behaviour did not cultivate our mindfulness or awareness, but rather it made us terrified of making a mistake. You tell your students that you spend most of your time engaging in Buddhist study and practice, but those of us who have attended you in private for years know this is not the reality.

We feel it is unethical that ours and others' financial contributions to you—believed to be furthering the dharma—are used to support this lavish lifestyle. Please stop living a duplicitous life. If you have no shame about your behavior then let it see the light of day. Allow the rest of your students to see who you really are, and let them make their own informed decision about whether you are the teacher for them.

4. Tainted our appreciation for the practice of the dharma.

Please understand the harm that you have inflicted on us has also tainted our appreciation for and practice of the dharma. In our decades of study and practice of Tibetan Buddhism with you, we trained our minds to view you as the "all embodied jewel" and the "source of all the teachings and blessings" of the Buddha-dharma. We trusted you completely. Yet, we struggled for years because your actions did not square with the teachings.

Today, for many of us who have left you, the Lerab Ling community, and Rigpa the organization, our ground of confidence in the Buddhadharma has been compromised. Some of us, who chose to depart abruptly Lerab Ling, left all of our possessions, because we were desperate to break away from your abuse and the community that supported it. Whether we departed abruptly or have faded away from you and Rigpa, we struggle to rekindle an appreciation for the transformative teachings and teachers we encountered. Often when we sit down to meditate and practice, we feel polluted with trauma from our experience with you; some of us relate to the Vajrayana with deep suspicion; and some of us are at work rebuilding from scratch the foundations of our study and practice recognising that your manipulation was intermingled with all that we were taught. Others of us seek conventional therapy as a means for processing. So quite contrary to your aspiration to bring the true dharma to beings, the effect of your methods is that our relationship to the dharma has been tainted. We now see clearly the many ways that you betrayed our trust, manipulated and abused us and our dharma brothers and sisters.

We are not showing a lack of trust and respect, being a "trouble-maker" with "negative talk" as you often assert when anyone has dared to object to your methods. In fact, we have trusted you too long, given you the benefit of the doubt over and over again. When we've attempted to raise these concerns you've shamed us, and threatened to withhold the teachings from all the students because we had "doubts." You have encouraged us to defame others, in particular in France, who have spoken out against you in recent years. We have seen how you hold the teachings "hostage" and demand that students show their devotion through continuous "offerings" in the form of money and free labor. You tell us this is how to become an authentic dharma practitioner. We do not believe this to be the path of the dharma.

With regards to your abusive behaviour, your sexual misconduct, and your lavish lifestyle, we see no clear or identifiable ethical standards or guidelines to which you are held. There is a vacuum of accountability. We hope that sending you this letter, sharing it with your peers, and the Rigpa Dzogchen Mandala students, will serve to fill that vacuum.

What you have taught in the last thirty years, and in particular *The Tibetan Book of Living and Dying*, has brought immense benefit to so many people including those who write to you today. If we are wrong in what we write, please correct our mistaken view. If your striking and punching us and others, and having sex with your students and married women, and funding your sybaritic lifestyle with students' donations, is actually the ethical and compassionate behaviour of a Buddhist teacher, please explain to us how it is. If, however, we are correct in our assessment, please stop your behaviours that we believe to be harmful to others.

In closing we want to acknowledge that most of the public critique of you that is found on the Internet is factual. Some of us, who have held positions of responsibility within Rigpa, struggle with our own part in having covered for you and "explained" away your behaviour, while not caring for those with traumatic experiences. Our past motivation to see all the actions of our tantric teacher as pure obscured us from seeing the very real harm that you are inflicting. We are each taking a long and serious look at our own behaviours, trying to learn from them, and supporting each other on our journey. We can no longer stay silent while you harm others in the name of Buddhism. Our deepest wish is to see Buddhism flourish in the West. We no longer want to indulge in the stupidity of seeing the Guru as perfect at any cost. The path does not require us to sacrifice our wisdom to discern, our ethics and morality, or our integrity, on the altar of "Guru Yoga."

Our heartfelt wish is that you seek guidance from the Dalai Lama, other reputable lamas of good heart, or anyone who can help to bring you back onto the true path of the dharma.

With deep respect for the dharma,

Mark Standlee, student for 33 years, Three Year Retreatant, former Director of the International Rigpa Online Courses & Rigpa US Teaching Services for 5 years, International Senior Instructor.

Sangye, student for 16 years, Three Year Retreatant, Buddhist monk for 14 years, Co- director of technology for Rigpa International.

Damcho, student for 15 years, Three Year Retreatant, Buddhist nun for 10 years, personal assistant to Sogyal Lakar.

Matteo Pistono, student for 19 years, former Rigpa US Board Member, author of *Fearless In Tibet: The Life of the Mystic of Tertön Sogyal.*

Joanne Standlee, student for 18 years, Head of Sogyal Lakar's household in US for 15 years, National Director for Rigpa US for 7 years, Director of Zam America for 5 years, Rigpa Instructor.

Graham Price, student for 20 years, Sogyal Lakar's personal attendant and driver.

Michael Condon, student for 21 years, Rigpa Instructor, Sogyal Lakar's personal attendant and driver in the US.

Gary Goldman, student for 23 years.

----

[1] Sogyal Lakar gut-punched a nun in front of an assembly of more than 1,000 students at Lerab Ling in France, August 2016.

[2] In December 2005, in a live-streamed teaching from the unfinished temple, Sogyal Lakar said that Ian Maxwell, one of his oldest students, was "an asshole" as Ian lay dying in the hospital in Paris. After Ian's death Sogyal Lakar said that Ian, "died spitting up blood" because he had defied him in the past. Sogyal Lakar regularly used this incident, saying, "Do you want to end up dying spitting up blood like Ian for defying me?" as an example to other students when he threatened them

with dire consequences if they did not obey his commands.

[3]Sogyal Lakar told Graham that his beloved partner, Elena, got sick (and died a year later) because Graham had shouted at him. In reality, Graham didn't even raise his voice.

https://behindthethangkas.wordpress.com/2011/11/20/13-dakini-janine/ is just one example

https://behindthethangkas.wordpress.com/2011/11/20/16-the-three-year-retreat/

"Gerard demanded an interview with Sogyal, who was initially wary, but then admitted he had had sex with Janine. He tried to shift the blame onto her—claiming that she had seduced him and that he was at first resistant, but later gave in to her demands."

Lerab Ling residential monastics Ani Drolma and Ngawang Sangye struggled for many years to fulfil Sogyal Lakar's ever increasing demands while receiving physical and emotional abuse. They asked for help from the community but were victim-blamed, and viewed as being unappreciative of the blessing of working close to the lama. There was extreme pressure to stay and conform. They both felt as though they had to "escape" the predicament as there was no arena in which to negotiate their position, or find resolution in how to tolerate their working relationship with Sogyal Lakar.

As a gesture for support and with an understanding for the many emotions and issues that could arise for individuals as a result of reading this letter we are sharing some resources and helpful links -

https://sanghacare8.wixsite.com/sanghacareresour
ces
*As well as a blog where concerned students can
connect with each other.*
https://whatnow727.wordpress.com/
(Now http://beyondthetemple.com)

***

What, I wondered, would happen next? How would
Sogyal and Rigpa management respond?

8
THE BLOG DISCUSSIONS BEGIN

The first post on the *What Now?* Blog I called, 'What the Hell are We Going to Do Now?' It didn't mention the word Rigpa or Sogyal Rinpoche, just started with the words, 'Concerned about a certain letter you read recently? Then I gave a few brief words asking people to be kind and supportive as they shared how they felt. Since we didn't want any of this getting into the public arena, I hid the blog from search engines and asked people not to refer to 'our organisation' or 'our teacher' by name, only by initial.

I also set up a Facebook group for 'more personal and private support' and added a note about that, telling people that they could ask to join it through the blog contact form. By the time I'd finished, it was late, so I went to bed. As I snuggled down beside my husband, I had a premonition that I'd be waking in the morning to a shit storm.

I was right.

What I didn't see was how long the storm would last and the extent of its causalities.

I turned on my computer, checked my email, and got my first shock. I'd forwarded the letter to a friend and she'd sent a reply that went something like this: *How dare you send this to me? Why would you share this slander?*

I stared at it, gobsmacked. It had never occurred to me that anyone wouldn't want to know what was contained in that letter, and it'd never occurred to me that they wouldn't believe it, or react against me as if I'd done something wrong in sharing it. Apparently the truth had upset her, and since I was the one who told her, she blamed me for her pain.

And 'slander'? Really? Why would eight people say all these things if they weren't true? And why would they, knowing the injunctions against speaking out within the Rigpa culture, and the likely way they'd be treated for doing so, stick their necks out by speaking out like this? They had nothing to gain by it, and a lot to lose. I figured that the only reason they would possibly do this is if what they said was true.

I'd thought this person a friend, someone who shared the same values as I, but clearly our friendship hadn't gone very deep if she saw my sharing this information as coming from a negative motivation.

Another response came through as a 'reply all' to everyone who'd got the email in Australia. It went something like: *How dare these liars hack our email list.* I knew that the eight would get some flack, but I hadn't seen that one coming! In an attempt to discredit the eight and divert attention from the contents of the letter, she erroneously assumed none of them had legitimate access to the email list.

I turned to the blog to see the results there.

What struck me straight up was the love and compassion evident in the responses—the trolls didn't hit until later. Most people expressed respect and appreciation for the eight students who had written the letter. People who had left years before and been isolated from the sangha expressed relief that it was finally all out in the open and they could at last speak about it with others. Commenters felt free to share their own experiences of Sogyal or Rigpa, and they responded to each other with real concern. Those who hadn't had any experience of this side of Sogyal expressed their utter devastation at the news. The following comment sums up how many felt, and echoed my own feelings on first hearing about the abuse.

> 'I have been a so-called good student since 2005, and did whatever SL told us to do. I saw him as living Buddha; I prayed to him all the time; I had dreams of him, and he has been the breath of my life. How could he betray me so? I am hurt, frustrated, confused, lost and very very sad. ... My devotion toward SL is so shaky I don't think I will be able to listen to him without feeling defiance. Since I have read this letter, I am not able to focus on anything; I'm just not able to practice at all. My mind is so disturbed. I feel very alone as if I had lost my parents all at once.'

And someone posted the first of what became an ever-broadening picture for me of the depth of the abuse. It also indicates the toll it took on those who knew about it but couldn't find a way to do anything about it.

> 'The problems [with Sogyal] started for me the very first moment I set foot in Dzogchen Baera [DzB] and encountered Sogyal Rinpoche [SR] and his outlandish teaching style in person. I somehow knew exactly what was going on with him from the word Go.

'All the trademarks of an abusive guru gathering an adoring cult following were falling into place IN PUBLIC, SHAMELESSLY, and even from the earliest days.

'I was so disappointed! I was so disappointed in myself too. I'd left my job without holiday permission to drive nine hours in the rain and the dark down to DzB to 'meet' SR for the first time. But when I arrived, as a recovering Catholic, I felt I had simply jumped out of the frying pan and straight into the fire. It was supposed to last ten days. I lasted two.

'In those two days, all the usual nonsense unfolded: teachings cancelled or starting hours late, people waiting in the shrine room in silent agitation for SR to come, when he did come, all the verbal abuse and brutal treatment that is now so familiar unfolded. There didn't even seem to be a train of thought in the teaching itself ...

'But there were reports desperately trying to be suppressed by the organisers about him shouting and throwing stuff at attendants in his cottage and a shocking report of 'something happening' to a young female first-timer who had somehow ended up in SR's bedroom!

'I demanded a refund of my money, jumped in the car and drove like a demon to beg for my old job back. Within weeks, there was a strangely quiet and dignified split in my Rigpa group. The young lady, her sister and friends left, and the rest of us stayed, bewildered and dreading what we'd gotten ourselves into. Turned out this young woman had been hand-picked by SR's female attendants from the

74

audience because she was his type and very much resembled his ex-girlfriend from France. Flattered at the chance to meet SR face to face, she went to his cottage with the group of women attendants that night. In his bedroom, SR was reclining surrounded by women all massaging a different part of his body. She was instructed how to massage his hand and say, 'Hello.' He flirted. I was afraid to ask what actually occurred. She was so shocked she ran away and never went back.

'In time, since I turned a blind eye to his carry on and got more and more involved in Rigpa, I came to see SR's real power as a true dharma conduit and powerful dharma presence in the world, a genuine mirror for the Buddha Nature to see itself. That is true. But I never accepted the abusive drama or the brutal abuse.

'I must admit, the sexual scandals were far too easy to dismiss as a non-monastic layman taking advantage of his rockstar status to get bewitched superfans into bed. At that time I couldn't bear to think of SR as a predator, and still don't know what to make of him. But the basic question remains: If it's not predatorial sexual abuse, what do these beautiful young women see in him sexually?

'In my senior roles at Rigpa, I tried my best to help those who came to me for support and advice as one scandal after another broke online, in the media and spread like wildfire through the wider sangha. I always hoped I was a positive force at that time and that nobody stayed in Rigpa because I was staying and they liked or respected me. I always made

sure I told people that this is what Rigpa have instructed us say if we were ever asked [there were guidelines, documents, sample Q&As] and that I would remain for the time being. But ultimately I instructed people to stay informed, follow their heart-minds, and move on if/when they felt it was right.

'However, in time I just drifted away quite naturally from that whole scene, but I've always felt ashamed of all I knew and that I never spoke out publicly. I have always wanted to share this testimony with others but, even to tell my other masters, I always felt it might create more harm than good.'

The Facebook group filled up fast, and I found myself too busy with it to continue my formal meditation practice. Moderating the group and the blog and responding to personal messages became my practice. The number of people that appeared to share their story of abuse or to seek support for their turmoil in the wake of the revelations required almost 24/7 support, and I found I had little time for sleep in those early days when I was the only group moderator. I could not abandon people who needed support, especially since many of them were the very people for whom Rigpa had provided no care in the past, so I found myself awake at three in the morning having conversations with people on the other side of the world.

Emotions ran high and conversations required a lot of moderating to keep discussions based on fact and not flying off into conjecture or personal attacks. Though much love and compassion was evident from some, a division in the group soon began to appear with some appearing to only be there in order to defend Sogyal and restate the 'party line' ad nauseam—as if we didn't all already know it! Their uncompassionate responses even to stories of the most heartbreaking suffering required a great deal of careful moderating, and I was extremely relieved when three other women came forward to assist in the moderating. We soon became a close knit and supportive team.

The letter by the eight was never intended to be public. It was supposed to raise the issue within the sangha so that Sogyal's behaviour could be confronted and dealt with within the sangha. However, on July 17, 2017, within a few days of the Dzogchen Mandala students receiving the email, someone leaked the letter to a Dutch online newspaper. It appeared a day later in a French online newspaper and in *The Lion's Roar* in English on my birthday, the 20th of July. I don't know who did it, but it wasn't one of the letter writers. Anyone who received the email could have forwarded it on.

Once the letter became public, the situation took on a different tone. The *What Now?* blog drew those who had been campaigning for decades to bring Sogyal's behaviour into the light, some who had taken an anti-Rigpa, and for some an anti-Tibetan Buddhism, stance. The moderators and I were concerned that the hard line of some of the commenters would send more moderate people away, and we had to moderate comments so that people stated their view without attacking others. It wasn't an easy task to hit the right line between censorship to protect people from abuse and freedom of speech.

The *What Now?* blog at that stage was primarily for people like me who had only just become aware of the abuse, who still had respect for Tibetan Buddhism, and who still had some hope that Rigpa would handle the situation in a wise and compassionate fashion. The blog focused on articles that would help us process the content of the letter, so we didn't want to alienate the very people for whom the blog was written. We purposely kept the tone of our posts moderate, hoping that it would be read by people who elected to stay in Rigpa or who were still deciding what to do, as well as those who took the first exit.

The public release of the letter also gave those who wanted to denigrate the eight letter writers ammunition. In an attempt to prove that the eight and their supporters were unscrupulous people who only wanted to 'bring Sogyal down', they spread the lie that the eight had publicly released the letter. They cast the eight as the enemy of Sogyal and Rigpa, encouraging all those who thought of themselves as good students to set themselves against these 'enemies'. This kind of discourse completely ignored the content of the letter in which the eight made it clear that they were merely asking for clarification from Sogyal, for Sogyal to stop his harmful behaviour, and for the sangha to deal with the issue. The tone of the letter is not that of people wanting to destroy anything. But this was ignored by those who wanted to vilify the authors. That vilification also became aimed at the public supporters of the eight—people such as me.

I remember speaking on the phone to one of Rigpa Australia's management team and they told me that in making the *What Now?* blog and speaking out in support of the eight, I had painted a target on my back. At that point, I didn't realise just how many people would want to fire at that target, but even if I'd known just how bad it would get, despite my personal desire not to be a target for aggression, I couldn't have stopped. My desire to help others navigate the treacherous waters of dealing with the issue of abuse by a lama was just too strong, and it quickly became clear just how important the blog and the Facebook group was in helping people deal with the fallout. I felt as if I had, through no desire of my own, landed in a role—that of the main facilitator of open discussion outside of Rigpa—that needed to be seen through, no matter where it might take me. I would gladly had handed that role to someone else had someone else stepped forward, but they never did.

I had the strange sense that all this really was a dream, playing out with us all as participants. It felt like something that had to happen and that the roles we all played were necessary for the overall fabric of the dream. The public revelations were necessary for the future of Vajrayana Buddhism in the West, and out of the turmoil, I sensed that something positive would come. I saw an opportunity for Sogyal and Rigpa to show the courage of a bodhisattva by admitting the truth of the attestations, apologising for the harm they'd caused, and vowing never to behave in such a way again. Then if they made moves to care for those harmed—some of whom had trouble finding work because they had spent years working in a volunteer capacity for Rigpa, and others who had spent hundreds, perhaps thousands of dollars on therapy—then they would show true compassion and be an inspiration to us all. If that happened, I could stay with the organisation and help them change for the better. At this stage, I truly felt that this was possible. I still believed then that Sogyal could wake up to what he'd done wrong and act according to the teachings.

I was wrong.

I met with my dharma friends via Skype again a few days after the letter came out. Due to our previous discussion, we felt able to formulate what we felt would be the appropriate response by Rigpa and Sogyal, a response that would allow them to retain some integrity and move forward with the possibility of regaining students' trust. I sent a letter containing our recommendations to Sogyal via one of his attendants, via the Australian Student Care Coordinator, and to Patrick Gaffney, Sogyal's oldest student. Though the Australian Care Coordinator assured me Sogyal received it, we never received any reply or response to our suggestions.

9
FEEDBACK AND SUGGESTIONS

Looking back on the feedback and suggestions that we sent, I find it interesting to note how, at that point, we all expressed our continuing love for Sogyal—seeing him in a compassionate Buddhist way—but later, after seeing how he responded to the letter and learning more about the depth of the abuse, that love became harder to retain.

It's also quite amazing to me now that we suggested him returning after a period of retreat and psychotherapy! I've since spoken with people who'd previously raised the issue of his behaviour with him and tried to get him to see a therapist, but without success. If he can't accept the help of mental-health professionals and actively work on his issues, students will never be safe around him.

Our suggestions seemed reasonable and obvious to us, particularly the point about Sogyal following the four powers of Vajrasattva—to acknowledge and regret the harm we cause, make some reparation, and vow not to repeat the negative actions in future. This was, after all, a key practice we'd been taught for healing and purification. The inability of Sogyal and Rigpa to follow those four powers did as much to send us away from Rigpa as did the abuse. Since not one of us remains in

Rigpa, I think I can speak for all those who expressed our thoughts in this feedback when I say that management never did manage to behave in a way that encouraged us to trust in them again.

I also posted our suggestions on the *What Now?* Blog. One commenter said:

> *'I went to a meeting with the sangha about the letter of the eight students. There were also some people talking about pure perception. SL did nothing wrong. The problem was that we could not yet see the pure perception. We talked on different levels. I did not know about the way they use pure perception in Rigpa. But it motivated me very much to stop with Rigpa. On the other hand I don't trust many sangha members anymore. It is a conspiracy of silence. Many were in Lerab Ling and it was beautiful. So I feel betrayed by people who knew and said nothing but stayed. Then one has to lie to oneself and make a construct of pure perception. Very unhealthy for your mind. I think not only Sogyal Lakar but also quite a few long term students need help against their brainwash ...*
>
> *'I do not know if any professional can help Sogyal Lakar. He has this behaviour for 30 years and never wanted to give up. He always got away with it. In fact in many European countries there are laws that could bring him to prison for his behaviour. He did a lot of damage to people.'*

And another:

> *'The female "sangha leader" to whom I brought some of my concerns about Sogyal Lakar's behaviour around the time of the lawsuit in the 90's, basically told me to "shut up" and*

*that I had no right to ask questions because I was obviously
an ignorant "new student" who didn't have a clue about
Sogyal Lakar's teaching methods, and didn't understand
that his every drool and hiccup and punch was a teaching
from the Buddha. I feel that the senior students who enabled
and hid his behaviour should either resign or go into mind-
heart cleansing retreat or therapy from therapists outside of
Rigpa. I left Rigpa at the time of the lawsuit. I am now
happily studying with another Tibetan teacher—one not of
the so-called "crazy wisdom" variety.'*

One comment on this post introduced me to the term
'narcissistic personality disorder' and I realised that those who'd
struggled with these kinds of issues for years had a great deal of
important knowledge to share.

*I am rather pessimistic based on my own cult experiences
with two abusive Tibetan Buddhist teachers. They both had
a type of a narcissistic personality disorder and Sogyal Lakar
seems to suffer from this too. To say it straightforwardly: the
healing he needs would need his admitting of his
wrongdoings and harm. For someone with a narcissistic
personality disorder this is a step they can't take—or if they
do it, they don't mean it honestly.*

*At the end I am pessimistic about changing Sogyal Lakar—
he might play or perform change—but it won't be real
change. His character—sorry to say it—appears far too
rotten and spoiled. There are anti-social or mentally sick
patterns that are far too deep and grave to achieve a real
change in his personality traits.*

However, though I am pessimistic with respect to Sogyal Lakar and his organisation, I think some people who wake up now will benefit from these activities by finally leaving the organisation and by settling with genuine and healthy teachers.

Though some declared that they couldn't trust any Tibetan lama, others left comments that assured people that there were healthy Tibetan teachers. These were of enormous benefit to people, like me, who needed to believe that not all lamas engaged in unethical behaviour. After being reassured that Mingyur Rinpoche was such a teacher, I joined an online course with his group studying Mahamudra, which is similar to Dzogchen. Receiving teachings from a teacher with a good reputation was a great support in coming to discover where Rigpa had gone wrong, and for keeping my appreciation for the dharma alive. Though I had set up these support systems for others, I was already reaping the benefits of them myself.

Other kinds of responses also began to appear. One commentator said that he'd figured it all out decades ago, that Sogyal was perfect, and that if people felt more burned than blessed by him then they'd either chosen the wrong teacher for them or stayed long after they should have left. He subscribed to the view that if your ordinary thinking mind wasn't blown through gentle and loving means then 'seemingly harsh methods might do the trick.'

He suggested that those writing the blog were on a witch hunt and that one day it would be over and we'd remember the blessing, teachings, transmissions, introductions, pointing outs and divine love that we received from Sogyal. The comment ended with a prayer that Sogyal remain in our hearts. Needless to say, such an attitude didn't go across well in some quarters.

The response from another commenter pulled out the farce in this view:

> 'This is a killer argument; it's calculated to silence criticism. It's not factual at all; it's not precise; it's not Dzogchen; it's just arrogant! You don't receive divine love from your master; the so called divine love is your one true being; it's the nature of your mind; it's you! See how dependent, addicted and subordinate you have been made … I will remember for the rest of my life, how I have been abused, but fortunately I woke up.'

And so the detailed and sometimes explosive discussions on the blog began.

10
SOGYAL'S RESPONSE

What was Sogyal thinking about the letter, I wondered? Had he realised he'd actually hurt people? Would he apologise? Would management resign? These seemed like the right things to do.

Some blog comments express our hopes:

'If this is handled in an open and compassionate way, in which students can be assured of transparency, it could strengthen Rigpa. Imagine the teachings that could come from this experience if it's not white washed and swept under the rug.'

And a response to that:

'Oh come on. Thirty plus years of getting away with it. I doubt he's gonna change now. He may say he is going to, but only when the cash flow starts to slow. This guy is sick, abuse is abuse; full stop. What's he done? Gone off to sulk (he's not teaching at the ngondro retreat). And this is not just Rigpa / Sogyal Lakar; all these lama's think they are better and beyond.'

I checked my inbox every day for some response from Sogyal and Rigpa management. A week later the sangha received a letter from Sogyal. I looked for the apology and found none, no indication of any acceptance of responsibility or of regret or concern for the students he'd harmed. The letter follows with my thoughts on it in italics:

July 20, 2017

Hello...

I'm writing to you as a dear member of our sangha, and therefore someone who has a special place in my heart. As you probably know, recently a number of people have been speaking out very critically about my behaviour as a Buddhist teacher. Some who have been my students, and whom I love, have expressed feelings of hurt and distrust from their experience of following me as a teacher.

I understand, too, that this news has given rise to a certain amount of pain and confusion within our community. I cannot begin to express to you just how much all of this saddens and distresses me.

It appeared to me that what saddened him wasn't that he abused his students, but that they'd spoken out about it.

I have spent my whole life trying my best to serve the Buddhadharma, to bring these teachings to the West, and not a day goes by when I am not thinking about the

88

welfare of my students, holding them in my heart, and feeling concern and responsibility for their spiritual path. It's clear now, though, that a number of people do feel very disappointed and hurt, and are looking for answers and changes. Please know that I take this very seriously and I will not ignore it. I am clear in my own mind that I have never, ever, acted towards anyone with a motive of selfish gain or harmful intent. This is unthinkable for me.

How can someone who has drawn blood on someone not realise that they have harmed that person?

At the same time, I need to hear and acknowledge the experiences that some of my students have spoken of, and over the last few days I have been reflecting very deeply on what course I need to take, how to address these issues.

Already, I am seeking advice from masters who have a genuine care and concern for Rigpa, such as Dzongsar Khyentse Rinpoche and Mingyur Rinpoche and others, about what we should do. And I will honour their guidance.

The letter writers asked that he take advice from HH the Dalai Lama, the one Tibetan Buddhist teacher who has made his stance on abuse clear, but his name is noticeably lacking here.

As I have mentioned to you before, according to astrological predictions, this year and the next two years are a period when obstacles can arise for my health and for my life in general. This was confirmed to me a number of years ago by Kyabjé Trulshik Rinpoche, and then again later by Orgyen Tobgyal Rinpoche. I have decided therefore to follow their advice and to enter into retreat as soon as possible. This is something I have been yearning to do for many years and I feel now is the right moment to do this. While I am on retreat, I intend to reflect deeply about myself, about how best to support students, and about the future of Rigpa.

At the moment, I am focusing deeply on the Lojong teachings—training the mind in compassion—and one verse in particular that guides me, and is continually on my mind, is:

"In all my actions may I examine my mind, and whenever a negative thought or emotion arises, since it endangers myself and others, I will firmly face and avert it."

I figured that if he'd been doing this all along, he wouldn't have lashed out at his students in anger in the first place. And why, I wondered, didn't he say he was practicing purifying his karma with Vajrasattva practice, especially considering that the whole sangha has been doing the practice for him with the aim of improving his health?

I am constantly watching my own mind, with mindfulness and awareness, so as to be truly compassionate in all my words and actions. So the teachings of Dzogchen and lojong are very much the focus of my own reflection and practice right now. In some ways, you could say that my retreat has already begun.

My being on retreat like this will open the opportunity for other teachers to take a more prominent part in guiding and advising the Rigpa sangha, and I will request them to do so. Simultaneously, it will also be the right time for me to hand over the work of Rigpa to my trusted students and to take a full step back.

These 'trusted students', however, enabled and covered up the abuse for decades.

If you just think about all the many extraordinary teachings I have given over the years, there is an incredible wealth of dharma. In some ways, there is not much more teaching that you need—there is enough for one whole lifetime, at least! So let's focus on putting these teachings into action, through reflection and practice.

Yet I will of course still be there for you all, sharing teachings and guidance from my retreat, and meeting with you whenever the time is right. I will plan this out therefore please don't for one moment think that you will be left alone or abandoned!

In a way, going into retreat now will be a real preparation for my own death. After all, you need to realize: life is impermanent. We all have to die one day. And we never know when. As one great master once put it, 'Teaching the dharma and helping people is wonderful, but remember: you have to die.' Every one of us will need to face ourselves when we die; therefore we really need to be prepared.

How is talking about his death relevant as a response to the letter by the eight students? It seemed transparently manipulative to me.

I am so grateful to you all, for your dedication, and especially for the love and support that you are showing to each other in this challenging time. It is extremely important now that we strengthen and build upon the deep spirit of friendship, openness, and genuine care that already exists in our sangha.

Where is the 'genuine care' in a sangha when people have faced abuse for decades without support or redress for those who raised the issue?

I encourage you all to reach out to one another, and look after one another, to listen to each other, and care for one another in the loving, compassionate and open spirit of the Buddha's teachings.

I know that many of you are wrestling with uncomfortable questions and doubts, right now. At the same time, please don't forget all of the good things and the bigger picture of our work. I know many of you have directly experienced the incredible blessings of the teachings, and the transformations they can bring, and that many of you feel love and gratitude towards me.

Don't ever forget the most important thing of all: these incredible teachings that we have shared together, and especially the priceless teachings of Dzogpachenpo. We have lived through such extraordinary moments together, where we all experienced the very deepest aspect of our bodhichitta, our buddha nature, the ultimate nature of mind. How can we not remember? We need to keep these teachings constantly in our minds and to hold them, so they will last long, long into the future. They cannot die.

I will also pray and practice for healing and understanding to prevail and, in the spirit of the great Kadampa masters of the past, take the suffering upon myself and give happiness and love to others.

This sounded like empty words to me. Truly taking the suffering on yourself would be saying, 'Yes, I did these things, and I'm sorry I hurt you.'

From the bottom of my heart, I encourage all of you to never ever give up on the teachings or on each other, but to focus single-mindedly on practising the genuine and unfailing dharma, fuelled by the vast motivation of bodhichitta, held within the profound and spacious view of non-duality and guided by the blessings of all the masters of our lineage.

These are the immediate thoughts I felt a strong urge to share with you right now. I will reflect further and have more to say soon.

With love & blessings,

Sogyal Rinpoche

But was what we learned the genuine dharma you said it was? Look what kind of people it produced. How is abuse and its cover up the actions of people practicing genuine dharma 'fuelled by the vast motivation of bodhichitta'?

***

I and others were very disappointed in this response. Though he said, 'Please know that I take this very seriously and I will not ignore it,' he didn't even attempt to reply to the issues raised by the eight or answer the questions they asked. Instead, he attempted to move our perception away from the problem—a method I would see regularly in further communications. I hoped that his 'self-reflection' would bring him the clarity to see that he must change his behaviour.

Looking back, given what I now know, this was a rather naive hope. One of the members of the *What Now?* Facebook group told me she asked one of his attendants if Sogyal was happy when in retreat in Australia. The attendant laughed saying, '*Our lama is doing everything else except retreat in Australia!*' Others said that from what they had seen from their time close to him, he spent his time having sex and massages and watching movies. Apart from his health issues, why would this new retreat be any different?

We discovered that he had immediately left France and gone to Thailand, which incidentally doesn't have an extradition treaty with France. Rather than going into retreat, it seemed to many as if he was simply running away and leaving a mess behind him. Where, I wondered, was the courage of the bodhisattva warrior that you'd expect to see from a great master?

The following comments left on the blog express the kinds of feelings people had about his response:

'I have just read SL's [Sogyal Lakar's] response to The Letter. He says, among other things, that he is going into retreat to reflect on the state of the sangha and because of expected obstacles and ill health, prepare for his eventual passing. And that all his great and valuable teachings will stand on their own and can now be utilized by all.

My opinions about SL may seem uncompassionate to all of you, but I don't view Buddhism as a passivist practice. It is a practice of integrity, courage, real devotion and the strength to face what one's dualistic concepts and conditioning don't want to face. SL is not going into retreat, he is going into hiding. If he had real integrity and compassion he would face the music at full volume. Teachings are not 'great' unless the teacher lives it. SL does not. I will not view his teachings for they are no example of what the lived meaning should be. But I will learn from his bad example. I wish the best for the sangha to wade through the mess he has left them.'

And:

'The letter of SL is offending to me: it does not take responsibility. It does not explain this behaviour. And on top he plays the card of death and retreat, frightening all those who depend on him. Instead of retreat, showing up is much more courageous, like a bodhisattva warrior, or/and getting advice from a Western psychologist (NOT involved in Buddhism). Addiction and Narcissism are heavy patterns.'

Sogyal's letter to the eight was very similar to what went to the sangha, and so I only reproduce here what was different to the above email.

'I have only ever tried to serve the dharma and to teach students to the best of my ability and I can sincerely say that I have never, not for one moment, had any intention other than a genuine wish to benefit others. My conscience is clear on this. But I have to see that hurt has arisen and my intentions and actions have been perceived in another way. You cannot imagine the distress this causes me. Therefore, from the bottom of my heart, I humbly ask your forgiveness.'

On first reading I thought he'd apologised—and some still think that's what he did—but on deeper perusal I realised that he only said that they had misperceived his actions and intentions and was sorry for that. His distress was that he'd been misperceived, not that he'd hurt anyone, so what was he asking forgiveness for? Certainly it wasn't for hurting them.

'Since reading your letter I have been thrown into deep reflection and I'm firmly resolved that if this is the way that my actions are perceived, then I do need to take real action.'

It appears that the only reason he sees to take real action is not because he'd hurt anyone, but because they'd misperceived his actions and intentions.

'As many masters have said, Rigpa is a very important vehicle for the Vajrayana and I don't want to see our sangha, or the greater vision of our work, which has been the collective effort of many great masters and many students, be harmed or affected in any way. If I am the problem, that can be solved. There's no need to bring everything down. I implore you to keep this bigger picture in mind.'

He thinks they want to 'bring everything down'? Did he not read the letter where they state their intention very clearly?

'I will gather some of my ablest students and ask them to tell me very frankly and openly what they think needs to change in order to prevent this kind of misunderstanding in the future.'

Misunderstanding? This isn't just a misunderstanding, this is about someone behaving in a criminal fashion!

'I would be happy to meet you one day if it might help in any way. I will truly listen and talk to you.'

He has their numbers, and up until this point of time eighteen months later, Sogyal has not contacted any of the eight.

***

97

The eight met, talked and replied to Sogyal, thanking him for his response, saying they were 'encouraged' by his 'willingness to engage in a dialogue' and that he was taking the issue very seriously. They asked him to 'seek counsel from His Holiness the Dalai Lama', and pointed out that in his letter he repeatedly mentioned the manner in which his actions have been 'perceived' whereas 'the critical issue here is not about our and others' perception; it is about how your actions have caused actual harm to many people.'

They also noted that 'you have not, in your response to us, nor has anyone within Rigpa, denied that you have done the things that we asserted', and:

> 'If anything we said in our first letter, or this communication, is untrue, then, being one of the most prominent Tibetan Buddhist lamas in the world, you are obliged to clearly and compellingly refute our assertions. If you do not refute them, are you not risking the Buddhaharma being harmed? If, however, our assertions are true, they must be acknowledged and fundamental corrections of behaviour must be made.

> 'Or, there is another way. You could say to the entire sangha, "This is who I am and how I act. I can use violence how I want. I can coerce students to have sex. I will have sex with any young woman I meet, even your daughters who you proudly offer to me in service. I can live and act as I wish. You make the choice if you want to study with me or not."

They reminded him that they 'harbour no ill-will toward' him. And said:

> 'We do not feel that we have broken samaya, trust, or our heart connection with you and others. We are clear that it is your actions towards us that have broken that trust. In your response to us, we had hoped that you would take responsibility and begin to try to repair this. However, instead of moving towards repairing, you ask for forgiveness for our misunderstanding, not for your actions. What kind of forgiveness is this?'

They also explained how they had not made the letter public, nor had they taken any media interviews despite receiving requests, and they reminded him that he hadn't answered their questions laid out in the original letter.

> 'Because of the gravity of the situation, we hope that you will act with a sense of urgency in the coming days and either explain to everybody how your behaviour, that we elucidated in the first letter, is acceptable, or else immediately refrain from such harmful actions.'

No reply to this letter ever came. And the central question—'If your striking and punching us and others, and having sex with your students and married women, and funding your sybaritic lifestyle with students' donations, is actually the ethical and compassionate behaviour of a Buddhist teacher, please explain to us how it is?'—was never answered. What I read into that lack of response was that he really didn't care, not about the eight or about any of his students.

II
RESPONSES FROM LAMAS AND OTHERS

The July letter to Sogyal written by the eight students was also sent to His Holiness the Dalai Lama, Mingyur Rinpoche and Dzongsar Khyentse Rinpoche, and I waited for their response, hoping that they would have some words of sense on the matter, something to show that basic ethics could not be thrown away or somehow superseded by Vajrayana.

The first public response on the matter of Sogyal's abuse came from the French monk Matthieu Ricard on July 29, 2017 on his personal blog. Matthieu assures me that he is not a teacher, not a lama, not a 'representative' or 'authority' within Buddhism; he is a translator, interpreter and occasionally a writer and speaker. However, he is knowledgeable about Buddhadharma and highly respected in Buddhist circles, so we truly appreciated his willingness to share his point of view.

He said:

'I know two of the authors of the letter and I consider them honest and trustworthy. The behaviour described in this letter and in the other past testimonies is obviously unacceptable—from the point of view of ordinary morality and especially from that of Buddhist ethics. This is all the more so given the considerable suffering that has resulted from such actions.'

Reading what he wrote—which backed up the Dalai Lama's point of view—was a great relief to victims and those who also knew the behaviour was unacceptable.

An extensive excerpt he gave from *The Treasury of Precious Qualities* by Rigdzin Jigme Lingpa made it clear that Sogyal was not the kind of teacher one should follow. Though most of us students didn't see what was going on behind the scenes and so couldn't truly examine Sogyal, I realised that had I really thought about it, I would have seen his unsuitability as a spiritual teacher just from the behaviour I had seen, and that the reasons I continued to go to retreats had a lot to do with it being a nice summer holiday and being with like-minded people. But now, I realised, a lot of them were not like-minded at all. I did not want to be associated with people who thought abuse was acceptable in any shape or form.

Matthieu Ricard also pointed out that His Holiness the Dalai Lama could not be held responsible because, unlike the Pope in the Catholic Church, he was not a central authority and that every teacher and dharma centre was entirely independent of each other. Teachers could ignore him if they wished and no authority checked that everyone was doing the right thing. Certainly Rigpa, who at the time of writing still have him listed on their website as a patron, ignored his advice that students of abusive teachers should speak up. They never sent any information to the sangha that showed His Holiness's perspective on the matter. On the other hand, critics of His

Holiness ignored this point of his not having any power over the behaviour or beliefs of other lamas.

The best informed people throughout this debacle were those who were active in the *What Now?* Facebook group—we shared everything, be it a fundamentalist or wider view.

His Holiness the Dalai Lama first made reference to Sogyal Rinpoche and the letter from his former students at the National Seminar on Buddhism in Ladakh, India on August 1, 2017.

> *'Many years ago in Dharamshala at a Western Teachers Conference, some Western Buddhist teachers mentioned some Zen masters and Tibetan Buddhist masters had created a very bad impression among people. Then I told them; these people do not follow Buddha's advice, Buddha's teaching. We cannot do. So the only thing is to make it public, through newspapers, through the radio. Make it public! These lamas, although they don't care about Buddha's teaching, they may care about their face [points at his face, indicating shame]. I told them at that conference, almost 15 years ago I think. Now, recently Sogyal Rinpoche; my very good friend, but he's disgraced. So some of his own students have now made public their criticism.'*

This was the beginning of several mentions of Rigpa or Sogyal that His Holiness made over the next six months, and in each instance he reiterated his position as he had stated it back in 1993. Those of us who sought a wider view than what we'd received in Rigpa found much support and solace from his words. His support for using our common sense and discernment in how we interpreted the kinds of beliefs that had been misused in the service of Sogyal's every whim was enormously heartening, and without it, many more would have left Buddhism entirely.

Mingyur Rinpoche's statement came out on the 9th of August 2017 in an article in *Lion's Roar* titled 'When a Buddhist Teacher Crosses the Line' and Dzongsar Khyentse's response appeared on Facebook on the 15th of August titled 'Guru and Student in the Vajrayana.' These two teachers had often taught at Rigpa, and were greatly respected by most of us at the time. However, since then Dzongsar Khyentse has published some ill-conceived Facebook posts which make him appear to many as misogynistic, sexist, emotionally immature, culturally prejudiced, self-serving, and lacking in any sign of compassion for victims. These posts, most of all a mock sexual-slave contract suggested as a contract between students and teachers, has lost him the respect of many and damaged his reputation as a teacher worth following.

He has, however, spoken more about the issues raised by Sogyal's abuse than any other lama—doing a tour of European Rigpa Centres early in 2018 on the topic—and I honour his willingness to engage with the topic, especially when other lamas simply do not want to get involved. He stuck his neck out when others were not prepared to do so, and at least attempted to clarify some essential points of Vajrayana, even though he confused many with his contradictions, and disappointed a great many with what came to be seen as a fundamentalist interpretation of Tibetan Buddhism.

He allowed me and others to ask questions by email during those talks, and even did me the courtesy of reading some of my blog posts on the topic of cults. Unfortunately, he misquoted me, mocked me for a view I didn't state, and misinterpreted other things I'd said. He also didn't respond fully to many of the students' questions, side stepping the core issues, and when pinned down on the crucial points, he upheld Sogyal's insistence that once you've taken a teacher, you must not criticise, must at least try to obey his every wish, and see his every action as enlightened action, no matter what it is. I suspect he and other fundamentalists feel that without these instructions Vajrayana will lose its transformative power. In my experience, however, the power of the Vajrayana does not depend on following these instructions—in my experience, the power of Vajrayana comes from doing the practices, not in slavishly following the teacher.

Dzongsar Khyentse's first statement on the matter of Sogyal's abuse was a rambling 10,000 word Facebook post without paragraph breaks that presented apparently conflicting viewpoints. One journalist accused him of having a 'foot in both camps'. He made a distinction between Sogyal as a 'Vajrayana guru' and him as a 'Buddhist teacher', which he said are 'totally different roles—even when both roles are fulfilled by one person'. This differentiation between public and spiritual perspectives is an angle that Rigpa (which he is now advising) also takes in dealing with public perception. They do what is required to satisfy the Charity Commission, but do not change the interpretation of Vajrayana that enabled the abuse, and so the same belief system that created this toxic culture in Rigpa still exists.

This tactic allowed him, on one hand, to condemn Sogyal's behaviour as inappropriate for a Buddhist teacher, but on the other hand insist that:

'The key point here is that if his students had received a Vajrayana initiation, if at the time they received it they were fully aware that it was a Vajrayana initiation, and if Sogyal Rinpoche had made sure that all the necessary prerequisites has been adhered to and fulfilled, then *from the Vajrayana point of view, there is nothing wrong with Sogyal Rinpoche's subsequent actions.*'

Though Sogyal had hit people before they had any empowerments, and women had even been coerced into his harem on their first retreat, many of those abused did fulfil 'the necessary prerequisites'. For those people, Dzongsar Khyentse's comments weren't at all helpful as he was saying that Sogyal had done nothing wrong to them. His words were a big disappointment to those who had previously thought Dzongsar Khyentse was a lama not afraid to challenge aspects of his religion. He simply reiterated the very beliefs that had caused the problems in the first place.

He identified the cause of the problem not as Sogyal's behaviour or the beliefs taught in Rigpa or how they were interpreted or put into practice, but that the students did not understand Vajrayana. The only blame he put on Sogyal was that he must not have taught his students properly—the suggestion being that otherwise they would not have complained. He did not categorically say that Sogyal's abusive behaviour was wrong, rather that it was only wrong if the students weren't 'properly prepared'. And though he spoke on the matter at various times after that, he never moved from this stance in subsequent comments.

The real problem is that Sogyal used certain teachings to his advantage at the expense of the well-being of his students. Due to secrecy and lies about his behaviour, students had no chance of a true evaluation of him. Then once within the organisation, they were subjected to what could easily be seen as brainwashing or gaslighting that altered their perception of his behaviour such that they saw it as acceptable. And if they joined upper management or the inner circle and experienced or witnessed abuse, the trauma-bonding dynamics further confused their ability to see what was truly happening to them. These are the real problems, not some misunderstanding of vajrayana.

In contrast, Mingyur Rinpoche's article, 'When a Buddhist Teacher Crosses the Line', was in-depth, nuanced and helpful. His compassion for the victims and his depth of understanding of the real meaning of the problematic beliefs shone through in his treatment of the topic of unethical behaviour by Vajrayana gurus, yet he never mentioned Sogyal by name or directly criticised him—thus staying within what is considered right behaviour in Tibetan society. He covered: ethics in Vajrayana—'Vajrayana practice is rooted in the ideals of nonviolence and great compassion. There is no Vajrayana without them;' finding a genuine teacher—'A genuine teacher should uphold their vows and precepts;' leaving a teacher—'If someone is being harmed, the safety of the victim comes first. This is not a Buddhist principle. This is a basic human value and should never be violated;' serious ethical violations— 'Physical, sexual, and psychological abuse are not teaching tools'; crazy wisdom—'We must distinguish teachers who are eccentric or provocative, but ultimately compassionate and skilful, from those who are actually harming students and causing trauma'; and Buddhism in the modern world—' It should go without saying that when schools, businesses, and other public institutions are expected to adhere to a code of conduct and the laws of the land, then spiritual organizations should be role models of ethical behaviour. And teachers even more so.'

What a relief! Mingyur Rinpoche's article heartened those who were seeking reassurance that unethical or abusive behaviour on the part of a lama was not an accepted part of Tibetan Buddhism, and people saw in it something totally authentic to the traditional teachings but with a healthy dose of common sense. And yet, when Rigpa sent out materials to students to help them understand the issue, they neglected to send either this or the notes from His Holiness's 1993 conference to students. With this lack, Rigpa made their stance clear: not only were they not giving any credibility to the views of two of the most respected Tibetan Lamas with a reputation for valuing ethics, but also they were withholding important information from members because it did not match their 'party line'.

Next Sangye heard from Orgyen Tobgyal Rinpoche who often taught Vajrayana at Lerab Ling. He replied to a letter Sangye sent to him, and after saying how he couldn't judge Sogyal, he then spent most of the letter talking about how much good Sogyal had done, and then finished by saying it was too late for Sangye to 'turn against him' after so long as his student and that to do so was a samaya breakage.

This makes the assumption that the letter indicates a 'turning against' Sogyal rather than the simple truth-telling that it was, and suggests that the eight would go to hell for speaking up. The words showed no compassion at all for the victims and plenty of support for the perpetrator. Later in the year, during a talk at the Paris centre, Orgyen Tobgyal Rinpoche said about spiritual teachers, '*Such great beings, whether it corresponds to western ideas or not, if they kill someone, it's fine,*' and, '*Beating hard increases wisdom.*'

In Lerab Ling during the Dzogchen retreat in September 2017, Khenpo Namdrol mentioned the matter of the letter. He also showed no compassion for the victims and did not address Sogyal's behaviour, instead he denigrated the letter writers, said they were possessed by demons, and attacked them for breaking the silence. He said that the letter was '*an attempt to not only just disparage the master, but to try to destroy him and everything that he's done.*' And yet the letter makes it quite clear that this was NOT their intention. For him, speaking out about the abuse was '*the poorest choice they could have made, forever.*'

At the end of his talk the assembly clapped, and someone in Rigpa with access to the recording consequently 'leaked' the video.

This was not helpful for anyone looking for a view that recognised that what Sogyal had done was wrong, but it must have been a great support to those who didn't want to re-evaluate the Rigpa 'party line'. The audience even clapped at the end!

He also expressed a common view we hear from some Tibetan lamas when they feel their religion is threatened: '*Never go off track just following your own whims or the customs of modern society.*' The assumptions here are: any desire for change from Westerners must be just a 'whim' and so not important; and following the customs of modern society—such as abuse being against the law—will lead you 'off track'.

Dzongsar Khyentse also promotes this line of thinking. In one Facebook post in early 2019 he said, 'Americans may today be damaging the dharma more seriously than the Chinese did during the entire Cultural Revolution.' Unfortunately, as comments on that post show, sycophants seem all too happy to lap up such ideas without examination.

We certainly must not change dharma on a whim, or to make the practice more comfortable for our egos, but that is not what's happening here. Addressing the issue of abusive behaviour is no whim, and why shouldn't Vajrayana conform to the customs of modern society where those customs are in line with the Buddha's teachings on non-harming.

Khenpo Namdrol even suggested that the eight were possessed by demons. Unfortunately, this man is another of Rigpa's 'spiritual advisors'.

As time passed, some Western Buddhist teachers added their opinion, but many, and practically all native Tibetans apart from those already mentioned, simply remained quiet, not wanting to get involved or put themselves in a position where they could be seen to be criticising another teacher. We did, however, find references to things teachers had said in response to earlier scandals and found an unfortunate tendency to point the finger to the victim. Sometimes this took the form of reminding him or her to use common sense and not to allow others to exert power over oneself. This kind of approach does empower the victim to act instead of being passive and allowing others to take advantage of oneself, but in a situation where there is a huge power imbalance and where the student feels unable to say, 'No,' because they are trying very hard to be a good student, it shows a lack of understanding of the complexity of the situation.

It does no good to, on one hand, say, 'You must do as your lama says without criticism or complaint,' and on the other hand say, 'You must use your common sense and not do or accept anything you don't agree with.' All you're doing is putting the student in a double bind. Such instructions cannot be given in isolation. They need qualifications such as: 'Do as your lama says *unless* he or she asks you to do something unethical or against the dharma.'

All too often, abusive behaviour on the part of Sogyal and others was given little or no mention by teachers, even where the teacher did say clearly that it was inappropriate or unethical. Robert Thurman on a podcast on the topic of abuse in Buddhism shared one often-mentioned idea that fostered spiritual belittling of victims. It goes like this: if a student was 'ready' for an advanced level of 'teaching', even if it was given by someone who was 'somewhat abusive but not perfectly enlightened', a disciple who was advanced enough in their spiritual practice to still see that teacher as a Buddha would be able to use this advanced level of teaching/abuse to 'transform their own faults'. So for that disciple the behaviour was not harmful because 'they had an advanced level of something they obtained from previous lives such that it is possible that they could use something dished out to them from an impure vessel to go beyond.'

This is a comforting point for those who did feel that they experienced some benefit from Sogyal's violence, but such an idea is assuming that abuse is a *legitimate* teaching method, even if only for advanced students. It also feeds students egos and leads them to victim blame: they pretend to be such an 'advanced' student because they want to be seen as a great spiritual practitioner, and they look down on those who consider they were abused, thinking that they were simply not spiritually evolved enough to see it as helpful.

Venerable Thubten Choden gave a series of talks, available on YouTube, inspired by the revelations of abuse in Rigpa which corrected misunderstandings of the relevant teachings and viewed the whole situation with compassion and wisdom. Later Venerable Jetsun Tenzin Palmo—the subject of the book *Cave in the Snow* by Vicki McKenzie—opened up on the topic in reply to an email request, and I found her clarity in laying the responsibility clearly at the feet of the guru most refreshing: 'Do not feel guilty about seeing and acknowledging where the boundaries have been overstepped by the teacher. The fault is with limitations and wrong conduct of the guru.'

There are teachers who see clearly. Those interested in the teachings of Tibetan Buddhism just have to find them.

12
THE *WHAT NOW?* GROUP

'Trauma isolates; the group re-creates a sense of belonging. Trauma shames and stigmatizes; the group bears witness and affirms. Trauma degrades the victim; the group exalts her. Trauma dehumanizes the victim; the group restores her humanity.' Trauma and Recovery, Judith Herman, M. D.

The *What Now?* blog was only ever the outer aspect of the *What Now?* group. Those in the secret Facebook group rarely ever commented on the blog. It was too public for most of them. The really deep conversations where we helped each other to process the revelations and what they meant for our relationship to the guru and to our spiritual practice happened in the Facebook group.

The *What Now?* Facebook group processing was invaluable for all of us involved, and I will be always grateful to those in the group, especially those who shared their research with us all. Members shared links to articles and books they thought would be helpful for healing and these became the basis for many deep conversations. I could never have found all those helpful quotes and articles myself. The group was an enormous assistance to me in my own processing, assisting me to examine the issues deeply and research relevant areas of which I had no

113

previous knowledge. It was a healing and educational process for me, which left me with many deep friendships forged in the fire of Sogyal's abuse.

Those of us not directly affected by the abuse had our eyes and hearts opened to the suffering of those who had in a way we never could have without that group. Because of our direct communication with the survivors, we couldn't have treated them as callously as Rigpa management appeared to do in their attempts to minimise the fallout of the revelations.

In the early days, we had a wide variety of views expressed in the group, and it soon became clear that some were trying to justify Sogyal's abuse by using the same thinking that had enabled the abuse and helped cover it up all along. Spouting the Rigpa 'party line'—that Sogyal was a crazy wisdom master and therefore even though his behaviour looked harmful it actually wasn't—tended to re-traumatise victims of abuse who'd had those same ideas preached at them as a way of condoning the abuse and shutting up the abused student when they complained about their treatment. This sent the abuse survivors right back into the situation that had contributed to their trauma. The moderators decided that above all we had to protect those who had been abused from being re-traumatised. The group's focus we decided had to, above all, be on supporting those who had been abused—a Sogyal supporter once accused us of doing this as if it were a fault!

Those who had been abused had never been protected within Rigpa, never had a place where their concerns were taken seriously, so it was vital that the *What Now?* group be a safe place for them to open up. We aimed to help them heal, and so whenever a conflict arose, we always took the victims' safety over and above anyone else's right to say what they felt. Some didn't like that bias, but I felt we were righting the wrongs of decades of neglect by Rigpa management.

An important first step in healing was for victims to realize they were not alone and isolated, to experience being heard and taken seriously and not shamed or made to feel guilty or inadequate as they'd been in Rigpa. We heard from many students who had left Rigpa years ago and were relieved to finally be able to talk about their experience with others. Some had never spoken about their treatment for over twenty years, and having a space to do so was a great relief for them. They said how lonely they'd felt leaving without such support.

We had to stop people from trying to convince victims that they hadn't experienced what they thought they had, so we insisted that everyone honour each other's experiences as being true—at least for them. We saw in some people's thoughts about crazy wisdom, pure perception, devotion, and samaya the same kind of attempts at manipulation of people's perception as that undertaken by Rigpa management. I remember telling people often:

'You don't have to tell us all this. We all know it. We were students too. The problem is that those beliefs enabled this abuse, so repeating them again and again simply doesn't help. It does not justify the abuse. It never did and it never will.'

For some, however, it did justify it. Their belief in the 'party line' was greater than their sense of compassion for people who'd been harmed.

If there was any truth in these beliefs that had enabled the abuse, I figured that we must have interpreted them wrong somehow. If we'd got them right, the result would have been people who exhibited wisdom and compassion, not people who didn't recognise harmful behaviour when they saw it, and who treated those who were traumatised with contempt rather than compassion.

Acknowledging the harm Sogyal caused was a necessary part of healing from trauma for victims, bystanders and ordinary students like me who were appalled by the revelations. The moderators were constantly having to remind people to have a bit of compassion for those who had been abused—mind boggling in a Buddhist community!

On the other hand, some people saw legal action as the only solution to the issue of abuse by gurus. They declared Sogyal's behaviour criminal and demanded that he be brought to justice in a court of law. Generally these were people who had left Sogyal and Rigpa many years previously, some after very distressing experiences, and whose attempts to stop his behaviour had had little effect. Legal action wasn't my first option for stopping Sogyal's behaviour, but I did see that if all else failed, a successful legal challenge would bring a strong message to other gurus as to what would happen if they flouted the law.

Most of the group didn't want to see Sogyal in a prison, and many didn't think it would help solve the problem of a community who saw the abuse as normal. Many of us were also very aware of the emotional toll legal action would take on anyone bringing a case for damages, and the injunction in Tibetan Buddhism against criticising one's guru meant that it would be very hard to get people to come forward.

Unfortunately, rather than allow others to have more moderate feelings on legal action, some members of the group tried to push survivors of abuse into setting legal action into motion. The moderators decided on a policy of not allowing calls for legal action in the group because we didn't want abuse survivors to feel manipulated into fulfilling someone else's agenda—manipulation on someone else's agenda had, after all, been what had happened to them in Rigpa. We needed to support people in making their own decisions, not push them into a decision someone else wanted them to make, particularly when taking legal action would likely result in some degree of re-traumatisation.

As Judith Herman says in her book *Trauma and Recovery*:

'In the matter of criminal reporting, as in all other matters, the choice must rest with the survivor. A decision to report ideally opens the door to social restitution. In reality, however, this decision engages the survivor with a legal system that may be indifferent or hostile to her. Even at best, the survivor has to expect a marked disparity between her own timetable of recovery and the timetable of the justice system.

Her efforts to re-establish a sense of safety will most likely be undermined by the intrusions of legal proceedings; just as her life is stabilizing, a court date is likely to revive intrusive traumatic symptoms. The decision to seek redress from the justice system, therefore, cannot be made lightly. The survivor must make an informed choice with the full knowledge of risks and benefits; otherwise she will simply be re-traumatized.'

This decision led some people who were pushing for legal action to treat me and the other moderators as their enemy, something I found kind of ridiculous considering that, just like them, I wanted to stop the abuse. Because we didn't push for legal action, they saw us as 'against' them and in their minds placed us in the same category as those defending the perpetrator. It's common for people to think that anyone who doesn't agree with them entirely is somehow against them, and I realised that if you'd been waiting twenty years to bring Sogyal's behaviour to an end, to see people who have only just become aware of the behaviour being less militant than you'd like would be frustrating.

In line with the thinking of the eight students who wrote the July 2017 letter to Sogyal revealing the abuses, we asked people to stick to the facts as they personally knew them. First hand and second accounts were permitted, but no third or fourth-hand accounts, no gossip or conjecture.

The thinking of some of the participants in the group in the early days astounded me. I naively thought that everyone would be as appalled as I was at the revelations, that everyone would realise that something had gone wrong. But some simply refused to believe the 'allegations'. They denied that any of it had taken place. Others had seen Sogyal hitting people or seen worse emotional abuse than most of us, or even been aware of the number of women groomed for his sexual proclivities but felt that since Sogyal was doing it with the aim to bring them benefit, that the result must be benefit. Many genuinely believed that the victim would eventually, in some future lifetime, reap benefit from their abuse. Others blamed the victims, saying that the reason they 'saw' it as abuse was because they didn't have the spiritual ability or capacity to use Sogyal's behaviour towards them as transformation.

Some outright attacked the eight students, calling them liars or making it seem as if they were seeking revenge for some perceived hurt that had no basis in reality. Some cast doubt on their mental stability, and others called them samaya breakers, insinuating (and in some cases being quite direct) that they would go to hell for speaking out against their lama. Some people exhibited classic passive-aggressive responses by appearing to be sympathetic but never missing an opportunity to use their passive words to slide a metaphorical dagger between someone's ribs in defence of Sogyal.

These were all tactics I'd seen used in Rigpa against those who had publicly spoken out about abuse in the past, and I recognised them for what they were—victim blaming designed to turn attention away from the actual problem of the abuse and its perpetrator, and onto the victim, making them out to be an unreliable witness. In most cases, I don't think people knew this was what they were doing, they were just following, without evaluation, the thought patterns and behaviour modelled by management and senior instructors.

Others spent a great deal of time trying to explain how the 'party line' was essentially blaming the victim for something done to them by someone else, but always Sogyal's supporters found a Vajrayana belief to counter any argument that showed Sogyal as a perpetrator of harm.

For some the only thing that was wrong was that eight people had upset their comfortable spiritual world. Those who had spoken up became their enemy, and by supporting the truth-tellers, I'd also made myself a target for their venom. The first arrows came in the *What Now?* group and blog or on personal Facebook posts, and often from people I'd thought had been my friends. It hurt until I learned to take a deep breath before reading any comments.

We made it clear on both the blog and the Facebook group that even though we wanted a space where people could say what they wanted, personal attacks were not allowed. We wanted minimal moderator intervention on the blog in order to not stifle conversation, but made it clear that though opinions were welcome, bullies were not. We first warned, and then, if they didn't change their behaviour, removed anyone who kept attacking people or belittling them.

An old Rigpa friend of mine eventually solidified the split in the sangha by creating the *Transformation* Facebook group which filled up with those who still subscribed to the Rigpa 'party line' and anyone who was 'on the fence' or just wanted to know what people were talking about there. Many found this split in the sangha deeply upsetting. We wanted to believe that as a sangha we had the capacity to hear each other and make the kinds of changes needed to heal what had become a highly toxic situation at the core of the community. Rather than trying to facilitate healing for those Sogyal had harmed, however, Rigpa seemed only concerned about healing the hurt the community felt due to the abuse being revealed to the world.

Though some friends created another Facebook group called *Bridging the Gap*, the gap never was bridged. And it's clear to me now that it never will be.

Gradually the composition of the *What Now?* group became more homogenous as those who denied any wrong doing on Sogyal's part left in favour of the *Transformation* group.

I'd expected pain, but I hadn't expected denial. It seemed weird to me that people who were training in seeing the nature of reality directly could so block their perception with their beliefs, but then I realised just how much of a challenge it is to question one's cherished beliefs, and that such denial likely hid fear. I could understand how someone would want to save themselves from the upset that those of us who'd accepted the abuse as fact were going through. How much more comforting it must be to remain steadfast in one's beliefs, even if they don't accord with everyone else's reality.

The *What Now?* Facebook group was secret, and no one could share what was said there outside the group, but the discussion in the group inspired me to write blogs in which I spoke not just for myself but for all those in the group. Not everyone supported what I wrote or said, though—far from it— and my attempts to remain moderate in my approach—to recognise the good in Tibetan Buddhism and advocate reform rather than discrediting the whole religion—was seen by some as weak, or as an indication that I was secretly working for Rigpa. (I had to laugh at that one, considering that Rigpa management considered me a thorn in their sides.)

One member expresses the view of most in the group:
'I want to say how very important and excellent the What Now? *group has been for me. We have really important and deep conversations on there, sharing our stuff and deep feelings around these issues, as well as sharing facts and suggestions. I feel safe there. I don't see my Rigpa sangha anymore, hardly ever any single person, and they were my*

main friends, and Rigpa was my life, and I have missed my sangha so much. And I have found What Now? *to be a really supportive and useful and altogether wonderful thing. People reveal so much and it is really so 'useful' to me and to others. And it's not soppy sharing; it's proper serious stuff, and deep suggestions and support. We are changing our mindsets/views really and going various ways but are still discussing it all together in a very special way. My whole world view has changed, and they are like a sangha.'*

13
SOGYAL'S RETIREMENT

Roughly a month after the revelations, Sogyal announced his retirement from the role of spiritual director of Rigpa. Many people I knew felt he should have stepped down immediately, as would have been the case in any business situation where such allegations had been made. His letter to the sangha was similar in tone to the previous one, ignoring the issue of his behaviour completely, and speaking only of 'shock and consternation' that the 'criticism' of him had spread across the internet.

Those with whom I corresponded were disappointed with this letter. For so long as Sogyal didn't have the courage to own up to his behaviour and show some compassion for those he'd harmed, rather than showing concern only for his reputation and the continuation of the business that pays his bills, he was only further proving his unworthiness of the role of spiritual teacher.

Soon after this, we finally received a communication from Rigpa management. This set the tone for all future communications, which rather than coming clean about what they'd covered up for decades, they attempted to minimise the fallout rather than actually deal with the problem on a fundamental level—one long term student's response to this was, *'They're circling the wagons.'* Management made attempts to change the culture with moves outlined in this initial communication, but none of it went far enough because underneath there was no willingness to admit that Sogyal had behaved wrongly.

Though initially I was heartened at the inspiring language and the three steps management planned to introduce, over time they consistently failed to live up to the expectations such soothing and inspiring words created. I came to see how their words were used more to manipulate perception away from the issue of Sogyal's behaviour than to communicate honestly.

Of course there were legal aspects to consider, but their legalise and PR speak—it's well-known in some quarters that Rigpa international paid huge amounts of money to a PR firm to help manage 'negative press'—did not impress students of a community whose mission was to teach wisdom and compassion. Here's the main points from the email we received with my responses in italics:

> The allegations that have been made against Sogyal Rinpoche by members of our own community, and which have spread widely in the media and on the internet, are of extreme concern to us all.

The allegations were what they were concerned about, not the abuse.

> We are fully resolved to meet this difficult situation responsibly, sensitively, head-on, and in a way that is completely consistent with the teachings and the spiritual values that we uphold.

In practice their response was insensitive, minimising, and consistent only to the Rigpa 'party line' not the spiritual values of the Buddha's teachings.

After careful consideration and advice from many parties, those of us responsible for the governance and management of Rigpa have agreed to take the following steps:

- We will establish an independent investigation of the allegations of abuse, including those outlined in the letter of 14 July 2017 to Sogyal Rinpoche.

- Immediately, we will launch an international consultation process to establish both a code of conduct and a grievance process for Rigpa.

- As swiftly as possible, we will institute a new 'spiritual body' to guide and advise Rigpa, as indicated by Sogyal Rinpoche in his letter.

Apart from the independent investigation all these steps fell short of expectations.

Channels will be established so that any sangha member has the opportunity to express their wishes, views and concerns.

We could express them, but we didn't receive adequate responses.

Let us be spacious and non-judgmental so that we can truly listen to each other with our whole being, and with compassion and understanding.

It's a pity people didn't pay attention to these last words. They sound so good, but few lived up to them. Even though those in upper management knew that the 'allegations' in the letter from the eight were true—as confirmed later by the independent investigation—they acted as if they weren't true. Did they need an independent investigation to tell them whether the behaviour outlined in the letter happened? No; they needed it to protect their finances by retaining their Charity Commission status as a non-profit organisation.

The other really sad thing about this approach is that they showed no compassion for the victims at all—not a smidgeon. And this lack of honesty and compassion for the abused in Rigpa's communications continued and lost them a huge number of students.

'What about those Sogyal had hurt?' we who didn't doubt the attestations asked.

Some I spoke to decided not to make any decisions or have any opinions on the 'allegations' until the results of the independent investigation came out. Meanwhile, Rigpa's further communications continued to suggest that the 'difficult situation' in which they'd found themselves was due to the publication of the 'allegations', not Sogyal's behaviour, and their attempts at healing, reconciliation, listening and compassion were limited to those who remained in their sangha. Those who recognised their treatment at Sogyal's hands as abuse had mostly all left already, so their attempts at healing did none of them any good.

Some in national management positions who had previously seen their treatment as a blessing did resign after re-appraising their experiences. Such a step wasn't taken easily, and they faced a difficult transition from devoted student who'd accepted their abusive treatment as part of Vajrayana to one who recognised that they had, in fact, been the victim of abuse.

I understand why some decided to simply ignore it all and continue as if nothing had happened. They didn't want their spiritual world shaken; they wanted to get back to the business of study and practice as soon as possible. And Rigpa management obliged them by apparently focusing on doing just that.

14
THE D.A.R.V.O RESPONSE

The group nature of the revelations, their dissemination to every member of the Dzogchen Mandala, and the internet, in particular the *What Now?* group, had a huge effect on the way the abuse scandal played out for students. During previous revelations about Sogyal's behaviour by individuals over the years, students had discovered the details and investigated (or not) related issues on their own, now they did it in a group. This gave all of us a much greater access to information than we would possibly have had on our own. Someone found an article and shared it. And I read every single one, which enabled me to write blog posts to educate those who didn't have time to read whole articles.

The wealth of material available on the topic of abuse on the web is vast and much of it of high quality, and I soon found much that helped me to make sense of the situation, including how some people reacted.

A blog post entitled 'DARVO: Deny, Attack, and Reverse Victim and Offender' by Esther Sweetman, that someone found on *Restored,* a website about abuse against women, was one such article. It refers to 'a reaction perpetrators of wrongdoing may display in response to being held accountable for their behaviour.' They may deny the behaviour, attack the person who spoke up, and reverse the roles of victim and offender so that the perpetrator plays the victim and makes it seem as if the true victim is at fault. So a guilty perpetrator may pretend to be falsely accused, attack the accuser's credibility or even blame them of being in the wrong because they are spreading false accusations.

This is a common reaction that you can see in high profile abuse cases where someone has outed a perpetrator on the internet. It seems naïve of me now to have expected Buddhist practitioners to be any different to anyone else when faced with a smear to their reputation or to the reputation of someone important to them, but I felt disappointed when I realised that many Rigpa folk had fallen into the DARVO response.

Denial in such cases comes in two forms: either 'it didn't happen or it rarely happened', and 'it wasn't harmful.' We saw both. First outright denial, and then, the qualification that if it did happen then it wasn't really harmful, rather people just thought it was. Though Rigpa management in their formal communications didn't deny the abuse allegations, they didn't treat them as anything serious either. It seemed clear to many of us that what they found serious was only that Sogyal had been caught out. Individual Rigpa students, however, had no problem with outright denial that any of it had taken place or that if it had, the case had been highly overstated by the eight and others.

Management didn't attack the 'whistle blowers' in their public communications, but individuals certainly did, and so did some people in roles representative of Rigpa. One woman reported how she'd gone to her local centre for the first discussion on the 'situation' and the leader of their centre read off the names of the eight letter writers and said, 'Liar,' after each of their names. In Rigpa discussion groups and Facebook pages we saw the usual Rigpa method of dealing with anyone who spoke publicly about Sogyal's behaviour: they were 'mentally unstable', 'carrying a grudge', 'didn't understand Vajrayana', 'out to get Sogyal', 'angry and bitter', 'had gone off', and so on.

In late 2017, the Lerab Ling Community filed a lawsuit for defamation on the French lawyer who was assembling testimonies from people harmed by their time in Rigpa. They said he made defamatory statements against Lerab Ling in the local newspaper, *Midi Libre*. It was widely seen as an attempt to silence anyone who called them a cult. Since French people don't look kindly on cults, the label was affecting their relationship with the local community. The suit turned them into the victim of defamation and made the lawyer their attacker. At the time of writing, this legal situation is still to be resolved.

Sogyal and Rigpa management in their communications were also adept at reversing the order of victim and offender in student's perception. They never failed to find an opportunity to remind people of all the good Sogyal had done or of the wonderful teachers who supported him and their wonderful plans for the future of the dharma while never mentioning his abusive behaviour, only ever referring to the 'challenging situation' or 'distressing time' and so forth. Many students soon gained the impression that by speaking up, the eight students and their supporters had done terrible harm to Sogyal and the dharma. They had brought the dharma into disrespect, and *they* were responsible for Rigpa's troubles—not Sogyal.

Poor Sogyal, the discourse went, he never meant to harm anyone. His motivation was pure. These people just want to bring him down and ruin everything we've worked so hard to build up.

Esther Sweetman says that:

This reversal of roles 'enables him [the perpetrator] to keep his reputation, roles and friendships intact while potentially continuing with the abuse unchallenged. It also serves to confuse onlookers—family, friends and church leaders/members, and couple counsellors (that is one of the reasons why couple counselling is not recommended in the case of abuse). Onlookers become confused and do not know what to believe and therefore choose to remain neutral or uninvolved; again another result that the abuser is hoping to achieve.'

But by having access to this kind of information, members of the *What Now?* group helped each other to see through the DARVO response and so be immune to its power. Without the back up of this kind of article, we would have been left only with our own vague sense that somehow the wool was being pulled over our eyes. But in light of this information, we could see exactly what was going on, and the result was a growing disenchantment with the organisation that we had previously trusted to have our best interests at heart.

Dzongsar Khyentse in a letter to the Rigpa sangha for Christmas 2018 also bought into this reverse-victim-offender approach, though so subtly that if you didn't have this education, you may not see what he was doing. A comment on the blog points out both the gaslighting—manipulating someone's perception—and the reverse-victim-offender play.

'As a former member of Rigpa who was sexually harassed by Sogyal, as well as having witnessed firsthand his abuse of others, to summarise Sogyal's behaviour as 'mismanagement' is so wide of the mark it beggars belief. The letter has also implied that somehow poor Rigpa members who have stayed on are the victims; it's completely turned the tables around, a perverse inversion, even though many of them were complicit and colluded in the knowledge that the abuse was taking place.

It's like Rigpa has become the martyr, as if [they are] Christians being thrown to the lions; again it's such a twisted avoidance and denial with no acknowledgment and a flat refusal to look at the crimes, and DZK has even gone as far as to honour their devotion. That makes sense, doesn't it? Honour and reward someone for following an abuser. How sick can you get! Now Rigpa is using the letter to make themselves feel exonerated and all virtuous.'

If we are not to get caught up with manipulative gurus then we must not take anything a lama or their organisation says at face value, particularly written communications which they can spend much time perfecting so that they twist devotees perception to suit their aims—which may well be simply to keep themselves enshrined on their thrones.

15
PERSONAL ATTACKS

I never intended to vlog on the matter, but I had a YouTube channel called *Living in Peace and Clarity* on which I used to interview people and ask them to share their happiness hints. I'd given up on the project several months earlier, but now I found myself at the end of a long day of editing other people's books—which is what I do for a living—wanting to talk about the abuse issue but not feeling like typing comments for the group. So I videoed myself talking about my concerns, questions and discoveries, and the YouTube channel, since it already existed was the obvious place to publish the videos. Not everyone affected by the abuse was on Facebook, and some people preferred to listen than to read. People said my vlogs reassured them that they weren't the only person going through what they were going through, so despite criticism from some quarters, I kept vlogging.

The vlog had a momentum of its own. I didn't plan it or even particularly want to do it, but I was consciously practicing trusting directions for action that came out of my meditation practice, and so I'd take a deep breath, let my reservations fall away and turn on the video camera on my phone. I only ever spoke as someone trying to process the fallout of the revelations, not as any authority, and certainly not as any kind of spiritual teacher, but though I mostly had a lot of support, some people criticised me severely.

Some seemed primarily concerned with protecting their guru and religion, and others questioned the motivation for my actions—something I re-evaluated often just to be sure I was doing all this in order to help, not harm. One person privately suggested I had no qualifications for saying anything since I wasn't a victim of direct abuse, and a couple accused me of using the suffering of others for self-promotion, a criticism that almost resulted in me not writing this book. I had to dig deep and draw out my 'warrior self' in order to bring it to fruition.

One of Rigpa's methods of disregarding or discrediting those who speak out is to label them as just an 'angry person' with some personal 'vendetta'. Because in Buddhism negative emotions are seen as something to be abandoned or transcended, some see any suggestions of anger in another as a sign of their spiritual failing, thus using it as a reason to judge and condemn that person.

Certainly, acting from the space of one's anger tends to be reactive instead of proactive and so can be counterproductive to achieving anything positive. As one of the letter writers told me, *'Histrionics don't get you anywhere. They're fine if you just want to vent, but if you want to effect meaningful change then you must be logical and dispassionate lest you give ammunition to those who you hope to affect.'* The ammunition is giving them a reason to disregard your point of view.

But a lot of people had every reason to be angry. It's a legitimate emotion given the harm caused and trust broken, and expressing that anger is important part of the process of healing.

Repressing one's anger is as unhelpful as spitting it out at everyone. We all felt angry at some point, but most of us in the group tried to keep it out of our communications—except for those moments when we simply needed to vent. We were very clear on the need to not let the group devolve into a festival of negativity, and though we had our moments, we did manage to keep rampant negativity from taking hold.

Despite my trying to maintain a level of equanimity in my social media interactions, some of Sogyal's defenders soon included me and members of the *What Now?* group in the 'just angry people' categorisation. Most of the people accused of 'being angry', however, didn't appear angry to me. They were simply being assertive in stating what they felt had to be said and repeating it because the truth didn't seem to be sinking in.

In the book *Be Angry,* His Holiness the 14th Dalai Lama talks about two types of anger:

'To be angry *on behalf* of those who are treated unjustly means that we have compassionate anger. This type of anger leads to right action and leads to social change. To be angry *toward* the people in power does not create change. It creates more anger, more resentment, more fighting.'

That pretty much sums up the kind of anger— assertiveness—I felt and saw around me and drives continuing activity around the issue of abuse in Tibetan Buddhism.

In line with the tone of the letter by the eight and HH the Dalai Lama's advice, most of the group seemed to want to still honour the good we received from our time in Rigpa. Honouring any good, however, was seen by some as indicating that I was somehow apologising for Sogyal, thus making me their enemy. On the other hand, if I didn't acknowledge the benefit I'd gained from my time at Rigpa, others doomed and dismissed me with the 'just angry' label. I realised that no matter what I said, I would have critics, and so I simply said what I honestly felt at any time and tried to be of service to others, to live up to my Bodhisattva vow.

YouTube seems to draw the worst comments. One person said:

> 'Don't push your rubbish idea too much. After so many years of learning Buddhism, you turned yourself into rubbish, seeing your guru as devil. What pure perception are you talking about? Do you mean to say tantrayana is seeing guru as devil? Don't give your childish talk. Learn more and expand your view beyond duality, after which you will not give such confused, childish idea/talk.'

Another said:

> 'Let it go, please. It is enough.'

And another:

> 'Sometimes it's better to say nothing.'

Those who thought I said too much would be surprised to know that I made a lot of videos that I never posted. Often I resisted saying anything, but then people asked what I thought about some development and I found myself answering with another vlog or blog.

The behaviour of Sogyal, Rigpa, students, and other lamas constantly amazed and appalled me to the point that if I didn't laugh I would've cried. Many found my ability to see the whole situation as somewhat ridiculous a relief in those dark times, a way to help us step back from the issues and not become too embroiled. Some, however, didn't appreciate my sense of humour. I had to giggle at the following YouTube comment:

> 'Tahlia please be coherent and respond point by point instead of shaking so much and giggling nervously. Must you inflict on us your disjointed garbage?'

The Vajrayana trolls had arrived and were out to get me. Having enough to deal with elsewhere, I stopped reading YouTube comments.

Ayya Yeshe talked about the tendency for some Buddhists to attack those raising reasonable concerns in a post in the *Survivors of Vajrayana Abuse and their Allies* Facebook group:

> *I have noticed how ill at ease with authenticity and emotion some Buddhists are in the spate of recent abuse scandals. Of course there is a difference between dysfunctional emotional dumping and a reasonable response to abuse. I wonder why so many Buddhists wish to burn at the stake, tone police, discredit and troll those who are simply voicing a reasonable response to oppression and abuse?*

> *So many of the teachings on the dangers of anger, the need for forgiveness and selfless compassion are being used out of context to bully survivors into silence. Those apologists, those who feel the need to suppress the cry of those who are broken hearted and fed up with degeneracy, hypocrisy, Tibetan xenophobia, patriarchy, the abuse of women and children, the millenniums of demonising women and excluding them*
>
> *...*

It all needs to come out. Like puss out of the wound. If it stays hidden, this tradition will rot from the inside and all the good things will be lost too. Tone policing, bullying, lecturing survivors on how they should not feel is just imposing the laws of cults and dysfunctional dynamics that make a fertile ground for abuse everywhere.

Don't talk, don't feel, don't trust.

Obey, Pray, Pay.

I for one am done with being silenced and told how to feel and shamed for telling the truth.

This is the only way we can let the dharma rise in the West again, like a phoenix from the ashes, with honesty, listening to survivors, accountability.

If you are tone policing survivors, imposing inauthentic standards from ancient texts, offering ancient quotes out of context without any sensitivity for the broken lives and abuse, you are part of the problem. What is it in yourself you don't want to feel or face? Why do you need to control other people's responses? Is your faith that weak?

Luckily I received plenty of care from other *What Now?* members. We all supported each other. This comment posted on the *Dharma Protectors* Facebook page sums up the feelings that many people expressed to me:

> *'Thank you for addressing the issue of abuse in Buddhism. It's long overdue and extremely necessary. Abuse by spiritual teachers causes profound psychological damage, impairs*

soteriological endeavours, and damages or destroys people's faith in the dharma.

A tradition ostensibly predicated on principles of compassion and wisdom should never tolerate abuse. Teachers who attempt to cloak their perversity and cruelty as "enlightened activity" should be exposed and we need to comfort their victims, not denigrate them.' Ex-monk and ex-Buddhist.

16
COGNITIVE DISSONANCE

The term 'cognitive dissonance' describes the feelings of discomfort that result when your beliefs run counter to your behaviour and/or new information that is presented to you. People tend to seek consistency in their beliefs, so when what you hold true is challenged or what you do doesn't fit with what you think, something must change in order to eliminate or reduce the dissonance or lack of agreement. Hence people tend to 'explain away' what doesn't fit.

We thought Sogyal was a good man; then reality presented us with information showing us that he was not a good man, and this challenged our cherished belief in him as a force for good. Could he be both good and bad? If we answer no, then we must either ignore the bad or ignore the good. If we answer yes, then does the good make up for the bad? Or does the bad outweigh the good? And so on.

Of course, we were playing with beliefs, which create our perception and distort reality until it conforms to our expectations and prejudices. Ego tries to protect itself—especially if our identity is based around the belief that the guy is good or that he is bad. The trick is to recognise our beliefs and see ego's games so we can step outside of them, or at least not get too caught up in them.

I had to learn to accept the discomfort of cognitive dissonance, of recognising that my dualistic mind would never work it out satisfactorily, and trying to do so only embroiled me in a confusing web of conflicting viewpoints. To step out of cognitive dissonance, one has to step outside of dualistic mind, so peace and clarity could be found in meditation practice, but I had difficulty explaining to others a perspective that held two apparently opposing realities.

If I spoke of the good, people assumed I supported the bad. If I spoke of the bad, people assumed I had forgotten the good. When I suggested that we needed to recognise both the good and the bad, I had some insisting that Sogyal had never really done any good and others insisting that he'd done nothing wrong. Still others said that on the absolute level of reality there was no good or bad, and assumed that meant there was no good or bad on a relative level as well.

It's easy for people who only hear about Sogyal through the story of his disgrace to see only the terrible side of him, and those who bore the brunt of his worst side have no reason to see anything good in him, but for those of us who were not emotionally, physically or sexually abused by him, we have good things to remember. We would not have stayed for decades, as many of my friends did, had we not gained some benefit.

I never believed Sogyal was enlightened, but when he taught Dzogchen—the teachings on the nature of mind—formally, in a shrine room, while in a state of devotion for his masters, I saw his Buddha nature, his wisdom mind, shining through, and in those times, I could relate to that part of him, that 'pure' part of him, with devotion. It was his wisdom mind, not his ordinary mind, and the Dzogchen teacher, not the flawed human being.

I held two views at the same time. On one hand, Sogyal with his Buddha nature revealed, and on the other hand, a petty, demanding and all-too-fallible boss. And I focused on the former because that *was the spiritual practice*, and like all his students, I ignored the indications of his behind-the-scenes activity, because allowing his harshness to bother you *wasn't the practice*. Being bothered supposedly meant that one's perception was simply not pure enough, but actually the opposite is likely true. The vision of those who didn't deny their gut feelings was perhaps purer because they were more connected to their inner teacher, to the wisdom and compassion inside, and less affected by contrived beliefs.

We were encouraged—or was it brainwashed?—to see his angry outbursts as wrath or compassionate anger, and his every action as a teaching, not as a sign of someone unable to manage their emotions. What happened to my critical thinking? My discernment? Realising how I'd been duped was em-barrassing.

Like a good little student, I'd offered up my discernment on the altar of devotion, to please the lama so he'd give me the precious nectar of the Dzogchen teachings—like a little girl pleasing her father for the reward of an ice-cream. Not only that, but I also helped others to see the way I did.

Forgive me for my complicity.

I rationalised that sometimes I must speak firmly to my child or she does not understand how important it is to correct herself. I would like to believe that this belief system was not

145

intended to control and coerce, but we in Rigpa certainly used it this way, not just the lama, but all those, like me, who didn't listen to those who cried out to be heard.

Forgive me for my complicity.

I expressed my shame in a blog post titled 'Confessions of a Devoted Student' and comments like the following one indicated that I was not alone in such feelings:

> *'You speak from my heart and I guess your explanation is true for every SR student who read the letter and is unable to close his or her eyes any longer. Yes, I feel shame and I can't understand why I believed all the stupid explanations of the instructors. The answer might be: because I wanted to!'*

Why didn't I see that students were being harmed? Because I saw the teacher in person only once a year, and only during a teaching, and because senior students told me those close to him had asked for this 'special training' and that they saw it as an honour to be treated this way. Surely, I thought, if they don't see it as a problem, then who am I to judge? And also over the years I didn't see any physical or sexual abuse, and emotional abuse is hard to quantify without a full picture.

In my second to last year with Rigpa, however, I did witness emotional abuse and recognise it for what it was. One evening during the annual Australian retreat, the Dzogchen Mandala students had been told to return to the shrine tent for a special teaching. We'd filed in and waited. Eventually Sogyal turned up, and instead of a Dzogchen teaching, he spent the whole time yelling at one of the people running the retreat for something she'd done wrong. She quickly became very distressed, sobbing in a truly heart-breaking fashion. He went over and over the same ground and never gave her any suggestions for improving, just laid into her for her failure.

I remember thinking, 'He's a bully. He's just a big bully.' And I realised that in any other situation I wouldn't have watched something like this without some protest. I've always stood up for the victims of bullies and always done what I could to stop bullying wherever I came across it. But here, I sat and simply watched these thoughts rise, then let them go, practicing not reacting. This was what we were supposed to do. If we hadn't come to terms with recognising this kind of behaviour as the activity of a crazy wisdom master then we had no place in the Dzogchen Mandala. But in this instance, I recognised that my thoughts and feelings had a point. I looked at the one hundred or so people sitting there watching the abuse, and no one showed any reaction at all. They looked like zombies, mindless, without any critical thinking faculties. Couldn't they see what I saw? Didn't they realise what they were witnessing?

No, they thought it was the enlightened actions of a mahasiddha. If you wanted Dzogchen teachings, that was how you were supposed to see it. But I recognised then that his behaviour had crossed a line, and I felt very uncomfortable watching it. To remain without saying anything to stop it went against the very fabric of my being. But he was scary when he was angry, and I didn't want that anger turned on me. No one did.

I sat next to a good friend, and she whispered to me, 'I don't see any teaching in this.'

'I agree,' I replied. 'This is not a teaching; it's emotional abuse.' I looked at my watch. He'd been at her for a whole hour. 'I can't watch this,' I whispered. 'I'm out of here.'

She looked at me in horror. 'What if he stops you?' He often stopped people from leaving or at least challenged them.

I shrugged. 'Then I'll give him an earful.' Part of me hoped I would be afforded the opportunity, the other part hoped he wouldn't notice. The other part won. I crept out of the shrine tent and escaped without notice.

Once outside I said to myself, 'That's it. I'm never coming back to another retreat.'

I felt that my time with Rigpa was over. In fact I almost left the next day, but my daughter was having too much of a good time on the beach, and she convinced me to stay. I didn't plan to return for another retreat, but I did come back, once more, the next year, in 2017, six months before I discovered the extent of his abuse.

I managed to forget that night during the following year. I pushed it out of my consciousness, likely because such a recognition threatened what I saw as the basis of my spiritual path—my relationship with my teacher. How many others had done the same with things they'd witnessed?

What happened to the eight and others is a great deal more damaging than anything I saw. Only when reading about trauma bonding and brainwashing techniques did I realise just how badly they'd been trapped in a cycle of abuse that was enabled by a system of beliefs that supported it as not only acceptable, but also normal. A belief system adhered to so blindly by those around this teacher that those who recognised the abuse for what it was had no support, but were made to feel that their perception was not pure enough and their devotion was not strong enough. They were made to feel that it was their fault!

I assumed that he did have sex with some of his entourage, but since he isn't a monk, I figured that that was their business so long as it was consensual, that the women could say, 'No' without fearing retribution for their refusal. I didn't consider the basic power imbalance and beliefs as a form of coercion.

When Mimi's story of sexual abuse by Sogyal first appeared in the Canadian Documentary *In the Name of Enlightenment*, which was broadcast in Canada on May 23, 2011, I didn't even look into it. Didn't read it.

I'm so sorry Mimi that I doubted you. That I didn't even listen to you.

I couldn't believe that he really would harm anyone. After all, he always professed that his motivation was to benefit all beings. Back then, though I thought Sogyal a little grumpy sometimes, I saw him as primarily a force for good, and I wasn't prepared to open myself to any cognitive dissonance. I didn't want my cosy security threatened. And many still don't. The cognitive dissonance that occurs once you accept that your dear teacher, who you revere, is abusing people is very difficult to handle.

Does his good work excuse the abuse? No. Nothing excuses abuse.

Was I stupid to trust that my teacher would live by the teachings he taught? Was I stupid to follow a religion that asked me to see *everything* my teacher did as enlightened action? Could I ever trust another teacher so deeply again? No. Never.

I do not regret following Sogyal for twenty years, and don't doubt the genuine experience and understanding I gained.

I do regret my blindness, however. And I have little faith left in 'the system' that allowed this to happen.

Separating the teacher from the man, and the teacher's deluded mind from the teacher's wisdom mind was, and still is, my way of handling the cognitive dissonance, but my respect for him as a teacher is tempered now by my realisation that any recognition I had of the nature of my mind might've had more to do with my qualities as a student than his as a teacher, and that we all gave him too much credit for an environment that was created by many people. Now that I'm aware of the power of suggestion and group trance induction techniques, the role Sogyal played in any of our realisations is, in my mind, much diminished.

I think we all gave him way too much credit, especially considering that the work of building Rigpa was all done by students—most of them working long hours for no pay. I still thank him for the teachings I received, especially the Dzogchen ones, but I'm also very aware now of how he twisted the interpretation of many of the teachings to create the situation where his students simply pandered to his desires.

It is possible to manage cognitive dissonance and see both the good and the bad in Sogyal and Rigpa, even if one side is far greater than the other. Though not as easy, it is far more realistic and healthy than feeling one must choose between 'all good' or 'all bad'.

Denial of harm is an unwise basis for maintaining devotion, however. As the Buddha said: 'Just as the clean kusha grass that wraps a rotten fish will also start to rot, so too will those devoted to an evil person.'

17
BELIEFS AND PERCEPTION

We don't see reality directly. We only see our perception of reality filtered through our beliefs and assumptions. So if someone doesn't think they were abused, were they abused or not?

According to HH the Dalai Lama, we practice Buddhism in order to develop 'a deep and heartfelt empathy for all beings coupled with a penetrating insight into the nature of reality'. We're aiming through meditation practice to see reality directly, without the obscurations of our beliefs, and our habitual, emotional, cognitive and karmic obscurations. Those obscurations are what obscure the truth, not just the truth of who we really are, but also the truth of phenomena as they exist beyond our flawed perception. To see clearly we must put aside all beliefs, and all our hopes and fears, and look at the bare facts of what presents itself in any moment.

We cannot see reality directly for as long as we hold to any belief about that reality. And yet some cling to Buddhist beliefs to such an extent that they blind them.

If someone punches another person in the stomach, it constitutes physical assault. And when around one-thousand people witness such a punch, the fact that it happened cannot be denied.

In the temple at Lerab Ling in August 2016, during the Dzogchen retreat of over **one-thousand** of the most committed Rigpa students from around the world, Sogyal Rinpoche/Lakar punched the nun Ani Chokyi in a fit of rage because she didn't do something quickly enough. This sent a shock wave through the sangha; though some had heard rumors of his violence, until then most had not witnessed it firsthand.

One friend had been sitting near the front. He told me, *'I could hear the wind being forcefully knocked out of her body and could clearly see the pain and hurt in her face as she doubled over and ran off the stage in tears. She came back a few hours later still in visible distress.'*

Sangye followed her back to her room after the teaching to check on her, and he told me that she was terribly upset and clearly hurt.

Sogyal did punch the nun. That cannot be denied because many witnessed it.

In a blog post called 'Rigpa Students in a Quandary' on the *Buddhism Controversy Blog* by Joanne Clark, she quoted from someone who was there: *'The next day Sogyal Lakar told the assembly he could stop hitting people but that it would affect the teachings. He's done this many times, [saying that] if you don't like how I act, I just won't give you the teachings; it's very sick and manipulative.'* This kind of manipulation is another example of the kind of behaviour undertaken by perpetrators of abuse.

His Holiness the Dalai Lama on pp. 209-210 in *The Gelug/Kagyu Tradition of Mahamudra* by HH Dalai Lama & Alex Berzin says:

'It is not healthy, of course, for disciples to deny serious ethical flaws in their guru, if they are in fact true, or his or her involvement in Buddhist power-politics, if this is the case. To do so would be a total loss of discriminating awareness.'

Nevertheless this is what many Rigpa students have done and are still doing. In a statement posted on social media over a year later, Ani Chokyi said that Sogyal wasn't in a fit of rage, that he had a 'single moment of wrath', manifesting in a 'soft punch' which she didn't experience as violent or abusive. She attributed her crying to something unconnected to the punch, saying that the 'incident sparked open an inflammation of a mental wound'.

So was it a 'soft punch' as reported by the person who felt it, or a 'hard punch' as reported by witnesses? Soft or hard, it was definitely a punch. Was it abuse or not?

Ani Chokyi in her statement also mentioned a 'long and loving hug' Sogyal gave her publicly earlier in the retreat and accused people of forgetting it 'in the midst of trying to prove abuse'. What she didn't realise is that such affection given by the same person as delivered the punch is actually further proof that she's in an abusive relationship. When interspersed with beatings and other forms of abuse, displays of love and affection keep victims of abuse 'trauma bonded' to their abuser through them thinking/feeling that the loving disproves, outweighs or makes up for the harm. The victims live for the moments of loving.

This kind of statement from people we'd seen publicly humiliated by Sogyal was common. They'd stand up in front of the retreatants the next day and tell us how what we'd seen as public humiliation was love because that's how they saw and experienced it.

I and the other students who returned year after year accepted that. Why? Because we didn't think it through, because it was easy and convenient for us to ignore the reality before us, and to assume that because the recipient didn't think they were being abused, they weren't. To wake up to the fact that what we were seeing was abuse, not an expression of love and not a teaching method, would, as we've now seen, rock the security of our spiritual practice—and no one wanted that.

But actually, what we witnessed regularly at retreats *was* public humiliation, just as the punch was a punch.

When women from a radical Islamic political group in Australia said in a video, posted on Facebook that Muslim husbands had permission from Allah to hit their wives and that such beatings are 'a beautiful blessing', *The Daily Mirror* in an article entitled 'Hitting Wives is Illegal, not "a Beautiful Blessing" Says Top Cop,' reported Police Commissioner of NSW, Mick Fuller, saying, 'The law doesn't distinguish between race and religion, when it comes to violence against women it is not acceptable in any shape or form.'

In other words, in the eyes of the law—and in the majority of people in Western society—a punch does constitute violence against the victim, and such violence is unacceptable regardless of whether or not the victim sees that punch as a blessing.

It's quite obvious really, but I found it impossible to get that idea across to some of my Rigpa friends. Some of them had experienced Sogyal's beatings as transformative, and in their mind their beating would never be anything other than an expression of wisdom love. They held onto this belief like a drowning person would to a life-saving ring. And I understood why: If you'd experienced this kind of behaviour for years, and handled it by thinking it was beneficial for you, to suddenly see it as abuse, and therefore detrimental to yourself and others, was a complete turnabout in the beliefs you held dear and in how you viewed yourself. It takes enormous courage to look at our cherished core beliefs and change them in light of reality. And it takes spiritual maturity to be willing and able to drop those beliefs even for a moment in order to see reality rather than our beliefs about reality. Those who speak up about their abuse have the courage of a true spiritual practitioner.

I'm not denying the perception of those who experienced aspects of Sogyal's behavior as transformative. Every moment of life is an opportunity for transformation. I can trip over a rock and the fall jolts me into wakefulness, but that doesn't mean it's due to any special quality in the rock. Nor does it mean that everyone who trips over that rock will experience something similar, or that the rock will stimulate some transformative experience if I trip over it again. And it certainly doesn't mean that one should throw the rock at people with the aim of bringing about a transformative experience. I only ask that people examine their interactions with Sogyal honestly, without the overlay of the beliefs that insist they see it as transformative. Only then do they have a chance to see reality as it is. When you look at the modern research into abusive situations, to consider that the behaviour outlined in the letter by the eight students is anything other than abuse is simply not in accord with reality.

155

Perhaps the strangest thing about the nun-punching is the acceptance of the witnesses who watched without apparent reaction. Many have stayed for years while experiencing this themselves, thinking such treatment means they are specially advanced practitioners and that this kind of behaviour—if they don't complain about it—will fast track their path to enlightenment. Looking back on this belief system now, it seems totally crazy.

Keen to get to enlightenment as fast as possible, we trained ourselves to obey our guru absolutely without complaint because we thought that was what would get us there. Because of this naïve attitude towards spirituality and the abuse-enabling beliefs, we accepted Sogyal's behaviour and an abusive situation became normalised. We saw it as normal, not a problem, just how things were, and if you wanted teachings from Sogyal, who seemed to have some spiritual power, then you accepted it as part of the package. It was the price we had to pay to get what we wanted. You either accepted it or you left.

Sangye told me that Sogyal *'routinely said that merely by displeasing him people were in grave karmic situations, so they had to build a new house, or make a pool or something to correct that— that's how he got the bigger house and pool at Lerab Ling,'* and he convinced his close students that people getting sick and so on was directly connected to them not obeying his instructions.

Sangye elaborated:

'He has made them believe his "magic trick", and they tell stories about all the magic, uncanny ways he calls you at times when you think about him. There are a lot of psychic, telepathic experiences that you get if you spend that much time and effort worshipping someone, and that really

reinforces that magical thinking. That got me. But, look, now I left, declare independence, and I'm not dead. But because his predictions don't come true, he'll explain that bad people seem successful but they just burn away all their merit in this life. This is also very standard stuff of cult leaders.'

Of course this scared people close to him into doing his bidding, whatever it was—and some did ethically dubious (sharing wives and girlfriends) or legally dubious (misuse of funds) things at his request—and those who remained simply accepted this culture as normal.

18
WHY THEY STAYED

The first thing I wondered about the culture of the inner circle was, why did those abused stay around for as long as they did? I found the answer in literature on the dynamics of abuse and the control mechanisms used by leaders of abusive cults.

On a personal level, I and other students like me who'd witnessed his petty, demanding and grumpy behaviour stayed because of the teachings. We heard truth from Sogyal, real dharma that resonated with us and that we could work with in our lives to make us better people. The mistake we made was to assume that because what he said when he was teaching dharma formally was wise and true that everything he said even when he wasn't teaching was always wise and true. It simply wasn't.

One of those who had been in the inner circle told me:
'While in public often Buddhist texts were read and quoted, in private, Sogyal just made it up as he went along, and turned his tantrums into teachings. Unable to divide one from the other, people took decades to find the spoiled, immature man playing the guru game in these confusing displays of selfish entitlement.'

And another explained this difficulty in separating truth from manipulation in more detail:

'In order to work with our egos, which anyone interested in self-improvement knows they must do, we were told that when the teacher did or said things that threatened our ego we weren't going to like it. (He said this repeatedly publicly but also strongly reinforced it in private; anytime any resistance came up, he'd say it was our ego.) So a template for sublimating our own common sense was foundational to his approach. Basically 'you can't trust yourself', which when it comes to our habitual patterns and behaviours is often times true. He told us that he was the only one we could trust, not our parents, friends, family; he was the only one who could see us clearly; he was the only one who could help us in a way that would last, that would create a paradigm shift. This was magical thinking.'

These are classic tactics of cult leaders. The student continued:

'Over 3/4 of what he said was absolutely true. We all know that we have blind sides, that others can often see where we're stuck; the fatal flaw was investing him with the power to "guide" us to the exclusion of all others. He actually emphasized the bit about not associating with non-believers.'

Isolating members from other influences is another cult tactic.

'Added to that he often times gave very good advice and pointing out instructions, which I definitely benefited from. The part that made no sense is that his instructions and advice were always designed to benefit him. Sussing that out, that he could be so very helpful but at the same time so very ignorant in some ways, is what was so very difficult and painful.

160

'It's like the moment you realize that your parent, the one who you owe so much, who cared for you when you were completely helpless, is no longer competent to make decisions for themselves. It's like having to take away your mom's car because she's a danger to herself and others. It's emotionally difficult to go against your mom's wishes. My feeling is that we basically took away Sogyal Lakar's car; he couldn't understand that what he was doing was wrong, was harming others. On one hand I like to imagine that if he were in his right mind, he'd be happy to be stopped, but it doesn't matter, once you realize that someone is a menace to others you're obligated to do whatever you can to at least warn others.

'The worst part is that many of us were completely altruistic; I literally gave up everything to do his bidding. It wasn't my first rodeo, and I had the deep desire to be able to be compassionate at all times to all beings; for me that was the embodiment of enlightenment. I never believed I would go to the Buddha realms or some kind of eternalistic reincarnation loop of successively positive re-births; I just wanted to learn how to be a good person, someone who could help others who were suffering. He used that desire to be decent human beings for his own selfish purposes'

As leaders of destructive cults do.

There's also another aspect to Sogyal's behaviour that worked on people emotionally, a well-researched dynamic of abusive situations known as trauma bonding, commonly used by leaders of destructive cults and sex traffickers as well as in domestic relationships. Traumatic bonding occurs as the result of ongoing cycles of abuse in which the intermittent reinforcement of reward and punishment creates powerful emotional bonds that are resistant to change. Sogyal apparently punished his students by belittling, humiliating, or beating them one day, and then rewarded them the next day by showing them excessive kindness—love bombing. The victim gains such validation from the display of love that they live for those times and work hard to please their abuser in order to receive that love. For people who have grown up in abusive households this kind of bonding seems to them to be a normal part of relationships, and the longer one is in such a relationship, the harder it is to leave.

In a *Psych Central* article called 'What is Trauma Bonding,' Sharie Stines, Psy.D explains:

'The environment necessary to create a trauma bond involves intensity, complexity, inconsistency, and a promise. Victims stay because they are holding on to that elusive "promise" or hope. There is always manipulation involved. Victims are prey to the manipulation because they are willing to tolerate anything for the payoff, which is that elusive promise and ever present hope for fulfilment of some deeply personal need within the victim.'

In this case, enlightenment.

'Victims hope the abuser will change. After all, there are good times in between episodes of abuse. There are reasons why the person loves or did love the abuser. Abusers can have a moody, Dr. Jekyll and Mr. Hyde personality. Dr. Jekyll is often charming and romantic, perhaps successful, and makes pronouncements of love. You love Dr. Jekyll and make excuses for Mr. Hyde. You don't see that the whole person is the problem. If you've had a painful relationship with a parent growing up, you can confuse love and pain.'

This describes the Rigpa dynamic perfectly. Stines continues:

'Only after time away from the unhealthy attachment can a person begin to see the destruction it caused. In essence, people need to "detox" from trauma bonds by breaking them and staying away from the relationship.'

But getting out and staying out of an abusive situation isn't easy. I heard several first-hand accounts from people who had to sneak away from Lerab Ling under the cover of darkness for fear of being stopped, and others were coerced to return or to stay when they tried to leave. Sogyal used threats of hell or illness falling on students or loved ones if they left, didn't return, or disobeyed him. Most had to make several attempts before they got away.

In many cases it took years for people to come to the point where they were ready to accept that Sogyal and their life in Rigpa were not what they'd thought them to be and to give up something to which they'd been devoted for many years. In true cult fashion, being involved with Rigpa at the inner-circle level left people disconnected from friends and family in the outside world, creating even more dependency on the abuser; this made leaving very difficult because it meant leaving the whole 'Rigpa family' behind too.

Victims also stay for financial reasons, perhaps because they have nowhere to live. They may also have no outside

163

emotional support. Stines explains this dynamic of entrapment further:

> 'If you're a victim of abuse, you feel ashamed. You've been humiliated by the abuser and your self-esteem and confidence have been undermined. You hide the abuse from people close to you, often to protect the reputation of the abuser and because of your own shame. An abuser uses tactics to isolate you from friends and loved ones by criticizing them and making remarks designed to force you to take sides. You're either for them or against them. If the abuser feels slighted, then you have to take his or her side, or you're befriending the enemy. This is designed to increase control over you and your dependence upon him or her.'

Sangye wrote about his journey of escape from under Sogyal's control:

> *'I used to feel a lot of spiritual and other fear. I had to slowly plan an escape—I was a monk so I had nothing. I had to completely restart, so I did various things to find some cash, and I basically ran away for a few months. I still had some idea that I would return to help with one last retreat. I told people where I lived in France at the Lerab Ling retreat centre for many years that I was going on a long retreat. ...*
> *I had tried to leave a few times and been commanded back. I had to really isolate myself and think.*
>
> *'I had stopped listening to audio teachings because I had this deep instinct to "deprogram", and I didn't at the time want to leave or know there was a problem. I just felt ... programmed ... and concerned in a way I couldn't even*

really explain to myself. So I posed a question: "Find out how your mind is if you don't listen to these teachings for some time, if it changes" ... Then I started to talk more to an outside friend on Skype in my free time. ... More and more events lead me to feel disgust until some lines got crossed, a well-known point where even though I was already resolved to leave, I was still there, dominated and forced to attend teachings. I was avoiding the temple and all the "meetings" but these were the highest teachings for the older students and mandatory, and some were, in fact, very good because of Mingyur Rinpoche [MR] visiting. Then Sogyal came and gave his diluted rambling on version of what MR taught and put on his grandiose act and punched a nun for no reason I could see other than perhaps a glint of defiance in her eyes. She ran off, and another nun left Lerab Ling in shock—all were brought back and forcibly made to testify that it was good and they understood. The eldest student made Sogyal out to be the victim, and said he was sad that we didn't understand. Even so, many people said, "You don't do that; you don't punch," confronting him in public from the front row.

'Later I learned about escaping that you don't tell anyone—I was kind of telling people, saying I was doing a retreat, and it involved getting as far away from Rigpa and nobody knowing where I was. Various emails chased me and asked how I was, with what I now see as obviously fake care and disingenuous concern. All they wanted was for me to turn up and be exploited as a backbone of the technical support I offered as my service to this "organization".

165

'One day the flashbacks started, emotional flashbacks triggered because I said on the surface of my mind, "I guess I'll say I'm going to come to retreat." Then a scream came from deep inside and I said, "Noooooo way", and then I said back to that inner child, "Okay, okay, we aren't going back." After that things got quite rough, but I also started to ask the hard questions.

'People kept trying to get me to go back, and I didn't want their money, or to see them. I said I would only communicate via email—no phone calls, no video chat ... that way I could have it in writing. Sogyal never wrote or sent any messages as this would have exposed his manipulation with evidence. However, I became scared of what he might do as some kind of psychopath which pretty much all narcissists are. They don't care for your health— that's why you get away from them.

'If it is an individual relationship, a student teacher relationship, please know that when you are ready, telling others in private or public will give you back your power to speak the truth. The most important is to get away if you are at risk—it can be dangerous. But on a spiritual level know that you will be protected and they don't have the power to hurt you with magic or spirits. They just don't. Those kinds of beliefs can be turned into your protection; just ask to be protected—you are the good one. Believe. And having meltdowns is fine; don't blame yourself—these people are master manipulators that can get at anyone. We have just been lied to and perhaps believed that lie.'

19
FURTHER REVELATIONS

Through posts in the Facebook group and private emails and messages, I began to realise that huge numbers of people had been adversely affected by either witnessing or being subjected to abusive behaviour. After we removed those who either defended Sogyal or attacked others, many people opened up in the group, and for most of us it became a place of true healing. Victims found loving kindness, acknowledgement of their experiences, compassion for the pain they'd suffered, understanding of their feelings and perspective, support for their decisions, and help in examining their experience through different frameworks.

Students found great solace in realising that they weren't the only ones thinking that Sogyal's behaviour was wrong.

The result for me of hearing all these perspectives was that it became much harder to retain any respect at all for the person for whom I'd previously had so much devotion. I felt I'd been sucked in by a fraud, and I had to work to maintain a balanced view that remembered the benefit he'd brought to me and others. My disgust deepened.

One man phoned me, saying that he had to tell someone to get it off his chest. He'd witnessed Sogyal 'laying into' the cook at the 2017 Great Lakes retreat in Australia. I asked him what he meant by 'laying into', and he replied that Sogyal had punched the cook about five times. I asked if it was hard; he replied, 'Very hard.' The event was witnessed without comment or reaction by a student who is still in a management role. The event bothered my informant on two levels: first that Sogyal had 'laid into' the cook, and secondly that the other student saw it as completely normal and perfectly acceptable.

Sogyal could show great kindness, but it could be quickly followed by extremely aggressive behaviour. People felt a lot of fear and apprehension about which version he would be on any day. When 'mistakes' occurred, he met with the people involved to have 'training' sessions, some of which were videoed and parts taken out and later shown to students as 'activity teachings' which were supposed to be direct realisations from his wisdom mind and therefore very precious teachings. Unfortunately, this gave a lot of power to what he said and did when not in a formal teachings session; it was all seen as the teaching of a crazy wisdom master, but they weren't actual Buddhist teachings, not like those he taught when in a formal teaching situation. As Sangye said, *'He just made stuff up.'*

Some of the slogans that came from these 'activity teachings' were astute and helpful—'Never assume' and 'Always check' are two that often come to mind—and so students made the assumption that it was all good. Add to that the injunction against criticism, and it was all accepted without complaint. Unfortunately, even the useful slogans could be used to criticise others or as an excuse for punishment; for instance, if Sogyal discovered that you failed to check exactly what he'd said when he gave an instruction, he'd publicly humiliate you or worse.

People told me that he struck them with anything at hand—often his back scratcher, but also a cardboard tube, a mobile phone, a statue and so on—and hard enough that it hurt and might leave headaches, bruises and even bleeding wounds. Apparently, he often punched people in the stomach, also hard enough to hurt, and often for little or no reason that the student could discern.

One student told me:

'He [Sogyal] came in and I was happy to see him, thinking that he now wants to say, "Hello." He came up to me, and I felt very joyful and open towards him, but he punched me very strongly into my guts. I was shocked. Why did he do this?'

In this instance, Sogyal had blamed this student for something that wasn't her fault. She continued:

'He then said, "I create such situations so that we can learn something!" I found it very heart-breaking that I was found to be guilty of something trivial and of something that was not my responsibility. I cried later and had very strong belly cramps as a result of the punch.

'When I returned to the temple, Sogyal said that now he could trust me (since I did not leave, despite knowing so much about what really goes on) and that he would be able to give the Thögal teachings (the highest teachings) to me now. I felt very frozen by the fact that this was the price he wanted me to pay: not to question his behaviour whatever it may be.'

A year later he punched her in the stomach again for no apparent reason.

One person said that he made her management group form a circle, then he walked around and punched them all in the stomach, supposedly to change how they were. When she asked that he not hit her, he hugged her instead, but said that hitting was better than hugging.

Otherwise intelligent people accepted this without complaint, which added to the bizarreness of the situation. When one student mentioned to someone that she thought Sogyal's behaviour was madness, she was summoned to speak to him and told it was her perception that was wrong, not his behaviour. Complaints were mostly ignored, but when other students tried to provide care for those who saw the abusive behaviour as problematic, they, without any malicious intent, tried to make the complainant see the situation through the filter of the Rigpa 'party line', which made the complainant feel that they were bad, had bad karma, and ultimately that the problem was just their perception.

One woman spoke publicly on a video published on YouTube about her experience. I found this event particularly disturbing. The video was in French, but a French friend provided a translation for me:

> 'There was a woman, undressed, in a room, who was with Sogyal, she was unwell, you know, psychologically; I think that she had severe mental health problems and he was leading her around by a rope around her neck. He was laughing and making braying sounds as if she was a donkey. The humiliation was unbearable and yet we were unable to react. I was a feminist; I wasn't the kind of person who could

170

be pushed around and yet here I was in a situation of great psychological violence, of humiliation for that woman and also of humiliation for us as well, because we didn't have the means to react normally anymore. His way of operating is to rape. He does it because he can, because people are under his control. Therefore people don't run out of rooms shouting: "I've been raped!" It's traumatic, therefore for those people, like for me for instance, it took me a long time to recognise that I had been abused.'

Somewhere during all these revelations, an ex-Rigpa friend reminded me that several years ago Sogyal had attacked one of my Rigpa friends (now ex-Rigpa) for no reason. He told me that suddenly, out of the blue with no provocation, Sogyal had become angry, had verbally abused this friend, and then beat him up badly. I was shocked to hear about the beating because when the victim had told me that Sogyal had attacked him, I'd assumed he referred only to a verbal attack. However, the ex-Rigpa friend who reminded me of this incident assured me that our friend been beaten, and I heard this confirmed later from another source.

This shows how we simply ignore anything we don't want to have to deal with. At the time, I didn't want my devotion shaken, so I'd assumed that my friend had overacted when he referred to how bad the 'attack' had been, and it had never crossed my mind that he meant a physical attack. But by June 2017, I was finally ready to hear what some people had been saying for years.

A great deal of money was spent on Sogyal's visits to centres—expensive food and perfect specimens of fruit and vegetables had to be found and cooked to perfection, and grapes had to be polished. Rooms had to be spotless and the best accommodation found. He would request furniture to be moved and then moved back, justifying it as creating the environment for the teachings to happen. Several told me this crazy environment felt like adults running around to try and please the whims of a small child.

One student in a position of responsibility in Rigpa told me:

> *'My main "issue" is his complete and absolute indifference to the sangha based on how he's allowed money to be used, and how he uses it himself. I finally woke up to the fact that he has no loyalty for the students who have put so much trust and faith in him by pissing away millions and millions of dollars on ridiculous things. I had to wake up to my own "magical thinking" when I realized he really didn't care at all about the sangha except in a very abstract way as the source of the money that fuels his ridiculous lifestyle. I could talk about the hospitality budget being over $1,000/day just on food and entertainment, about spending another $1,000/day on accommodations, about always flying first class, about paying Rigpa international $3,500/day for Sogyal's fees and teaching team that travels with him on top of covering all the expenses, on top of recording all the teachings and giving them back to international for free.'*

Another said:

> *'SR had a million in Euros in his personal safe at Lerab Ling, plus other currencies, plus gold and jewellery. I have heard similar accounts of money in safes at other Rigpa locations as well as safety deposit boxes and an offshore account.*

'And cash was literally packed in suitcases for taking to India. Many people were asked to carry large sums of money from one country to another, bundles of the limit of cash you could carry, and then he'd collect it all up after he arrived.'

I didn't doubt these stories because I, just an ordinary student, during retreats saw his pettiness and insistence on the best. If his tea wasn't the right temperature, it had to be taken away and a new cup made—not just reheated. He insisted that his papers and cup be set a certain way in a certain place on the table and that table had to be in the exact 'correct' spot on the dais. But what he considered 'correct' placement one day, he might consider incorrect the next day, so his attendants could never possibly get it right, and then they were publicly belittled for their failure. They were supposed to 'tune into his wisdom mind' and know what he wanted. Students jumped at his every command, something I did myself when he asked me once to bring him something—I didn't want to be the brunt of his anger.

He shamed people in public—over their weight, their relationships, their emotional state. I saw a lot of this. He asked at one retreat if anyone wanted to be a boyfriend for one girl, saying that she 'needed a good fuck.' I would never remain with a teacher who said this kind of thing now, but at the time, I laughed nervously with everyone else. When those around you accept things without question, it's easiest to do the same, especially when there is a religious belief system supporting that acceptance. And when you're keen to receive the most powerful teachings, the reward delivered to the most devoted, you tend to not express anything that might make it appear that your devotion is questionable.

173

Some people reported that several years ago, around the time that Mimi's story had become public, they attended trainings given by a senior instructor —similar to the 'Representing Rigpa' one that I'd attended—where they were told that it was important we all agree that the allegations against Sogyal weren't true; that Sogyal is a crazy wisdom master and the issues perceived by those who complain is a matter of perception and lack of devotion. One student quoted above reported being shocked when she was directly told in one of these sessions that *'If we had no devotion, we would not be allowed to hear the prized Dzogchen teachings any more. The cult showed its true face more and more to me. I half-heartedly played along, while feeling more and more alienated from the whole community.'*

I learned that not only had this abusive behaviour been going on as long as Sogyal had been teaching, but also that in 1992, 1994, 1996, 2007, and 2013 people had confronted trustees and national directors with specific details of the abuse. Not only did those confronted do nothing, but also, according to one student …

> *'They used legal threats to shut people up, and they hired PR companies in multiple countries to "spin" the stories. I have no doubt that these tactics were directed by SR, and I've heard during the garden meetings the way in which the whistle-blowers of abuse have been labelled as having 'gone a bit off'. The tactics used to try to convince students that the whistle-blowers' views were wrong was to speak in exaggerated terms of SR's greatness, to love bomb them, or to publicly discredit them (as I was) or to use legal pressure.'*

One person said they *'had met with Rigpa management and given confidential and anonymised case examples which reported such issues as rape, sexual harassment, sexually transmitted diseases, abortion and an appalling litany of complaints,'* and had made a clear call for accountability which had been ignored. And the levels of physical violence appeared to escalate over time. Drolma told me:

> *'I could not give a figure to the number of times I was beaten by Sogyal, from being gut punched (and it was so far from being soft: it was so strong that the wind would be fully expelled from my lungs and I would double over) to being slapped on the face, hit on the head with anything, or being kicked (and yes these were all done with force and aggression). (And this is only one aspect of the abuse I received.) It was usually daily and often numerous times a day. I was in constant fear of displeasing him and strived to do everything to perfection and with equanimity and also with a wish to try to help avert the wrath from being inflicted on others. To use Sogyal's analogy of the "football team" if any one of us dropped the ball, then the whole team would suffer. This meant that I worked often till exhaustion, and so my logical mind was never given enough space to objectively step back and appraise what was going on. I was trauma-bonded.*
>
> *'At a few points in my time at Lerab Ling, I reached my limit of coping with Sogyal. During these periods, I would feel tormented for a number of months—being repelled by the sound of Sogyal's voice and unable to be around him without squirming in my skin. Yet I always blamed my impure perception and believed I was not fully committed.'*

Two acts close together changed her perception: one of Sogyal acting in an unsympathetic, frustrated way toward an elderly woman at a time when she was vulnerable, and when he was having issues with one of his girlfriends, this student 'took the fall' for the team and he beat her in frustration. At that point she realised that Sogyal was also a human being—

> 'an aspect that I had been blind to as I'd tried to see all his actions of those of the Buddha (as, of course, I'd often been taught). So, then, just like the flick of a switch, I recognised that "this is abuse". And with that, I started to reflect on all the ways in which I had allowed it to happen. It was like in The Wizard of Oz when the curtain is finally pulled back and you realise there is no 'all-mighty Oz', there is just a little man shouting into a microphone …'

When delivered by a master, behaviour that is not conventionally kind is traditionally seen in Tibetan Buddhism as a way to crush the student's ego, but the very idea of one's ego needing to be 'crushed' rather than simply transcended indicates a violent approach that, even if it was helpful for eighth century Tibetans, is not helpful for the majority of people today. There are non-violent ways to help a student recognise their grasping at a fabricated self. Drolma continued:

> 'It's hard to say at what point it passes from merely being unpleasant into being traumatic, but cumulatively it is very traumatic and soul-crushing, rather than ego-crushing. For some of us there have been periods of time, when we were repeatedly beaten and treated like an abused and unwanted dog.

'Humiliation was also routine, and would often be done in front of entire gatherings. It might include talking about something very personal from a student, something said confidentially in trust, and then used to ridicule or criticize them in front of everybody.'

This, I learned, is also a common control tactic used in cults.

'Then one might be compelled to sit at his feet and be told nice things and given hugs—"love bombed"—but these only happened on stage, in public. Behind the scenes it would be straight back to hitting and humiliation.

'For me the worst psychological abuse was the "Rigpa Therapy". There was a therapy formula which was used with a few people who were working closely with SR. During the session, the Rigpa therapist (who was also a Rigpa student and wanted to please the lama) would tell you that your problems were all just projections based on issues with your parents and nothing to do with SR hitting you, sexually abusing you or whatever. One "Rigpa therapist" told me, "The things I hear from women in these sessions, if I was to hear them in the real world, I'd have to report them." That was the problem in a nutshell: people believing real world principles no longer applied.'

20
A TOXIC CULTURE

These words by Sangye helped me understand what the culture was like in the inner circle of Rigpa:

> *'I was exposed to subjugation over time, beatings, punches to the face and stomach, and hit with objects randomly. The super pinch where he takes a fist full of your flesh and twists. It wasn't so hidden—people I hired who I tried to protect were also hit as if just to prove, "I do as I please".*

> *'Sogyal would fly into a rage—especially over something like money and who spent what. People had to justify that they were "worth it". "Showing how much you cost" became an annual ritual of being presented with a bill—like being told you are less than human. You are a slave—you must obey completely and be worth the price of feeding and housing you, and you're lucky to get that.*

> *'Life around the teacher in his 'household' leads to a lot of strange behaviour and recovery time from intense reactions [to the abuse]. Sogyal has parties, and people have to comply like robots; they must attend and create the right atmosphere for the teacher, drinking alcohol, of course, because "we are Vajrayana students."*

179

'Funny things happen, like mentally unwell people trying to visit, and they have to be kept away. The teacher may want round-the-clock guardians or at least ensure the place is locked down to protect all his things and stop someone from sneaking in. It doesn't seem so bad until you're seeing all the levels and privileges that Sogyal calls "showing you how to take care of people" as he pushes a bell to have his personal cook come running. He yells at them or speaks kindly according to the latest food, checks on them preparing meals for group lunches and visitors, and asks them to make a plate for an exhausted retreat manager having a breakdown or one of his companions for the morning.

'The intercom took over from the bell so he could just yell, 'Where is the food,' or a name over and over, and if the person takes more than twenty seconds to arrive, more yelling. It's madness ... if any of you had to be around it, you would quickly stop thinking that things are what they appear to be at the teaching venues. If Sogyal wants something and can't get it, he is relentless and enlists people to find it, acquire it or cajole someone to let him use their luxury house if they can be convinced. He sees himself as a great CEO, but he is mostly just a drain on resources, but also the main attraction to get bums in seats at retreats. Retreats supposedly don't make any profit, but without them, there seems to be a big problem making financial ends meet. Of course, large amounts of the retreat cost are to placate Sogyal.

'Most denialists were not in the household. The silence of those who know about the household is stunning; they don't *say it isn't true, because it is true. They just redirect attention away. Tuning in to the teacher means becoming an extension of his need to turn something on and off, or facilitate calls or video chats where you hear him berating and manipulating person after person. Then you are told to get out while he has private conversations with women and then come back when he was done. It became obvious there was no spiritual value or real wisdom of dharma, and I realized I was just a slave giving more and more.*

'There were times when nobody could be around the house so Sogyal could walk around naked or half-dressed and be massaged to sleep, daily two or three times by the multiple masseuses that he kept around for that duty. He even had a special massage room—rather than use it as accommodation. He would also send his masseuses to his girlfriends' houses, and he'd take one or more to his study apartment. We often had to work through the day and through the night—people eating breakfast in a rush before his voice commanded them, yelling into some phone or intercom. Sogyal rented another place with a beachfront view at Blueys Beach as well as the house Rigpa Australia built for him to "save money so we don't have to rent". He rented or used a student's house for his girlfriends. Two of those places were mostly empty other than when Sogyal went there during the afternoon or night time, usually alone with just one woman. At those times a driver was on call to pick him up.'

The following, written by another *What Now?* member, indicates how an ordinary student experienced this toxic culture.

181

Apart from sharing an example of the kind of public behaviour Sogyal displayed, it shows how students tended to blame themselves for not seeing a situation 'correctly', for not having enough devotion, understanding, or pure perception to see the abuse as acceptable—as the older students did. The following testimony also shows the mental bind students were put in and the effect of extensive chanting practice in putting students in a more easily manipulated state of mind:

> 'A very distraught woman approached Sogyal during a teaching; she had come in from a side door, was very vocal and clearly not in a good frame of mind. She begged not to be removed and to be allowed to approach him with prostrations, but Sogyal verbally banished her from his presence, very coldly and critically. Quite literally saying, "Remove her from my presence; I cannot stand to see her; get her out of my sight." I didn't know about the crazy wisdom ideas at the time, and was very shocked by his tone and that no one was assisting her or calming her down, and his very unkind and cold words were making her worse. She was eventually led away. This was in front of a full audience of students, and [at the time] the theatricality of it all dumbed down my sense of revulsion at the treatment of this woman, who I did not know. And there was no one to ask about it.

> 'So I was already compromised by having accepted without any proper discrimination the idea of wrathfulness, which I had otherwise only encountered in reading about different forms of deities. The clear implication was that Sogyal had the power to transform from one kind of emanation to another because he was such a high teacher.

'I should have challenged myself on the veracity of this and didn't, but also didn't really buy into it either, and in my mind that became a matter of me not having enough faith. So as I write this I can see how several times over, just in relationship to this, I was putting myself at the centre of the dilemma as an aspirant student who was constantly failing rather than an individual whose credibility was being stretched. Now I know that all my misgivings at that retreat were not about me being a failed student but about me failing to see in the right way the ethical bind in which I had been placed.'

The following comment on the *What Now?* blog during October 2017 was frighteningly perceptive, not only in its analysis of the situation but also in its prediction of the outcome in terms of Rigpa's behaviour:

Rigpa had, and still has, a collective psychological problem because long-term members hold beliefs that are far removed from those held by most members of modern society, whether religious or secular, and they've held these beliefs for a very long time. By now they're no longer psychologically capable of abandoning them.

Generally, even if people are members of a religious faith, if rational, they understand their obligation to live within the law, and observe a normal moral code. They may disagree in some areas and even be resentful, but since their faith probably has a code that isn't too different, the conflicts are usually minimal.

183

According to modern understanding and morality, the bizarre belief that an exploitative serial abuser like Sogyal can also be enlightened and that his actions are motivated by wisdom and compassion for those he abuses, isn't a religious one, it's the serious delusion of a cult member.

The abuser is likely a sociopath and a narcissist and the belief a version of Stockholm Syndrome, a codependence between abuser and abused and a survival strategy by the victim. In this context, it's a means of dealing with the cognitive dissonance of being constantly treated cruelly by the person they believe can relieve their suffering and transmit wisdom.

When this dynamic is also justified by scriptural references of any kind, it means abuse has been integrated on a philosophical and institutional level and although such perverted reasoning, even if backed up by magical tales from the past, can be dismissed from a modern secular point of view, its hold over the minds of both abuser and abused shouldn't be underestimated.

So what seems to be an ethical difference is, in fact, a psychological dysfunction that could be described as bordering on mental illness. A person may seem to be rational and fully functional, but if they've lost the ability to tell the difference between cruelty and kindness, it's no longer safe to assume they are.

The fact that abuse has not only gone unchecked but also been actively enabled for so long and that various lamas are now being drafted in to provide scriptural justification and suppress criticism by talking about demonic possession and threatening critics with hell realms is confirmation that this is a very deep-seated, collective psychological problem among many of Sogyal's older students.

Trying to deal with a collective psychological problem of this magnitude by presenting a set of rational moral requirements to a group of irrational people and waiting for them to comply is bound to be futile.

Judging by the way the Rigpa management is reacting, preventing further harm will have to involve a degree of forced cooperation rather than negotiation, and the only realistic way to do this is through the courts and financial authorities.

Absent this, Rigpa will delay, but may make some token gestures, possibly in time, even present an entirely fabricated new 'reformed' face to the world, draft in compliant lamas and carry on as a money-making business with exactly the same dysfunctional mind-set as before.

Unfortunately, this is exactly what has happened.

21
SEXUAL ABUSE

Though it was only part of the picture of Sogyal's abuse, the phrase 'sexual abuse' appeared often in headlines, presumably because it was more newsworthy than the alternatives. The vulnerability of people in a sexual relationship makes abuse in that situation particularly abhorrent. And when the perpetrator is a spiritual teacher—who by definition should care for his students and be a good role model—it's even more disturbing. The trust students place in a spiritual teacher and the power he has over them makes them even more vulnerable to his demands and leads to greater trauma when that trust is betrayed— something akin to the trauma experienced by a child abused by their father.

Like most students, before I discovered the actual nature of many of the relationships Sogyal had with women and investigated the factors that obviate consent, I assumed that Sogyal's girls were in a consensual relationship with him, which was what we were led to believe. The power difference between a teacher and student makes it difficult for students to say no, however, thus true consent is not possible. This is why teachers engaging in sex with students is not acceptable in Western culture.

However, in Tibetan Buddhism, sex is not seen as something opposed to spirituality, as Westerners often see it, but something that when following practices of sexual yoga can be utilised to assist the practitioner to attain realisation of their true nature and assist the guru in having a long life. Because of this, Tibetan gurus have long enjoyed sexual relationships with students, and this culture and belief system make it even more difficult for a woman to resist a guru's advances. Of course they want to help extend their guru's life! Of course they want that ever-elusive enlightenment promised by sexual yoga. These factors can make it appear that the women have willingly given their consent, but actually they make it even more impossible for there to be true consent. Such beliefs tend to coerce them into sexual relationships with the lama.

In her book *Trauma and Recovery*, Herman says:
'Conventional social attitudes not only fail to recognize most rapes as violations but also construe them as consensual sexual relations for which the victim is responsible.'

And even when the woman is genuinely a willing participant—one well-known guru claimed that women actively seek sex with him—are these gurus all practicing true tantric sex where the partner gains spiritual benefit? I think that's highly unlikely given what I now know about Sogyal and other high-profile lamas' bedroom behaviour. I know of one girl that Sogyal sent to another lama for sex. She didn't want to go, but eventually capitulated to her teacher's request. This was confirmed by the independent investigation. In the report Karen Baxter said, 'It is alleged that Sogyal offered one of his

188

female attendants to another lama for sex. I heard evidence that this happened on more than one occasion.'

One ex-student reported:

'Obviously some women willingly had sex with SR, but many others were heavily coerced into it with promises of spiritual benefits for themselves, or the dharma in general by prolonging his life, or the better passage of a dead parent through the bardos, or that they were the reincarnation of such-and-such. These "special" women were young, slim and pretty, of an identifiable physical type. Often these would be women who were totally new to the dharma and Rigpa and really knew nothing about anything. Certain women were just his whipping posts and scapegoats. He would use them sexually, abuse them physically, and humiliate them publicly. Some of these ended up in psychiatric institutions. One killed herself.

'Since the letter came out, many women have sought me out and confided in me personally, and other extremely disturbing accounts of sexual abuse have come to my attention through various channels. I have now had several extremely credible accounts of rape taking place over the last forty years. The women were in different countries and at different times, but the stories have a lot in common. Most of these women have no ability to deal with the kind of exposure going public would bring and therefore don't speak out. Some have gone to the police. From what I've heard it seems safe to assume that there may have been dozens of instances of rape across the years. But since these are crimes spread across different countries and any police force needs a

weight of testimony to take it to trial, it is hard to build a case.'

And that is just Sogyal. I read several first-hand accounts published in closed Facebook groups by women abused by gurus other than Sogyal. Their testimonies show that the way Sogyal behaved is the common mode of operation for Tibetan gurus, a mode that has nothing to do with true tantric sex and everything to do with manipulation and coercion.

In the book *Karmamudra: The Yoga of Bliss, Sexuality in Tibetan Medicine and Buddhism* the author Dr Nida Chenagtsang says, 'Sexual misconduct is very common amongst high level lamas,' and this was confirmed for me by two people who'd lived in Tibetan communities in exile long enough to learn that gurus having sex with a parade of young women was common practice. When I eventually realised just how widespread sexual abuse by gurus is in Tibetan Buddhism, I decided I would no longer consider myself a Tibetan Buddhist. I wanted nothing more to do with a religion that permitted, and even encouraged, such abuse.

I highly recommend the above book to anyone who is in a position where they have or might be approached by a teacher offering them karmamudra practice or demanding sexual favours. As Dr Chenagtsang says on page 53,

'There are some Tibetan Buddhist gurus today, both male and female, who have sex with many of their students and call it karmamudra, but I think that these teachers do not really know what karmamudra is and simply want to have sex with attractive young men and women. Some of the stories you hear about what these teachers do with their students also suggests that they don't really have much idea about how to have good quality or consensual sex either … But of course the problems start when such teachers get a lot of power and start abusing it and demanding their needs be met. All sorts of suffering follows.'

As I know all too well.

Given the widespread abuse of the notion that sex with a guru can be beneficial, this general acceptance of sex between teachers and students cannot continue. The book I mentioned above makes it clear that the reality of sex between gurus and students these days is likely far removed from a genuine tantric relationship, and so students would be best served by taking sex with their teacher out of the picture. Codes of conduct should expressly forbid it as anything else provides loopholes that can be abused—lamas can use dating apps for their assignations, and for genuinely loving relationships, sex can be delayed until they no longer have a student-teacher relationship. It is unlikely, however, that lamas will willingly give up such 'perks' of the job.

Many people came forward in the *What Now?* group and shared their experience of abuse. Some reported seeing women coming and going from Sogyal's room at all hours of the day and night, others mentioned isolated incidents of sexual harassment and still others hinted that they'd experienced prolonged sexual abuse. However, in the early days no one spoke in detail about their experience; so many months passed before I gained a clear picture of how Sogyal acted with the women in his 'lama care' team. When someone finally told me their story, I was deeply shocked because how he behaved in this intimate relationship seemed to indicate a real lack of concern for others, not to mention a very cult-like dynamic at the core of the Rigpa community.

Let's be clear on what we mean by sexual harassment: 'Sexual harassment and behaviours that fall under this category include: inappropriate touching; invasion of privacy; sexual jokes; lewd or obscene comments or gestures; exposing body parts; showing graphic images; unwelcome sexual emails, text messages, or phone calls; sexual bribery, coercion, and overt requests for sex; sexual favouritism; being offered a benefit for a sexual favour; being denied a promotion or pay raise because you didn't cooperate. And of course, some women experience what more aptly could be described as sexual assault: being forced to perform oral sex on a man in a position of power, a man in power forcing himself on the woman either orally, vaginally, or anally, being drugged and rendered unconscious or incapable of defending oneself.' Beverley Engel, *Psychology Today*, 'Why Don't Victims of Sexual Harassment Come Forward Sooner.'

According to Engel victims of sexual harassment don't speak up due to shame over what happened, a tendency for victims to blame themselves, denial or minimisation as a protective mechanism, fear of the consequences, low self-esteem and/or feelings of hopelessness and helplessness, and some may have a history of being sexually violated and so see it as 'normal'.

Engel says:

'Many don't disclose, because they fear they won't be believed, and until very recently, that has primarily been the case. The fact that sexual misconduct is the most under-reported crime is due to a common belief that women make up these stories for attention or to get back at a man who rejected them. Victims' accounts are often scrutinized to the point of exhaustion. In high-profile cases, victims are often labelled opportunists, blamed for their own victimization, and punished for coming forward.'

Rigpa's policy in reaction to public testimonies of sexual abuse appeared to be to discredit the person who spoke out—we were told in the special 'Representing Rigpa' session that Mimi, who spoke publicly about her sexual abuse, wanted revenge because Sogyal broke up with her and that she was merely a 'woman scorned'.

Given the added injunction in Tibetan Buddhism against criticising one's teacher, and the likelihood of Vajrayana-style character assassination, the likelihood of victims of sexual abuse by Tibetan Buddhist teachers sharing their stories publicly or taking legal action becomes even less than in a non-religious context. By the time victims have processed their experience sufficiently to have gained the self-esteem and emotional distance required to consider a court case, the statute of limitations would have passed in many countries. Legal action would also involve such a high degree of re-traumatisation that the prospect would be too much for most victims, especially since they know they couldn't trust that devotees wouldn't lie to protect their guru. Unfortunately the result is that the perpetrators get away with their behaviour, and so the abuse continues.

What follows is a written report sent to me by a woman who worked in Sogyal's care team. In it she shares her conversations with one of Sogyal's girlfriends. Of course, we haven't used her real name, and it includes allegations of the kind of sexual misconduct investigated by the Lewis Silkin independent investigation.

'I talked with and made friends with Sandra while she waited to go onto "night-shift" with Sogyal, and at some point I questioned why he does not sleep with his main attendant. She laughed and she said: "No, he does! He sleeps with all his so-called attendants. With me, too."

'She told me that Sogyal had asked for her phone number when they'd met first, saying that she was an old student from his previous life and they needed to stay connected. She started being close immediately. She worked in the lama kitchen in Lerab Ling and he would come in from behind, grab her breasts, push her towards the sink and say that this would liberate her of her karma of rape.

'She started sleeping with him. He would just say: 'Undress, walk around.' Then the whole thing would only last a few minutes, nothing special, no pleasure, but she felt special to be his consort and to have been his student in a past life. It was said that she had been a yogini (spiritually realised female) living in a cave close to Terton Sogyal, the so-called previous incarnation of Sogyal. Sandra also feels that her

194

practice is very advanced and that it gets enhanced by sleeping with Sogyal.

'The attendants have to watch porn videos with Sogyal, and they themselves are erotically filmed and photographed at his request by other Rigpa students. Sandra had to strip in front of him or in front of all the people gathered, e.g., in a living room or at garden parties, and dance like a prostitute in lingerie. Everybody attending the party witnessed this.

'Sogyal forced anal sex on Sandra. Once while in bed with her, he banged her hard in hatred saying, "I hate you; I hate you." She cried a lot afterwards.

He made the girls gather and line up and asked Sandra to lick the genitals of each of the girls. These kind of orgies seemed to happen sometimes. One of the girls said she didn't want it and left the room. Sogyal accepted that, and I told Sandra that she can say, "No," just as the other girl did, but she told me that he does not accept any "No" in her case. That he would beat her for being so stubborn and having such a great ego.

'When he went to the cinema with Sandra, Sogyal rubbed her vagina all the time, and it would be sore afterwards. Sogyal sometimes wanted Sandra to lick his balls to calm him down, sometimes for so long that her neck would hurt afterwards. He wanted blow jobs, and she had to show other girls how to do it right. Sandra was somehow proud to be the "mature sex-girl" that shows the others what to do and how to accept the heavy training.

'Sogyal never used condoms; Sandra would sometimes suffer from vaginal yeast infections. And every four weeks she had to go to Lodève, the nearby town, for full body waxing. All girlfriends have a driver who takes them there.

'Sogyal would tell Sandra to come over to his chalet and to wear this or that dress, and sometimes he didn't let her eat and sleep. He also rejected her when she was menstruating. He told her that she was there to give him long life, and she is very happy to be there for that reason.

'In the temple, Sogyal publicly criticized Sandra most of the time, belittling her, and nobody was aware that she was actually one of his attendants doing night-shifts. Emotionally she would often feel left out, not acknowledged, looked down upon by the inner circle and rejected by Sogyal. A push-and-pull game: he ignored her, then seduced her again and so on.

'Sandra received severe beatings. The girls around say that she is one of the worst beaten girls. One time, she had an open wound from a blow that Sogyal made to her head using a telephone. There was a gash on her scalp and the doctor who was on site at Lerab Ling was called to stop the bleeding. Sogyal didn't allow anyone to call an ambulance. As a result of this incident, Sandra was concussed for three days.

'Sogyal also physically assaulted her by beating her with his hands and kicking her with his feet. These beatings would be to the belly, on the head, on the back, beatings with sticks, and beating with a wooden back scratcher. Sandra was told that she purified negative karma on behalf of her nation. She said that she was liberating her ego, initially tightening up in fear, but now she can stay more and more soft, and it doesn't hurt her as much as before.

'Sogyal asked her for two years in front of another lama to sleep with that lama. She had to walk up and down in front of them, and the lama who is married did not venture to say: "I am married. Stop it." When he, Sandra, and I met outside the temple, I noticed that he just smiled at Sandra in a way that I found disgusting. But instead of saying, "No", or learning from it, she would tell me, that it was her final "test", and that she was horrified because she wouldn't be allowed to say, "No". I disagreed strongly with her. Her ex-boyfriend also knew of this request of Sogyal to sleep with the other lama, but he advised her not to tell anybody about it.

'Sandra was asked to give a blow-job to a senior student. The man was very uncomfortable with that and at one point he requested for it all to stop.

'One of the things that Sogyal told Sandra is that she should eat his shit and drink his piss. Sandra wouldn't, but she explained that that was due to her lack of realisation.

'He asked Sandra to leave any boyfriend she had who wasn't a Rigpa student. He also told her that an ex-student was dying of stomach cancer because he wanted to be his own Dzogchen guru and spoke badly about Sogyal sometimes.

'Sandra sometimes ran away from Lerab Ling, she told me, especially once in the beginning of the "training". She said a "troop" of lama carers were sent after her, and when they found her on site, she was told never to tell anybody what was happening in Lerab Ling with Sogyal.'

The woman who shared this information with me listed twenty previous girlfriends of Sogyal whom she personally knew. However it must be noted that he did have 'dates' with women and not sleep with them—one woman told me that was her experience, and that he hadn't propositioned her—and women were able to, and did, say, 'No.' One person told me that if they were in his close circle, however, they may later receive a beating for no apparent reason. We must be careful not to assume that this kind of experience was the same for all the women around Sogyal.

According to this ex-member of the inner circle, sharing girlfriends and wives with Sogyal is common place for those in the inner circle, and he tells them who should have sex with who. She spoke of a couple being made to have sex in front of Sogyal.

Here's a testimony from the Lewis Silken Independent Investigation Report:

'He suddenly asked me to lick and touch his genitals. He said it in a jovial way and I wasn't sure if he was serious. [The other student] smiled and said, "Yes, do it". I tried but I freaked out, and he said, "Oh, that's OK," and he dismissed me. The next day I felt very uncomfortable and said I was not well and stayed in bed. A couple of hours later I was called and told he wanted to see me in the garden straight away. I went to the garden reluctantly, and he started screaming abuse at me, saying, "You think I'm attracted to you; why would I be?" He was aggressive, and it was terrifying. I was not used to being yelled at. I started to cry and felt panicked. I said I didn't think that, but felt bad because I had failed him and his test. He immediately turned nice and said, "Oh no, you did well." I felt shaken and was not OK with it. I had no one to talk to.

'I then went to [another country] with him [as part of the lama care team] and I was leaning over to give him something. He put his hand down my top and touched me. He said my nipples were young. I felt shocked.

'[Some time later], I attended a retreat and was feeling better and more on track. I was alone with him in the shrine room and he asked me to give him a blow job. I tried to be a good Buddhist and see it as a teaching. It was an out of body experience. I didn't want to do it but I did. I didn't

do it for long, and he then dismissed me. It felt like a power play, he didn't seem particularly aroused.'

The following story from the biography of Lingza Chökyi translated by Bryan Cuevas in *Travels in the Netherworlds* (Cuevas 2008, pp. 48–50) shows why women in the grip of the Tibetan Buddhist belief system are afraid to say, 'No,' to a Tibetan lama's request for sex or to speak out if they feel they have been taken advantage of.

'The young lady from a well-to-do family, named Chödrön, had sought out Buddhist teachings from numerous esteemed lamas. One of them, the itinerant Zhönu Gyaltsen, asked her to be his "secret consort," but she refused. The request caused her to lose faith in the lama and leave the gathering before receiving the complete instructions. Later, she told girlfriends about the incident. In Yama's assessment, since Zhönu Gyaltsen was a master of esoteric teachings, Chödrön had breached her tantric commitments (Skt: samaya, Tib: dam tshig) on several counts: not complying with the lama's request, not completing the training in his teachings and (worst of all, it seems) speaking about the incident with other women. When Chödrön protests that if the lama was realized, it was inappropriate for him to take a sexual interest in her, Yama counters that when Zhönu Gyaltsen died, numerous relics and miraculous signs occurred, attesting to his high degree of realization.

Positioning her as a gossip, he avers that she caused numerous others to lose faith, thereby harming the lama and his disciples. He concludes, "It is a greater sin to

200

denigrate and slander lamas and teachers than it is to murder a thousand living beings," and condemns her to suffer the torments of the hell realms.'

I found this story in an online article written by Holly Gayley (Department of Religious Studies, University of Colorado) called 'Revisiting the "Secret Consort" (gsang yum) in Tibetan Buddhism.' It appears in the Religions section of the MDPI website. She goes on to say about the story:

> 'As a literary representation of normative ethics, we should read Chödrön's disturbing tale as prescriptive (rather than descriptive): conveying how women should or should not act regarding the sexual advances of Buddhist lamas. Therein is a potent message that capitulation to the teacher's wishes is virtuous and defiance has dire consequences as does breaching the secrecy that typically surrounds such encounters. Nowhere is it questioned (and the tale is attributed to a female delok from the sixteenth century, Lingza Chökyi) whether a realized master could act unethically or whether his sexual advances may have harmed Chödrön. Her tale raises questions about religious authority, misconduct, and secrecy that remain salient as ever today.'

Note that in the Lewis Silkin independent investigation, the conclusion came to for the allegations that Sogyal used his position to coerce, intimidate and manipulate young women into giving him sexual favours was that there was a 'significant weight of first-hand evidence which leads me to uphold this allegation'. The report also includes a statement that reveals patterns common to many sexual abuse situations with Tibetan lamas. These are the patterns women need to watch out for:

> 'In the first, women undertaking lama care (i.e. acting as attendant to Sogyal) were told, upon entering his room, to lock the door and take their clothes off, whereupon Sogyal proceeded to have sex with them. As described to Witness B, they did not feel they had a choice in the matter, and submitted to him in a state of shock since he was their master.

> 'In the second, Sogyal would talk about marriage with the female student, indicating that she was very special. She would then find out later that he was having sex with multiple partners. On one retreat, a student told Witness B that she estimated that Sogyal Rinpoche was having sex with seven women including herself.

> 'In the third, women found themselves attracted to Sogyal out of curiosity, knowing him to be sexually active. However, once involved, they frequently found themselves unable to extricate themselves from the relationship.'

22
TO STAY OR NOT?

A big question for Sogyal's students was whether or not we would stay members of the Rigpa sangha. Some people never wavered from their devotion to Sogyal and commitment to his organisation; others remained because they weren't sure of the truth of the revelations; out of those who decided Sogyal couldn't be their teacher anymore, some of them left Rigpa immediately, but many waited to see how Rigpa would respond before eventually breaking their ties with the community.

The Rigpa community, or sangha as we called it, was important to its members, like a spiritual family. In the last few years, I'd only gone on retreat to see my sangha friends, because I'd come to the point where I knew Sogyal's teachings so well that I could think the words he was going to say next as he said them.

Many students, including me, had put a lot of time and effort into making Rigpa the organisation it had become—one dedicated to bringing the supposedly authentic dharma to the West—and we'd developed many friendships as a result. In the first six months after the letter came out, no one I knew wanted it all to fall apart; however, later many decided that if Rigpa was only going to continue to propagate the beliefs that enabled the

203

abuse—and it appeared that they had no desire to change on that fundamental level—it was better that they disband. In the early days, most hoped Rigpa could reform and grow stronger without Sogyal, and many were willing to stay and help make that happen.

One comment on the blog in August 2017 expressed the initial hopes shared by many:

> *'Please, all of you, stay together as a sangha, and help Rinpoche to correct whatever was harmful. He is going on retreat to reflect. What you all created together is a model to us all, your three-year retreat, publications, love, brightness, devotion, monastics. Teachers are human, and subject to the exact same things we are, both good and bad, and everyone is redeemable; I'm confident of that. Please don't leave and dismantle all that you all built with such heart. I think that sangha needs each other more than ever now. What happened—the hurt, reported abuse of power etc—is done; may everyone heal swiftly.'*

However as time passed, it became clear that Sogyal didn't seem to think he had anything to correct and so he wasn't going to change—just stay away until the heat died down—and the sangha, despite their attempts at greater listening and care, tended to ignore ordinary students who kept demanding better of management. More of the people I knew left.

I left as soon as I realised that ethics simply wasn't as important to many Rigpa students as it was for me. I asked myself what kind of people I wanted as companions on the spiritual path, and I knew that it was vitally important for me to be alongside people who had no doubt that ethical behaviour was the foundation of an authentic spiritual path. I wanted to walk alongside those who practiced kindness and compassion, not those who couldn't recognise abuse as abuse, or those who appeared primarily interested in protecting their lama, their organisation, and their religion. And I didn't want to take as my companions people who closed their eyes to the pain of others, or practiced blind devotion. I wanted to be surrounded with people who were willing to examine and question, and demand answers where they weren't forthcoming, and in Rigpa, despite the attempts at change, I kept hitting ceilings beyond which my questions would not be answered and my concerns, though they may have been listened to, were not given any consideration.

I felt that remaining in Rigpa would mean I was, on some level, condoning not only Sogyal's behaviour but also the blind devotion that had enabled him to behave as he wished with impunity. I wanted nothing more to do with unquestioning devotion, especially when it was so badly misplaced.

The members of *What Now?* became my new spiritual community.

My realisation that Rigpa wasn't the right spiritual family for me strengthened as I grew aware of the mechanisms by which Sogyal apparently controlled and manipulated his closest students and which they, in turn, used to manipulate ordinary students. Others, however, went through a similar reflective process and chose to stay in Rigpa regardless of their feelings about Sogyal. The Rigpa organisation is full of good, hard-working people who are genuinely studying the dharma and who are acting with the best of intentions on the basis of whatever guidance they're receiving from instructors and teachers they trust. I completely respect their decision to remain, honour those dedicated to genuine reform, and pray that their trust is not misplaced.

They say that large ships take a long time to turn, but I have no faith in the captains of the Rigpa tanker. And I don't have the patience to keep banging my head against a brick wall, aiming to make a dent, when all I get for it is a headache.

23
PRACTICE REPERCUSSIONS

What happened to people's spiritual practice during this time? It varied considerably. Some kept doing the same practices—though not many of those I interacted with—several, like me, kept up the Vajrasattva practice for a while, but then it fell away as our disillusionment with the religion grew. The general lack of willingness from Buddhist teachers to become 'involved' or to provide guidance that was of any genuine use on the matter of abusive gurus contributed to a large extent to students leaving Tibetan Buddhism. More often than not, all that those hungry for reassurance that the religion didn't condone abuse received was more of the same kinds of teachings that Sogyal had used to enable the abuse in the first place!

The problem with Vajrayana practice in the case of guru abuse is that one's guru is central to the practice, especially in the practice of Guru Yoga where the student merges their mind with the wisdom mind of their master. Someone who has been abused by their guru could hardly be expected to do spiritual practice with the perpetrator of their trauma as the central focus. To even attempt it would simply traumatise them all over again. Many of those not directly abused, however, struggled to try to continue their Vajrayana practice. I often had people ask me how they could continue their ngondro—Vajrayana pre-liminary practices—when they couldn't bear to see Sogyal's face and the word 'lama' brought up his image in their mind.

I reminded them that the lama they were supposed to visualise was not Sogyal Rinpoche, but Guru Rinpoche, the teacher who'd brought Vajrayana to Tibet and who, in practice, was a symbol for all the gurus and enlightened beings. But, unfortunately, Sogyal had tried to get us all to believe that he *was* Guru Rinpoche in the flesh, which meant that in our minds they were one and the same, or at least so closely related that one couldn't even practice with Guru Rinpoche without him being associated with Sogyal. In this way, Sogyal's behaviour stained the whole practice and turned many students away from the Vajrayana.

Some got around this unfortunate association by using an image of the Buddha as the guru in practice instead of Guru Rinpoche, and some used the Tibetan syllable AH which helped them get away from seeing the guru as any single person. I also discovered that Vajrayana practice worked quite nicely if I substituted the word 'Buddha' for 'lama', while recognising that the word 'Buddha' also referred to my own Buddha Nature. That way I 'cut out the middle man'.

The centrality of the guru concept in Vajrayana and Dzogchen practice meant that once group members had seen that our outer guru was unreliable as an anchor for our practice, we reaffirmed the ultimate meaning of guru in the tradition, and turned our attention to the guru within, the true nature of our mind, the recognition of which is the whole point of practice. For the most long-term students, this happened the very instant we gave up our outer guru. With no outer guru to demand our devotion and servitude, those of us who had trained in Dzog-chen automatically took refuge in our inner guru, and realised that we had relied on our outer guru for too long.

Leaving Sogyal was incredibly liberating.

Many of us had the same realisations at around the same time. We saw how, though Sogyal diligently taught us that the ultimate guru was within and that our whole task was to recognise that inner guru, in practice he fostered a kind of dependency on him. Devotion to the outer guru in Vajrayana is merely to facilitate recognising and realising our inner guru, but while being told to turn our minds in, not out, he encouraged us to look outwards—to praising him, serving him, seeing him as our saviour, always wanting another teaching, always looking outwards for the final moment that Sogyal would give us the key to our enlightenment. But in fact he'd already given most of us the key. His failure was that he didn't then tell us to go away and use it, instead he kept us always looking for a new key.

And so for many of us, after leaving Sogyal our practice became what for us Dzogchen practitioners it should have been all along: looking inwards to our true nature, every moment, day and night, like the unceasing flow of a river.

Far from dropping our practice and abandoning the dharma as some accuse us of doing, we used the circumstances of our disenchantment to deepen our practice, though with a different form. The devotion that opens us up to the nature of our mind, we discovered, ultimately has nothing to do with a person.

Cut loose from the restrictions imposed on us by Sogyal and Rigpa, we gave up set ideas of what spiritual practice entailed and took that freedom to follow the guidance of our

209

inner guru. We shared links to video teachings by a variety of teachers, including psychologists and scientists, and we revelled in our freedom to listen to whoever we wanted and entertain any idea we found interesting—but we stayed well clear of falling into another guru trap.

Many of us gave up formal practice for a time, and some gave up Buddhadharma entirely. Most of us didn't chant mantras or prayers, or do visualisations, but life became practice. If we did any formal practice, we turned to something uncomplicated, like compassion practices or sitting practice—Shamatha, Vipassana, Dzogchen—and focused on being authentic dharma practitioners in our lives, on being kind, compassionate, mindful and aware. Some turned to engaged dharma and social activism.

Some of us, myself included, found a unique form of personal spiritual practice emerging, something that, though an outcome of our years of Tibetan Buddhist study and practice, was free of cultural and 'religious' baggage. And some of us found ourselves maintaining or returning occasionally to Vajrayana. I wasn't the only one who found deity practices free of negative associations. For me, these deities were simply unstainable, their pristine purity far beyond the capacity of anyone or anything to taint my relationship with them, a fact I found most comforting. Even when I was most disgusted with the behaviour of some who called themselves Tibetan Buddhists, I never once lost my love of essential Vajrayana practice beyond its cultural trappings.

Our search for enlightenment became less urgent when we realised how one's hunger for it can lead one astray. Pretty much everyone felt that being a kind and decent human being was far better than giving a guru complete power over you in the hope that you'll 'get there faster'. From our present point of view, the promise lamas gave that with Tibetan Buddhism we could 'achieve enlightenment in one lifetime' sounded like nothing more than a hook from a dodgy spin doctor. Many, if not most of us, and certainly myself, have been left deeply suspicious of anyone who remotely appears to be taking on the guru role. That doesn't mean that we aren't open to a slow realisation that someone does actually warrant our trust, but we'll not be rushing into anything, and we'll be looking out for warning signs.

24
RECOGNISING TRAUMA

'Trauma is perhaps the most avoided, ignored, belittled, denied, misunderstood and untreated cause of human suffering.' Peter Levine.

When I asked for contributions to this book from the *What Now?* group, one woman said:

> *'One of the big barriers I see [to genuine change] is that most people in Rigpa cannot put themselves in the shoes of a trauma victim/survivor and understand what it's really like, the extent of damage that has taken place, and how that damage continues into the future.'*

The dynamics of guru abuse are similar to those in domestic abuse situations, victims are just less likely to realise they're being abused because of the spiritual beliefs that help the perpetrator to deny their actions and blame the victims. Domestic abuse is often thought of as physical abuse, but emotional abuse is also a serious form of domestic abuse. Had we been educated on the dynamics of emotional abuse before entering Rigpa, we would have recognised it immediately. But, of course, anyone not in the inner circle didn't see the full picture.

In an article titled 'The Truth about Domestic Violence and Abusive Relationships' on her blog, psychotherapist and relationship expert, Darlene Lancer, LMFT says, 'Victims of abuse often live in denial.'

Many people who were emotionally, physically and/or sexually abused are still in Rigpa and still run Rigpa, but they don't think Sogyal's actions harmed them. Perhaps they found enough benefit from being close to Sogyal that it overshadows for them any pain, confusion, or trauma caused by his actions. Or perhaps their devotion to him and their belief that his actions were beneficial for them is such a core belief in how they see themselves and their place on the spiritual path that it is unthinkable for them to consider any other possibility. The results of a different perspective might shatter their perception of themselves as advanced spiritual practitioners who could 'handle the heat'. To set aside their beliefs and look at their experience directly without the conceptual overlay of thinking 'this is wisdom love' and evaluating truthfully the result of their *every* interaction with Sogyal takes incredible honesty and courage, as does looking at their experience through the lens of the literature on trauma and destructive cults.

Until those who've been verbally abused, beaten, and sexually harassed step outside their indoctrination, they have not recognised the trauma they've experienced, and so they don't recognise it in others. This is a major issue for them in developing the compassion and understanding required to relate to those who have left knowing they have been abused. Is 'putting themselves in the victims' shoes' too confronting? Would recognising the depth of the trauma and its repercussions make them see it in themselves?

I understand completely why one would resist putting themselves in the role of a victim. It is certainly more reassuring for one's ego to maintain the illusion of being an 'advanced' practitioner blessed by the actions of a crazy wisdom master. Perhaps, however, they could manage the term 'survivor' or simply don't apply a label, rather just recognise that they may have been harmed more than they realise by his conduct.

Judith Herman MD's book *Trauma and Recovery: The Aftermath of Violence-From Domestic Abuse to Political Terror* provides a helpful framework for re-evaluation, and it was of major assistance in helping survivors to understand the dynamics involved, realise that they had been abused, and to recover from their trauma. It was also a key source for the education of those of us who supported the survivors.

This excerpt from the book—reprinted by permission of Basic Books—describes exactly the situation in which those working close to Sogyal found themselves:

'Psychological trauma occurs as a result of a distressing event or series of events involving feelings of intense fear, helplessness, loss of control, and threat of annihilation. We are traumatised when no action we could take will help resolve the situation. When we can't effectively resist or escape, our system of self-defence becomes overwhelmed and disorganized. Our physiological self-preservation system goes into permanent alert, a state of hyperarousal, the first symptom of post-traumatic stress disorder in which the traumatized person startles easily, reacts irritably to small provocation, and sleeps poorly. …They cannot resume the normal course of their lives, for the trauma repeatedly interrupts … both as flashbacks during waking states and as traumatic nightmares during sleep. Small, seemingly insignificant reminders can also evoke these memories, which often return with all the vividness and emotional force of the original event. Thus, even normally safe environments may come to feel dangerous, for the survivor can never be assured that she will not encounter some reminder of the trauma.'

Thus safety is of vital importance to survivors healing from trauma, which is why when someone didn't feel safe in the group, the moderators took action. Those who espoused the Rigpa 'party line', by thinking that those who recognised their treatment at Sogyal's hands as abuse had simply misunderstood Vajrayana, constantly undermined survivors' self-esteem by denying their experience and their evaluation of it—exactly what they'd been subjected to by Sogyal and the Rigpa culture. We removed such people from the group, not because of our difference of opinion, but because the beliefs they promoted re-traumatised survivors and undermined their healing.

I see now that any real concern for survivors' healing, any true compassion, required one to give up defending Sogyal and the Rigpa belief system and to recognise the damage both had caused. Recognising the damage meant recognising the flaws in the belief system, and those in power in Rigpa are apparently not prepared to go there.

But it's not just what's said that can be unhelpful for healing, it's how it's said. The moderators—regretfully and after much deliberation—also had to remove a couple of people who'd been abused decades ago from the group because they

216

were pushing other victims to take legal action and belittling anyone who professed any gratitude for their learning while with Sogyal. Other abuse victims told the moderators that these people made them feel bullied, even re-traumatised, because being forcibly told what they should think and do was reminiscent of how they'd been treated in Rigpa. Some said that they couldn't trust that they wouldn't use something said in confidence in the group if it suited their agenda for legal action, and so we had to remove them to ensure a continuing feeling of safety in the group. I wish we'd been able to provide a place for everyone, especially because these people had been so terribly hurt by Sogyal and Rigpa, but it simply wasn't possible to keep everyone happy, so the four moderators made democratic decisions based on what we felt was best for the group as a whole.

At the same time those of us not directly abused were trying to understand just what it had been like to be in Sogyal's firing line. Herman's description of prolonged repeated trauma describes the experience of students in the 'inner circle' exactly:

> The perpetrator 'seeks out situations where his tyrannical behaviour will be tolerated, condoned, or admired. The perpetrator's first goal appears to be the enslavement of his victim, and he accomplishes this goal by exercising despotic control over every aspect of the victim's life. But simple compliance rarely satisfies him; he appears to have a psychological need to justify his crimes, and for this he needs the victim's affirmation. Thus he relentlessly demands from his victim professions of respect, gratitude, or even love. His ultimate goal appears to be the creation of a willing victim. ... Fear is also increased

by inconsistent and unpredictable outbursts of violence and by capricious enforcement of petty rules. The ultimate effect of these techniques is to convince the victim that the perpetrator is omnipotent, that resistance is futile, and that her life depends upon winning his indulgence through absolute compliance. The goal of the perpetrator is to instil in his victim not only fear of death but also gratitude for being allowed to live. ... Terror, intermittent reward, isolation, and enforced dependency may succeed in creating a submissive and compliant prisoner. But the final step in the psychological control of the victim is not completed until she has been forced to violate her own moral principles and to betray her basic human attachments. Psychologically, this is the most destructive of all coercive techniques, for the victim who has succumbed loathes herself. It is at this point, when the victim under duress participates in the sacrifice of others, that she is truly 'broken.'... Survivors frequently recall that what frightened them most was the unpredictable nature of the violence.'

If you have no experience of the kind of prolonged terror experienced under the control of an abuser or no understanding of the kinds of manipulation and control used on victims of guru abuse, you might think that in similar circumstances you'd show greater courage and resistance than the victim. This leads to the common tendency of others in the community to assume that the victim must have some defect in their personality, but research indicates 'no evidence of serious psychopathology before entering into the exploitative relationship.'

As is common in traumatised people, survivors of guru abuse that I've been in communication with, not just from Rigpa but also from other Buddhist communities, reported feeling utterly abandoned and alone without any form of care or protection; something which, afterwards, left them with a sense of disconnection which pervaded other relationships. And the inability to satisfactorily resolve the traumatic situation in which they found themselves leaves the person prone to shame, doubt and guilt. These feelings often arose in our group discussions.

Herman says that guilt comes from trying to learn some useful lesson from disaster and to regain some sense of power and control; thinking we might have done better might be preferable to accepting that we were utterly helpless. 'Feelings of guilt are especially severe when the survivor has been a witness to the suffering or death of other people.' And this is something all of us who witnessed even the less obvious forms of abuse had to come to terms with. At the time, we were relieved it wasn't us on the receiving end of Sogyal's bullying, and we also felt terrible that we could do nothing to help the person being abused, at least not without opening ourselves up to the same treatment.

Traumatized people lose their trust in themselves, in other people, and in this case, the religion that has failed to protect them. Experiences of humiliation, guilt, and helplessness batter one's self-esteem, and intense and contradictory feelings of need and fear compromise their capacity for intimacy. Trauma destroys the identity of the person the victim was before their traumatic experience. This is why reconnecting with who we were before is so important for healing.

Admitting that Sogyal had actually harmed a lot of people, that the behaviour we'd tried to see as enlightened action was in fact abuse, was painful for those in leadership roles who had supported the culture of abuse by teaching students the Rigpa explanation. The group situation allowed such students to apologise, something that was vital for their healing and the healing of others. This testimony from a student higher up in the organisation than I, expresses these feelings well:

> *'I have been really uncomfortable defending Rinpoche's way of training and behaviour and feel doing so has not been good for my personal sense of integrity. I have been really distressed for years hearing about experiences of students that felt they were abused and harmed. I felt pressure to see things purely and to not criticize the teacher.*

> *'I also realize now that I was numb and out of touch with my emotions and was not able to clearly see what was happening to others and myself. This is actually really scary. I hope this way of training has helped some people, but my experience shows me that there may be others like me who will not process their experiences possibly for years to come.*

> *'I know that I have been afraid to speak up and remove myself from supporting this harmful behaviour not to even speak of stopping it. I feel like I have supported and allowed to continue a way of training that has had very damaging side effects for some and that some people did not have the means to deal with it and turn it into growth and learning. At least not yet. I have also put doubt on the credibility of*

*descriptions of behaviour by Rinpoche because of fear that
to the outside world it would clearly look like abuse. I would
like to express my sincere apology to all those who feel
harmed, and I am reflecting how I can contribute to right
that. Like I said, to help people heal and ensure that such
experiences do not reoccur in the future.'*

And from another student:

*'I am deeply grateful to all the positive that has come from
receiving the Dzogchen teachings from SR and the
recognition and truth of that can never be sullied or
removed from my heart. I listened to a short teaching this
morning and just cried because it hit me that I don't even
want to hear any more teachings from him.*

*'I am so saddened and disgusted by all the harmful
behaviour, and attempts to conceal and deny it, by both SR
and Rigpa the organisation. I apologise for any part I may
have played in condoning it, that may have upset another
person (including my own children and family).'*

Some Buddhists say that even in highly traumatic
situations, trauma is not experienced by great spiritual
practitioners, and they cite those Tibetan Yogis who came out
of Chinese prisons after decades of incarceration and torture
with great realisation and no ill-will towards their torturers.
However, the dynamics of spiritual abuse in the inner circle is
more akin to a domestic abuse environment than that of an
incarcerated yogi.

And Herman says as a result of her studies that, though personal resilience does affect the impact of traumatic events to some degree,

> 'Individual personality characteristics count for little in the face of overwhelming events. There is a simple, direct relationship between the severity of the trauma and its psychological impact ... Only *a small minority of exceptional people* appear to be relatively invulnerable in extreme situations. Studies of diverse populations have reached similar conclusions: stress-resistant individuals appear to be those with high sociability, a thoughtful and active coping style, and a strong perception of their ability to control their destiny.'

But Sogyal and Rigpa took away that ability to control their destiny.

Though different people react differently to traumatic situations, the effects of trauma reside in the body and brain, even if unacknowledged, and will have long-term impacts. People with Buddhist belief systems may not be aware of their post-traumatic stress syndrome but that doesn't mean they don't suffer from it. They may ignore their symptoms or not speak of it to anyone in their keenness to 'not dwell on it', but even if they don't recognise the symptoms in themselves, they will suffer long-term repercussions for being in what any psychologist would recognise as an abusive and traumatic situation.

The book *The Body Keeps the Score: Brain, Mind, and Body in the Healing of Trauma* by Bessel Van der Kolk makes it impossible for us to deny the profound extent of trauma and its impact on our lives. One of the world's foremost experts on trauma, Dr. Bessel van der Kolk has spent over three decades working with survivors. In *The Body Keeps the Score,* he uses recent scientific advances in neuroscience to show how trauma literally reshapes both body and brain, compromising sufferers' capacities for pleasure, engagement, self-control, and trust. Trauma physically affects the brain and the body, causing anxiety, rage, and the inability to concentrate. Though our minds try to leave trauma behind, our bodies keep us trapped in the past.

Though mindfulness is one tool that can be used to help trauma victims, Buddhism is not therapy, and therapy of some kind is required to help the abuse survivor examine what happened to them such that they can assimilate their experience and move forward with their life.

Long term verbal abuse can break people emotionally and mentally, make them unsure of themselves, unable to recognise their true value, and unable to trust anyone or anything. Sogyal confused this breaking people down emotionally and mentally with breaking down one's ego. However, the ego that needs to be removed in Buddhism in order to reveal our true nature is our grasping at the idea of an inherently existing self, not our basic sense of self or healthy ego that we need in order to navigate the conventional world. What he was really doing was crushing that basic healthy sense of self, destroying people's self-confidence and self-esteem, not assisting the recognition of how we grasp at our false idea of ourselves, which we can do far better when not put in circumstances that stimulate our fight or flight impulses. In such extreme circumstances as we see in Sogyal's alleged behaviour, when we are completely helpless, we are far more likely to dissociate—a common response to traumatic situations in which one disconnects from one's thoughts, feelings, and sense of identity. The dissociation triggered by abuse can be experienced, as Herman says, as a:

> 'state of detached calm, in which terror, rage, and pain dissolve. Events continue to register in awareness, but it is as though these events have been disconnected from their ordinary meanings. Perceptions may be numbed or distorted, with partial anaesthesia or the loss of particular sensations. Time sense may be altered, often with a sense of slow motion, and the experience may lose its quality of ordinary reality. The person may feel as though the event is not happening to her, as though she is observing from outside her body, or as though the whole experience is a bad dream from which she will shortly awaken. These perceptual changes combine with a feeling of indifference, emotional detachment, and profound passivity in which the person relinquishes all initiative and struggle.' [Judith Herman MD, *Trauma and Recovery.*]

This describes a state that could easily be mistaken for some kind of spiritual experience. But dissociation is not the same as 'resting in the recognition of the nature of mind'.

Because dissociation is a common, and useful, automatic response to traumatic situations, some who remain in Rigpa are likely to have dissociated when subjected to beatings and, in order to make sense of the situation, may think that a dissociative state is a spiritual experience. Several abuse survivors mentioned to me that they spaced out, even to the degree of no longer feeling as if they were in their own bodies as the only way they could cope with the abuse.

Darlene Lancer LMFT in an article on her blog titled 'The Truth about Domestic Violence and Abusive Relationships' says:

'Emotional abuse is insidious and slowly eats away at your confidence and self-esteem. The effects are long term, and can take even longer to recover from than blatant violence.'

A survivor of abuse in another sangha posted this in a survivor's group about the effect of emotional abuse:

'They didn't hit me, but they destroyed all I was as a person. I didn't even realise it was abuse, because it wasn't physical. It was the mental abuse that wore me away like an eraser removing a pencil mark on a piece of paper. It never really goes away. It fades, but you still know that traces of it are left behind. I live with those traces every single day.'

I watched that kind of destruction in progress, and all I managed to do was creep out of the shrine tent because I couldn't watch it anymore. Was it truly not a problem for the victim, or was she unknowingly traumatised by it? She certainly appeared traumatised

The following conversation in our *What Now?* Facebook group from early in 2019 (published with permission) shows some of the long-term results of emotional abuse.

Student A:

'I have an intense fear of doing things wrong that I acquired during my time working with SR. He would constantly

criticize, humiliate, or be punitive if you didn't get things "right"—according to his wishes and preference. But those wishes and preference would often change without notice.

'This fear crops up whenever I am doing something new and different or something big, or almost anything where there might be mistakes. I'm glad I'm becoming conscious of it now, so I can heal it.

'Many people just cannot grasp how deeply these seeds get planted and how your trauma brain then gets easily activated—over and over—as a result. It's such a deep gut experience of fear.

Student B:

'At the end of the day, he taught me nothing through these tactics when I worked with him — anything positive was offset by the negative. Or worse yet, was so woven into the irrational and childish behaviour that it was crippling to me. Now I am having a very hard time doing anything. The legacy is toxic.

'At one point, I used to think he was training me to be more mindful in the moment — 'visualize don't conceptualize' was actually great advice. Unfortunately, he didn't do that himself, or he would have known what people were up against, what the reality of a situation was in practice. But that also requires empathy. Otherwise 'visualizing' is just a fantasy.

There is also the problem of ownership. If you don't own what you tell someone to do, and then fault them (intensely) for not doing something different than you said, especially when you are very demanding about people doing things to your exact specifications, then you are creating a very dysfunctional working relationship. You are not 'working with people's egos' when you can't work with your own and admit your own mistakes. We all learn by example. And his was no way to learn how to be.

'In your case especially, when he was telling you that you were ruining his work, and even when you did exactly what he said, you were made to be wrong. That is some fucked up shit right there. Please know that. You were trying to get right what he was making impossible to get right, and you were doing it for him, and ostensibly for the dharma. And now you are recognizing that it was all too wrapped up in his pathology to ever be right.

'May we all learn deeply from this that this is not the way, and never be pulled into that kind of shit ever again. May we work with kindness and true perception and empathy wherever we go and whoever we become, always. And never again get sucked into a narcissist's delusions of grandeur.

Student C:

'You write "Now I am having a hard time doing anything. The legacy is toxic." I am too. For the first time in my life I can no longer self-motivate. I didn't get what many of you had from working far closer in, but I feel like the spiritual stuffing has been knocked out of me. I am looking at things *again, but really I am not motivated much. I used to believe in something more, and now I don't know, and as all the creative things I did were fed by this 'something more', I feel rudderless and without direction. I do not even know where to start. I can be positive for everyone else, but a lot less so for myself. I have a lot going on in my life one way or another that contributes, but in my more dour moments I wonder whether Rigpa has left me broken.'*

Though those directly abused suffered the most, everyone in the community suffered spiritual abuse by having their trust in their guru shattered. This post from an ex-Shambala student expresses the bind in which even ordinary students of Tibetan Buddhism find themselves where a teacher and community are not 'walking their talk':

'The core damage, for me at any rate, has come out of a severe double-bind effect. Tibetan Buddhism introduced me to the notion of basic goodness — and then stomped all over it, tearing it to pieces. Cognitive dissonance multiplied. Eventually it short-circuited my mind, my basic funct-ioning.

'The teachings told me I needed to trust myself, trust in my clearest and sharpest intelligence and understanding. Then the teachers and senior students undermined this, over and over and over again. Which was correct, the teachings or the teachers? The problem was, I was also taught that the teachers 'were' the teachings. And everybody had taken loyalty oaths to the hierarchy in any event, so they all followed suit. Nobody would ever contradict a teacher.

'So at that point the question became: which was correct, the teachings or, effectively, the community? But then I was 'also' taught that the community was the 'lineage', that the teachers were representatives of the lama, who in turn represented the protectors and all the buddhas and bodhisattvas. In other words, and pardon my Anglo-Saxon, I realized that I was fucked. Totally lost. Condemned. But no one is condemned — that is what the teachings say. Yet, in fact, I was condemned. But no one ... and yet ... But no one ... and yet ...

'It has been very difficult for me to entirely shake loose from what has been appallingly destructive conditioning, leading to paralysing self-doubt and self-condemnation.'

The pervading belief system in Rigpa created a culture that conspired to silence and discredit victims, which added another layer of trauma, and every time people levelled these same arguments at victims, or treated the victim in a similar fashion, it triggered this secondary trauma, thus harm was heaped upon harm. This extract from page four of the pdf version of *Trauma and Recovery*, by Judith Herman, describes how perpetrators in general try to escape accountability. According to several first-hand reports, it is also an accurate description of Sogyal's mode of operation.

'In order to escape accountability for his crimes, the perpetrator does everything in his power to promote forgetting. Secrecy and silence are the perpetrators' first line of defence. If secrecy fails, the perpetrator attacks the credibility of his victim. If he cannot silence her absolutely, he tries to make sure that no one listens. To this end, he marshals an impressive array of

229

arguments, from the most blatant denial to the most sophisticated and elegant rationalization. After every atrocity one can expect to hear the same predictable apologies: it never happened; the victim lies; the victim exaggerates; the victim brought it upon herself; and in any case it is time to forget the past and move on. The more powerful the perpetrator, the greater his prerogative to name and define reality and the more completely his arguments prevail.'

The sophisticated and elegant rationalisations Sogyal used were what I've called the Rigpa 'party line'—beliefs I will discuss in the next section of this book.

Drolma told me, *'At the time that I left, I was not aware of, nor connected to anyone else that had been able to turn their perception of their experience around to see it as it was: abuse. Sogyal discredited me to the people that I left behind. I found that the people that I'd previously counted as my friends within Rigpa could no longer be trusted not to betray my confidence as they all reported back to Sogyal. I felt exceptionally vulnerable and unsafe.*

'I returned to Australia in June 2011 and the disconnect I felt was mammoth. The [Rigpa] "family" that I'd left either rejected me or kept a polite stance: "We won't talk about what's just happened, will we? And besides, Sogyal has changed: since you left, he's stopped hitting people and is so much more loving!" The family that I returned to in Australia had no concept of what I'd come from or the trauma I'd experienced. I was full of shame and felt like I'd failed.'

25
GASLIGHTING AND INSTITUTIONAL BETRAYAL

'Gaslighting, like all abuse, is based on the need for power, control, or concealment. ... The term actually refers to a deliberate pattern of manipulation calculated to make the victim trust the perpetrator and doubt his or her own perceptions or sanity, similar to brain-washing.' Darlene Lancer, MFT, 'Gaslighting 101: Signs, Symptoms, and Recovery.'

Gaslighting can be so subtle that the victim isn't aware they're being manipulated. It's a malicious form of abuse designed to alter the victim's perception in a way that serves the perpetrator's agenda. Gaslighting is illegal in the UK.

Whistle-blower gaslighting is one term that has been applied to retaliation against people who report misconduct. Whistle-blowers (I prefer the word 'truth-tellers') are further traumatised by the emotional manipulation routinely used to discredit and punish those who report misconduct. According to a paper titled 'Institutional Betrayal and Gaslighting: Why Whistle-Blowers Are So Traumatized,' by Kathy Ahern, PhD, RN,

'Whistle-blower gaslighting creates a situation where the whistle-blower doubts her perceptions, competence, and mental state. These outcomes are accomplished when the institution enables reprisals, explains them away, and then pronounces that the whistle-blower is irrationally overreacting to normal everyday interactions. Over time, these strategies trap the whistle-blower in a maze of enforced helplessness.'

The paper goes on to state that the effects of whistle-blower reprisals include anxiety, sadness and distress, 'akin to the grief associated with the death of a loved one' and even disabling post-traumatic stress disorder (PTSD) symptoms that first start with self-doubt and then escalate 'in a spiral to a loss of sense of coherence, dignity, and self-worth.' One student expressed this culture of truth-teller gaslighting in Rigpa by saying:

I saw the systematic use of bullying and manipulation— used consciously and intentionally by some core people in the organisation, but for others (probably most people) taking part in it either unconsciously or backing this method up in good faith because they are kept in the dark of things having gone wrong. The bullying method has a lot of varieties, but mainly I've seen this: People, who have been directly affected and/or tried to speak up, address concerns and so on, both directly to Rinpoche as well as to people responsible in the organisation, have been ridiculed, shamed, made silent, singled out and isolated, been given many direct and even more indirect messages about 'being the only one having concerns', 'troublemaker', put in category with 'other lunatics' (as well as lacking devotion and pure perception and so on). This has often happened in subtle and hidden ways so it takes time to discover, as does most adult bullying. Part of the method has also been to point out people's personal issues.'

This wasn't something that occurred only in relation to the eight letter writers. It had been going on for years. While in Rigpa, I'd heard such allegations made against every person who had ever criticised Sogyal or Rigpa in any way.

Sangye continued to share his experiences on Facebook, and some in Rigpa used the manner of his writing as a way to discredit him. And yet, as Herman said in *Trauma and Recovery*, 'People who have survived atrocities often tell their stories in a highly emotional, contradictory, and fragmented manner which undermines their credibility.' In light of my deepening education on the dynamics at play here, I realised that Rigpa's standard response to truth tellers constituted further abuse of those who'd already suffered at the hands of the organisation and their leader.

In her article 'Gaslighting 101: Signs, Symptoms, and Recovery,' on her *What is Codependency?* Blog, psychotherapist and relationship expert, Darlene Lancer says:

'The perpetrator often acts concerned and kind to dispel any suspicions. Someone capable of persistent lying and manipulation is also quite capable of being charming and seductive. Often the relationship begins that way. When gaslighting starts, you might even feel guilty for doubting the person whom you've come to trust. To further play with your mind, an abuser might offer evidence to show that you're wrong or question your memory or senses. More justifications and explanations, including expressions of love and flattery, are concocted to confuse you and reason away any discrepancies in the liar's story. You get temporary reassurance, and increasingly, you doubt your own senses, ignore your gut, and become more confused.'

It appears to me that not only were those directly abused subjected to this kind of treatment but also the whole sangha are victims of gaslighting both in sessions with Rigpa instructors and in Rigpa management's communications to the sangha, which actively distort members perception of events. For example, they spoke about a 'press campaign' levelled at Rigpa and Sogyal. There was no campaign, just a bunch of different people speaking out about their treatment, and yet, in true gaslighting fashion, Rigpa persisted in suggesting that those who were speaking up had somehow organised a 'campaign' 'against' Rigpa and Sogyal. An idea that was then used to discredit the whistle blowers and their message.

In their communications, Rigpa management appears to manipulate members' perception of the 'situation' by never referring to the abuse or the harm Sogyal's actions have caused, emphasising the good they and he have done, limiting information, misrepresenting events, and reassuring members that they've changed. However, their actions never quite lived up to the reassurances. They said one thing—often in inspiring language—then did something that wasn't quite what they said they'd do, and then reported that they'd done what they said they'd do. Rigpa's website listing saying Sogyal and they have apologised is one example.

Here's how it worked for the ordinary attendee at a retreat: After every event of public humiliation, the victim

234

would stand up later in the day or the next day and say how they experienced Sogyal's verbal abuse as love and care. It made us think, 'Well, if they aren't bothered by it, then it's not a problem.' This was teaching us that good and bad, and right and wrong are a matter of perception and that what's important for your happiness is how you think about something, not the event itself. There is some truth in that idea, of course; which is why we could believe it. However, in this situation that concept was used to control and subdue us, and to make us come to see abuse as kindness.

Even after witnessing something distressing, there was no point complaining to anyone because we knew we'd just get the 'talk' about it being crazy wisdom, and your complaint would likely be reported to Sogyal in which case he might single you out for that same treatment—fear is a powerful method of control. While watching the public humiliations we were also told 'don't make stories,' and 'they're just thoughts and emotions; don't get caught up in them' which led us to ignore our gut feelings that what we were watching was wrong. They were training us to not honour our own perception and reframe the abuse so we'd see it the way they wanted us to see it. Encouraged by Sogyal to remain in meditation during these displays, those watching were likely in some kind of trance or meditative state in which one is highly responsive to suggestion and psychological manipulation.

And then if you wanted the 'highest' teachings, you had to at least appear to be so devoted that you accepted everything Sogyal did as enlightened action, and we all wanted those teachings so we did what was needed to get them, which included not having an 'issue' with the abuse. Sogyal used to mock anyone who complained as them having 'issues' and he completely denigrated 'issues' as being just fabrications of the mind with no basis in reality. We believed the spin until we saw how bad his behaviour truly was. The revelations jolted many of us out of the brainwashing, but others remain held by it, and they're pretending to be healthy. My heart bleeds for those who haven't become aware of this manipulation, but you can't rescue people who don't want to be rescued.

An example of this kind of gaslighting can be seen in a video, recorded in Ventura in 2015, in which Patrick Gaffney said the following:

> *'I've known Rinpoche for over forty years now, and so I can say with full confidence that I've never seen him do anything which wasn't compassionate or didn't come out of love, or come out of a deep wish to care for people. And so one huge key to who Rinpoche is, is care, or caring. And in his teaching—apart from destroying our concepts, apart from introducing us to our nature of mind—one of the things he is doing is teaching people how to care for, not only themselves, but how to care for one another. And you'll see this, a caring, not [just] in the teaching, but also in his interaction with people. Teaching how to care.'*

I think I've described the actual situation and the effects of Sogyal's behaviour on abuse victims enough for you to see how incredibly twisted it is to call public humiliation teaching people how to care for ourselves and others.

Gaslighting is a form of emotional abuse, and it's hard to see when you trust someone. Having love and respect for someone, as we did with Sogyal and Rigpa, is a strong incentive to believe the lies and manipulation, and gradually you lose trust in your perceptions. You no longer trust that what you see as humiliation is humiliation. You subdue your own instincts in order to see it as 'care'. Darlene Lancer, LMFT, says in 'Gaslighting 101: Signs, Symptoms, and Recovery':

> 'We use denial, because we rather believe the lie than the truth, which might precipitate a painful breakup. This is especially true if all the bad behaviour was out of sight, and memories of the relationship were mostly positive. We lose not only the relationship and person we loved and/or shared a life with, but also trust in ourselves and future relationships.'

And so we denied what we didn't see personally, minimised what we did see, and finally took a very long time to recognise the depth of the lies.

One student directly abused told me:

'I have flashbacks to things I allowed to be done to me that are horrifying, things that he said to me publicly in the shrine room, no one ever stepped in to stop him. One time he hit me so hard before a teaching I couldn't stop crying; I sat in the shrine room balling my eyes out. NO ONE asked if I was okay; I got multiple emails saying how happy people were to see how deeply Sogyal was working with me—the asshole had just brutalized me in a small meeting; there were people who knew exactly why I was crying. Why didn't anyone say/do anything?

'Personally, I think that it's due to his perversion of the teachings, taking something whole and real and beautiful and warping it to suit his sickness. We all felt the power and authenticity of the teachings and somehow that got conflated

with Sogyal's abuse. Many of us who stuck with it despite great personal cost did it because we had faith in the wrong thing.'

Gaslighting is a tactic that Rigpa appears to use consistently in every communication with the sangha and their manipulation of the truth goes so far as to include actual lies—as revealed in a detailed post on the *What Now?* blog titled 'Lies Damn Lies and Lerab Ling'.

We noted that the word 'abuse' was never used, yet the word 'allegations' was used a lot. The word 'compassion' is used to suggest that they are giving a compassionate response, all while nothing was being done to support the many people left traumatised.

Back in 2016 a press release by Lerab Ling in response to a highly critical book on Sogyal and Rigpa said, 'Both Rigpa and Sogyal Rinpoche categorically reject the assertions of abuse and cult-like behaviour that have been made in this book.' Then after a local newspaper put out a piece about Lerab Ling, the Press Release was re-issued, now with an explanatory letter which complained, 'For several weeks, Rigpa and Sogyal Rinpoche have been the victims of a malicious media campaign based on the publication of a highly critical and extremely prejudiced book ... We are deeply shocked and dismayed at the way Lerab Ling and our spiritual director, Sogyal Rinpoche, have been depicted. In no way does this picture correspond to reality.'

All the while, it seems, the behaviour outlined in the letter by the eight and confirmed in the Lewis Silkin Report continued. Rigpa said one thing and did another, and made themselves out to be the victim.

You might think, 'Oh yes, but this was back in 2016. Rigpa is better now.' Are they? At the end of 2018, the phrases 'media campaign' or 'press campaign' were still being used in oral presentations to discredit Rigpa's critics. And even after the findings of the independent investigation vindicated the contents of the letter by the eight students, senior students were still calling the 'allegations' 'unfounded' (meaning not true) in video presentations shared with the sangha.

The sangha Connection newsletter that came out after the report on the independent investigation was released in August 2018 refers to the victims of physical and sexual abuse committed by Sogyal without using the words 'victim', 'sexual', 'physical', 'abuse', 'harm', or even the name 'Sogyal Rinpoche'. Instead they use the phrase 'those who are hurt' to cover all of this. Using the present tense 'are hurt' instead of the past tense 'were hurt' means that you are not referring to injury or trauma that occurred somewhat in the past, you are referring to feelings experienced in the present. Thus the 'harm' is once again minimised in the reader's mind to 'a feeling of harm', not an actual harmful event. This seems to me to be gaslighting in action.

As Jo Greene states in his blog post on *What Now?* titled 'Missing the Connection':

'Instead of saying "those who Sogyal hurt"—which has a definite sense of cause and effect, with the cause of the hurt identified—a word is substituted to create the bizarrely neutered "those who are hurt" as if the nature and cause of the hurt are unknown. And that's without even changing "hurt" to the more appropriate "harm".'

239

Hurt is a feeling. Harm is something caused by abuse.

Space is always given in communications to saying how much good Sogyal has done and reminding students of his links with other lamas. As Jo Greene says:

> 'A person with compassion would understand how inappropriate it is to recite these affirmations any time the issue of the bad things he did is tiptoed towards. It is insensitive and has upset many of the victims a great deal.'

Take a look at this excerpt from a sangha connection email: 'Friends who have left Rigpa and may have an unresolved ethical question or complaint that impacts on their peace of mind' can contact the new Rigpa councils for support. Again the minimising of severe abuse into something that 'impacts on their peace of mind.' As Jo says:

> 'That's a very delicate and low-key way to refer to matters such as having your ear half ripped off, or having a piece of furniture smashed over you and then being compelled to do degrading sexual acts, or being ordered to give a blow job whilst trying to carry out your professional duties. The Rigpa leadership know who these people are and they know how to contact them. Would compassion not consist of getting in touch and offering support rather than telling victims to write to an email address?'

Members of an organisation, and especially a religious one, trust that the organisation will have their best interests at heart and will act with integrity. Institutional betrayal occurs when an organisation betrays their members' trust, and Rigpa did this in their mishandling of the revelations of abuse. We expected better from them. We expected they would show sympathy and concern for the abused, that apologies would be forthcoming and resignations immediate, and that they would be willing to look deeply at the causes and make fundamental changes to the enabling belief system.

But no, instead, they went for a more subtle form of cover up—denying or minimising the abuse—and Band-Aid solutions that look good but lack any underlying conviction that what Sogyal did was wrong. Add to that the manipulation of members' perception through soothing and self-congratulatory communications, and promises of noble-sounding undertakings which their consequent actions do not live up to.

What we came to realise was that the people in positions of power put finances first. Not people. Not enlightenment. They sacrificed the truth-tellers because they criticised the man who brings in their biggest income. We all wanted to believe that Sogyal and Rigpa had our best interests at heart, but it became obvious to us that the interests of the organisation he founded came first, before the rights of any individual within it. Rigpa management valued the reputation of the organisation over the well-being of members or any commitment to ethical conduct and Buddhist values. This realisation hit us hard, but after months of false assurances and actions not meeting their words, we came to see that it was true.

I saw, in the reactions of even ordinary students not directly abused by Sogyal, signs of distress, grief and trauma created through the betrayal of trust by both Sogyal and Rigpa. Institutional betrayal in a religious community is called spiritual abuse, and we were all spiritually abused, betrayed by a person and an organisation we trusted.

This betrayal hit the ordinary student so deeply that some wanted nothing more to do with the Tibetan Buddhist religion, even to the extent of finding images and terminology that reminds them of their involvement offensive. The deeper the betrayal and the worse the abuse, the more likely it is that such reminders will trigger a painful flashback. One student examined this reaction in herself:

'Like so many of us, I find myself increasingly triggered and annoyed by my friends' online posting of imagery, portraits, videos and quotes from the "heavies", but also and even from any Tibetan Buddhist teachers at this point. I've been asking myself what exactly it is that revolts me so much, and what it is in the images or words themselves that is traumatizing to me. What I realized is that what's more triggering to me than the content itself is the recognition of my former self. I'm disturbed by my unpleasant identification with the person posting. For me, the triggering is less about the offensive abusers' faces, the tired and trite dharma phrases, or the sacred art reduced to cookie-cutter images; it's more about the discomfort of seeing my younger self, a parroting acolyte, in these ongoing posts.'

Rigpa management needs to understand that in addition to their organisational cover up the abuse for decades, it looks to me as if they're accountable for gaslighting, institutional betrayal, reprisals against whistle-blowers, and failure to protect people from Sogyal's abusive behaviour.

26
SPIRITUAL BYPASSING

In *The Gelug/Kagyu Tradition of Mahamudra* (pp. 209-210) His Holiness the Dalai Lama says:

> 'It is not healthy, of course, for disciples to deny serious ethical flaws in their guru, if they are in fact true, or his or her involvement in Buddhist power-politics, if this is the case. To do so would be a total loss of discriminating awareness. But for disciples to dwell on these points with disrespect, self-recrimination, regret or other negative attitudes is not only unnecessary, unhelpful and unproductive, it is also improper. They distance themselves even further from achieving a peaceful state of mind and may seriously jeopardize their future spiritual progress. I think it best in this circumstance just to forget about this teacher.'

Unfortunately, however, it's not easy to simply forget, and such emotions in cases of abuse are natural and need to be given space to rise and their validity recognised before they can truly fade away. Otherwise we risk repressing them, and they will keep returning to haunt us. If we don't process what happened to us, we cannot heal, and working with our emotions is a huge part of healing. We must walk the line between dwelling on our emotions and repressing or ignoring them. Meditation practice teaches us to watch the emotions rise and let them fade without getting caught up in them, which is great training for remaining calm regardless of what arises in us, but we also must honour the validity of our feelings and examine the situation that caused them in order to assimilate our experience into the totality of our life.

It takes time for students of abusive lamas to be able to forget about such teachers, and the longer one has studied and practiced under them, the harder it is to simply forget. Having nothing more to do with them is easy, once you've left the abusive situation, but can one ever forget someone who for decades played a pivotal role in your life?

Joanne Clark states this well in her blog post 'Rigpa Students in a Quandary' on the *Buddhism Controversy Blog*.

> 'When a relationship between a student and her tantric master goes bad, I mean really bad, trauma to the student can run very deep. In my own case, I could no longer think straight. I was an abject, slumped-over, stumbling human being, smoking in the dark and making plans to commit suicide. Speaking out and investigating were absolutely essential steps for me. I needed to hear that I still had a voice and a functioning mind. I needed to understand what had happened.

> 'After years of subverting my own wisdom to justify my lama's actions, I needed to recover that wisdom so that I could regain my self-respect. I needed to investigate and better understand where my lamas had gone wrong so that I could stop blaming myself for everything, stop my "self-

recriminations". So it took me time to arrive at a point where I could "just forget about" my past teachers.

'The Buddhist path demands brutal honesty and huge courage. If we are to have the courage of the bodhisattva, we need to be unafraid to face ourselves and our lamas with that honesty. For myself, I worked hard to stay clear of anger, ill will or disrespect towards my lamas. That was my main goal as I moved forward to health and strength. I know that's threatening and hard for some, particularly those who are survivors of sexual assault. Emotions are going to be powerful and we can only do our best.'

The need to investigate the situation and see it from a framework free of the beliefs that kept us stuck in that situation is a vital part of the healing. It's nice to think we might be able to simply 'drop it' all and be done with it, but there is psychological work to be done, and 'dropping it' prematurely might be spiritual bypassing of the issue rather than a healthy response.

'Dropping' happens naturally when something has run its course after achieving its purpose—for instance thoughts or feelings that perhaps the hitting you're experiencing might not actually be doing you any good will continue to arise until you examine whether that thought or feeling is true or not. In Buddhist meditation, however, we learn to not pay too much attention to thoughts and emotions. Meditating this way brings us a measure of peace by helping us to not get caught up in, or dwell on, rising thoughts and emotions, but the resulting spaciousness and ability to focus mainly helps with mental reactions and issues, rather than physical or emotional ones—at least not directly and not without being directed towards self-examination and physical awareness. Because of this, it's easy to use meditation techniques to bypass our problems, issues and feelings rather than to help us deal with them.

This is known as 'spiritual bypassing'. We ignore our issues in the name of spiritual practice, but they don't go away, and one day they arise with a vengeance and kick us in the butt. Unfortunately, in Rigpa many of us became masters of spiritual bypassing—isn't that what we did when we gave no credence to the feelings bubbling up inside us while we watched Sogyal publicly humiliate someone? Our thoughts dissolved when we paid them no attention, but a gut feeling remained, and we ignored it, too. We didn't listen to our own wisdom. We sat like zombies, thinking we were advanced practitioners because we didn't react, but perhaps we were really just numb, naïve and scared.

The Rigpa meditation instructions facilitated spiritual bypassing because they gave no credence to our inner wisdom or to the feelings in our body. The instructions are to let thoughts and feelings arise and let them go, but never were we taught to acknowledge or give any weight to those thoughts and feelings before letting them go. Letting go became something we did, not something we allowed to happen naturally, and so it became an active method of repression or bypassing.

Sogyal often accused people of too much thinking. He blamed thinking too much—'making stories' he called it—for all our ills, and we came to consider thinking a bad thing. We took instructions meant to free us from being ruled by our thoughts to the extreme of repressing them, and we were not corrected because it suited Sogyal not to have us think for ourselves and especially not to use our critical thinking faculties. One student wrote:

> *'After 25 years of trying I was faced with realizing that I didn't know how to work with myself, my mind, my heart. Looking back I can clearly see I was heading towards physical and emotional breakdown.*
>
> *'This turned out to be the beginning of a personal healing journey. I am understanding now that one main reason of why I was heading towards breakdown was because I was trying really hard to repress a lot of pain and conflicting emotions that were starting to surface because I did not have the understanding, skillful means and support to deal with them.'*

A commenter on a Facebook post said:

> *'I know one thing, I spent way too much time being still, endless hours of stodgy sitting and Shamatha and mantras (with no result other than credentials), when I should have been dancing into joy and openness.'*

27
FURTHER PSYCHOLOGICAL PERSPECTIVES

Gaining a psychological perspective on what we'd experienced was very important for freeing us from the beliefs that held us in Rigpa. Our study of the literature, widely available on the internet, on trance states and induction, trauma, cult behaviour and recovery, codependency, disassociation, narcissistic personality disorder, spiritual bypassing, and gaslighting gave us a different framework through which to view and evaluate our experience.

> 'All this teacher-student relationship stuff used to make sense. The best way for me to understand what happened is that it became mixed with "trance induction" and "peak experience" along with suggestion. Hypnosis is real, and suggestion can make us see what is not there or believe we experienced what we, in fact, merely manufactured for ourselves to experience to complete the task assigned. Then we are asked to be grateful for being guided. Which mostly we are. We tell ourselves, "This is probably what I was looking for, no … not probably; it must be. I am where I am supposed to be," and almost, as if by magic, the lama says the same thing. He or she seems to know what you are thinking, but it's only because they suggested it anyway and lead you there—you are seemingly not alone. They are in

there with you, guiding and acknowledging your thoughts, and it becomes deeply personal. So much so that you go on a long journey of trust.

'My trust has been massively broken, but the journey continues, and I think maybe the bathwater that they wanted me to discard was worth keeping, and the baby was the infantile lama. Either way it became a very contrary and solitary mission to chuck it in.' Sangye.

Group Hypnosis and Trance states

A hypnotic trance state, being a calm state of altered-consciousness, can easily be thought to be meditation. 'Hypnosis' and 'meditation' are both rather nebulous terms and therefore not easily compared, but we can say that the main difference is that meditation is self-induced and *with full self-awareness*, whereas hypnosis is usually induced by another person (unless it's self-hypnosis) and the person is in a state of trance, amnesia or unconsciousness.

Hypnosis is an artificially induced altered state of consciousness, characterized by heightened suggestibility and receptivity to direction, and abusive cults use methods to induce and prolong trance states to make devotees easy to manipulate.

Hypnotic gaze induction is a trance induction technique used by hypnotherapists, and you can find instructions for how to do it on the internet. It involves 'maintaining eye contact with someone but in an inviting manner rather than an aggressive one.' The hypnotherapist subtly communicates the hypnotic trance state by 'accessing an altered state of consciousness himself, and directing the subject to follow you in a non-verbal but powerful way.' (Tony Mask, 'Five Secrets of the Hypnotic Gaze Induction,' *Hypnosis Unlocked*.) The result is that the person who gazes into the hypnotherapist's eyes enters a trance state.

When we sat in meditation with Sogyal, especially during an 'introduction to the nature of mind', he told us to look at his eyes, saying, 'Eyes here,' while he pointed at his eyes and looked at us with the soft gaze recommended for hypnotherapists. We sat and stared at him for large periods of time. And we used the same 'soft' gaze in our meditation practice. Apparently, anyone doing this for long enough will eventually enter an altered state.

I recognised the difference between true meditation and trance states in my latter years in Rigpa. When in a group situation with Sogyal, or when the group was doing a chanting meditation, I felt peaceful and relaxed, but also dull and sleepy. I found it hard to feel strongly about anything, and had trouble staying awake. But when practicing meditation alone at home, or even simply when I walked away from the group, my mental state became crystal clear and wide open—the state I had come to know as meditation. In my early days, I expect that I had mistaken the group trance state for a spiritual experience, but after many years of diligent practice, I could recognise the difference between that and the awareness and clarity of true meditation.

Rigpa retreats also used methods known in cult literature to extend trance states and make devotees easy to manipulate. In a paper called *The Manipulation of Spiritual Experience: Unethical Hypnosis in Destructive Cults* by Linda Dubrow-Marshall, and Steve K. Eichel, they stated:

'Continuous lectures, singing and chanting are employed by most cults, and serve to alter awareness. The use of abstract and ambiguous language, and logic that is difficult to follow or is even meaningless, can also be used to focus attention and cause dissociation (Bandler & Grinder, 1975). Information overload can occur when subjects are presented with more new data than they can process at given time, or when subjects are asked to divide their attention between two or more sources of information input or two or more channels of sensory input; this tactic is almost identical to the distraction or confusion induction methods in hypnosis (Arons, 1981).'

Our retreats consisted of hours of video teachings as well as Sogyal's daily two to three-hour visits. Often we would be trying to follow three different strands of teaching topics as well as having meetings and meditation practice sessions, including a couple of hours of chanting practice. People often got 'information overload' and felt 'overwhelmed', something Sogyal used to mock people for, saying they should 'get over it.'

I don't believe that those running the retreats did any of this with any ill intent or awareness that this was a cult tactic. They simply followed Sogyal's wishes and, presumably, felt that the more teachings we got the better, even though the diet was far too rich for most people to digest.

Chanting, of course, is part of the tradition, but in Rigpa it was all done in Tibetan which made it meaningless for most people. The amount of instruction given on these practices was minimal and, I suspect, inadequate for the majority of students.

252

I only did them at home, where I could practise in English and at my own pace, making sure I fully actualised the practice, rather than just parroting words.

The above paper explains how these methods make participants more pliable, less critical, 'more dissociated from him/herself and more apt to accept spurious and even preposterous notions as "facts".' Another reason why we found ourselves sitting there watching abuse and accepting it as if it were perfectly okay.

The above paper states 'spiritual experiences can be secularly produced rather than divinely inspired, especially with the aid of a willing subject and a reasonably facile natural or trained "hypnotist". … Manipulated pseudo spiritual experiences may be the rule in cults.'

When I first read this kind of information, I found it very disturbing. I didn't want to consider that my spiritual experience might not be what I thought it was, but when I finally did get up the courage to re-evaluate, I realised I had sufficient knowledge and experience to ascertain the difference between a trance state and a true meditative state. Dubrow-Marshall and Eichel do say that 'true spiritual experiences may occur.' It's up to us Rigpa students to look carefully at the teachings on overcoming obstacles at a Shamatha level and at a Dzogchen level, distinguishing the nature of mind from its look-alike states, and then self-evaluate with uncompromising honesty.

The true nature of our mind is not an altered state; as even Sogyal used to tell us, it is an *unaltered* state. It's our natural pure awareness recognising its own nature, its empty essence, cognitive nature, and unconfined energy. It could never be called 'unconscious' but is rather an extremely refined state of conscious awareness.

Narcissistic Personality Disorder

I'd never heard of narcissistic personality disorder until I went on this journey of discovery, and though I would never presume to give any kind of diagnosis, many noted that the attributes of narcissistic personality disorder were reminiscent of Sogyal's behaviour. The closer people were to him, the more apparent this became.

It's important that students and potential students of any guru look at the literature on how to spot a narcissist, because similar views have been expressed about other high-profile gurus. Where a teacher displays symptoms of possible narcissistic personality disorder, it is important for students to consider the possibility that being a student of such a teacher will expose them to the risk of narcissistic abuse. Understanding narcissistic personality disorder helped members of the group to understand the dynamics of the abuse and to feel compassion for Sogyal as someone with a possible personality disorder.

Darlene Lancer, in an article on her blog titled 'How to Spot a Narcissist,' lists the following characteristics:

1. Has a grandiose sense of self-importance and exaggerates achievements and talent;
2. Dreams of unlimited power, success, brilliance, beauty, or ideal love;
3. Requires excessive admiration;
4. Believes he or she is special and unique, and can only be understood by, or should associate with other special or of high-status people (or institutions);

5. Lacks empathy for the feelings and needs of others;
6. Unreasonably expects special, favourable treatment or compliance from others;
7. Exploits and takes advantage of others to achieve personal ends;
8. Envies others or believes they're envious of him or her;
9. Has "an attitude" of arrogance or acts that way.'

I don't have space here to go into the specific ways in which Sogyal apparently displayed these characteristics, and though students who were not close to him may not have seen these qualities sufficiently to recognise some of them, I have heard reports from people who were close to him that he meets all these characteristics to some degree.

Literature on narcissists indicates that people with narcissistic personality disorder are masters of verbal abuse and manipulation, even to the degree that they can make their victims doubt their own perceptions—gaslighting—and their mode of operation looks very familiar to those who Sogyal abused. One of the things we found really helpful to understand about this disorder is that narcissists very rarely take responsibility for their behaviour—which would explain Sogyal's lack of genuine apology. Instead narcissists deny their actions and further the abuse by blaming the victim. Guilt does not bother them.

It can be empowering to understand that narcissist's rage, arrogance, and self-inflation are merely defences to avoid hidden feelings of inferiority. Scared of feeling weak and humiliated, they aim to increase their control and authority, while creating doubt, shame, and dependency in their victims.

What turns a child into a narcissist? Some of the childhood scenarios that can lead to narcissistic personality disorder describe aspects of Sogyal's upbringing. Elinor Greenberg, Ph.D. says in an article in *Psychology Today* on 'How Do Children Become Narcissists?' that:

> 'Excessive idealization of a child as flawless and special can lead to the child having a Narcissistic adaptation in later life. ... If children believe that their parents only value them because they are special, this can contribute to an underlying insecurity ... The children may become ashamed when they see any flaws in themselves. This can lead them to keep striving for perfection and proof that they are flawless and worth idealizing.'

Tulku's are supposedly reincarnations of great teachers and are brought up in an environment where they're idolised as such, but what if they aren't a reincarnation of a great teacher? What if they're just an ordinary child with this pressure put on them, living in an environment where *everyone* around them treats them as little gods? The tulku recognition system is highly open to manipulation, especially for children of rich families as in Sogyal's case—the monasteries want a reason for the rich family to support them.

Another factor Greenberg says is that, 'The child is raised in a family that is very competitive and only rewards high achievement.' One retreat Sogyal told us about his childhood, about how he was beaten—quite severely it seemed—if he didn't recite his lessons perfectly at the end of the day. He also talked about how he playacted being a lama, like his master, using village children as his disciples. Greenberg continues:

'Some children grow up in a Narcissistic household where there is an Exhibitionist Narcissist parent who rewards them with praise and attention as long as they admire and stay subservient to the parent. … Their role in the family is to uncritically worship the greatness of their Narcissistic parent without ever trying to equal or surpass that parent's achievements.'

Sogyal boasts how Chokyi Lodro Jamyang Khyentse, a highly revered lama, was like a father to him, but as you'll see in chapter thirty, he was also fond of beating people. Greenburg continues:

'Too much parental idealization may lead to an unbalanced view of the self. When this happens, the child then perceives *any flaws* as unacceptable and strives to be seen as perfect. It is a short hop, skip, and a jump from this to full blown Narcissism. In some homes, becoming a Narcissist is often the only sane solution.'

Unless, perhaps, the child is genuinely born with some kind of spiritual realisation.

Codependency

Darlene Lancer's book *Codependency for Dummies*, Second edition defines codependency as 'A lost self … A codependent is a person who can't function from his or her innate self and instead organizes thinking and behavior around a substance, process, or other person(s).' (p. 31, John Wiley & Sons, Hoboken, NJ: 2015).

Abuse survivors may not want to look at their role in their relationship with their abusers, but once they feel strong enough, it's helpful to look at the behaviours and feelings common in the types of unhealthy relationships referred to as codependent and see which, if any, describes aspects of your relationship with the abuser. Education on any patterns that apply to you will help you to avoid falling into similar patterns in future. It's likely that at least one or more may apply—I recognise a desire to please as one relating to me—and some may see themselves in all the codependent behaviours. This doesn't mean you have to label yourself codependent or take it as a shortcoming, or that it makes you somehow to blame. The term codependent is really just a tool for self-understanding and growth.

Codependent behaviours can keep us trapped in a dysfunctional relationship, but they aren't responsible for us being abused. Victims are not to blame for the abuse in any way at all. The perpetrator has total responsibility for the harm he caused and any codependent tendencies in play don't change that.

Here is one student's reflection on codependency. This also shows the fearlessness of members of the *What Now?* group and the depth of their examination of the issues and of themselves:

'One main pattern of codependency is to stay silent to not provoke the abuser. We ALL did that, let's face it in its full catastrophe. We allowed an abusive community. Whenever someone stood up, we were denounced and all were told that we were having psychological problems! The abuse of the sangha was even greater because we all could have started to

protect. We did not; we acted out of our manipulated minds and patterns of codependence.

'To look after one's own health was considered "not being capable", "being weak", "being selfish"—a classic misinterpretation of compassion for others which we find only in cults.

'I was part of it and was not part of it by protesting. Nobody stood up to help me, though two others witnessed how I was punched in my guts. They were both so scared themselves! It is really horrible.

'It is actually not true that abuse was only seen in the inner circle. The emotional and verbal abuse was in every open teaching—called "wrathful compassion". Perhaps we can start speaking about these accounts in which we were allowing abuse and when we were in fear. Then this group can grow and face its own "unconscious spots", our own demons, and then we can help each other to heal from this guilt, although it is very important for healing not to be hard on ourselves since we were blinded by the cult talk.'

In her article 'What is Codependency' on her blog of the same name, Psycho-therapist and relationship expert Darlene Lancer says of codependency:

'Core feelings include: denial; low self-esteem; painful emotions: shame, guilt, anger and resentment; anxiety and fear, depression.

'Core behaviors include: dependency; intimacy problems; dysfunctional communication; dysfunctional boundaries; control of oneself and/or others (includes caretaking)

'Core feelings and behaviors create other problems, such as, people-pleasing, self-doubt, mistrust, perfectionism, high-reactivity, enabling, and obsessions. Codependents are usually more attuned to other people's needs and feelings than their own. To quell anxiety about rejection, they try to accommodate others, while ignoring their own needs, wants, and feelings. As a result, they tend to lose their autonomy, particularly in intimate relationships. Over time, their self-worth declines due to self-alienation and/or allowing others to devalue them.'

Recognising some of these tendencies in myself, helps me to see how I could just have easily been trapped in the same cycle of abuse as my vajra brothers and sisters.

28
ABUSE BY OTHER LAMAS

As time passed, I came to realise that the issue of abuse was not limited to Sogyal and Rigpa, and my disenchantment with Rigpa became a disenchantment with the whole religion of Tibetan Buddhism.

First, some members of Shambala, Chogyam Trungpa's group, spoke out about the 'intergenerational sexualised violence' and several students accused their teacher Sakyong Mipham of sexual abuse. Shambala management pretty much followed the Rigpa mode of managing the fallout from these revelations, thus furthering my and others' disenchantment with the religion.

In one forum one person said of the Sakyong that he was a terribly sick and dangerous man. This person said he (or she) was one of the very few people who had gotten close enough to Mipham to witness first hand 'his mental illness and confusion, desperation, and very real sociopathy.'

I learned that abuse was one of the legacies left by Shambala founder Chogyam Trungpa. One of Trungpa's 'wives' began sharing on Facebook first-hand accounts of his abuse of people and animals. These were confirmed by others while his most outspoken supporters claimed they had never

261

seen such things. I'll recount only one here. It's from John Perk's memoir about his time as butler to Chogyam Trungpa, *The Mahāsiddha and His Idiot Servant*.

'One night after supper Rinpoche said, "Get Myson [a dog] and bring him in here." I dragged the shaking dog into the kitchen and following Rinpoche's instructions I sat him on the floor and covered his eyes with a blindfold. I set up stands with lighted candles by either side of his head. Myson couldn't move his head without being burned. Rinpoche took a potato and hit Myson on the head with it. When the dog moved, the fur on his ear would catch fire. I put out the flames. Now and then Rinpoche would scrape his chair across the tiled floor and whack him again on the head with a potato. ... "That's how you train students," Rinpoche calmly stated to me.'

And then I saw more and more people, most of them women, reporting in Facebook groups on their own experiences of abuse in a variety of different Tibetan Buddhist organisations. Here is one such comment:

Unfortunately I have since also experienced unethical, deceptive and harmful behaviour within my own sangha which has sadly led me to withdraw from the organisation and "break" with my lama who is held in very high regard within Tibetan Buddhist circles. I have had to abide by my own ethical standards and for that appear to have "lost" everything. However, I could not have responded any other way and still remain true to the dharma as I understood it. I could not live with the conflict or hypocrisy.

'I have been adrift really since then, questioning the apparent chasm between what Tibetan lamas preach and what they appear to practise. I also do not understand the apparent complicity of the lamas in each other's misdemeanours and harmful actions. They seem not to answer to anyone really ... How much suffering would have been averted, had a sincere, transparent and workable approach been taken at the outset of these serious issues?

'As horrific as the situation is now for all involved, I am hoping that one outcome may be a ripple effect, bringing into the light the abuse and hypocrisies within other Tibetan Buddhist groups so healing may occur there also.'

The need for a support group for victims of abuse in Vajrayana communities other than Rigpa became so acute that new Facebook groups emerged to deal with the demand. We kept our *What Now?* group just for Rigpa students because the specific nature of our shared experience provided a ground for our discussions not shared by those from other sanghas.

Another woman told me that her ex-teacher, a former monk and so-called geshe, *'abused sexually an enormous number of women, including me, his translator. ... Whoever knows the true facts about him are immediately included in the blacklist of his worst enemies. I have been accused by him of theft of his money, prostitution, breaking and entering his apartment, casting a spell on his wife, transforming a boy in her womb into a girl and, yes ... Mafia and drug trafficking.'*

I read all too many posts such as this in these groups. All the stories of sexual abuse I heard had the same patterns as those in the stories I shared in the earlier chapter on sexual abuse. The following comment speaks about a high-profile, popular lama and is not the only story about him indicating a lack of concern for ethical conduct. Many, however, won't speak openly for fear of retribution because, as one student told me, 'he has a lot of money and a reputation to protect':

> *'I was about 21 when I met the man who would be my lama for the next 16 yrs. Despite him being attractive to women, I only wanted the dharma. I was young and, yes, pretty and very open and committed to pursuing the dharma wholeheartedly. Within a short time he was paying me quite a bit of attention, making me feel special and close— enquiring after me—pursuing me, actually. I had many occasions alone with him. He told me how much merit I had, promised me many amazing things for my future and really seemed to care.*
>
> *'He was an incisive, well-spoken and entertaining teacher, humorous, seemingly self-deprecating, mysterious and wise—otherworldly. Very magnetising. He drew me in until he began to speak of sex and said it was a path I was qualified for—a spiritual thing. He also said my biggest obstacle was not thinking I was sexy! When I asked about other women, he said it was something he did with just a few women and that it was hard work—whilst also keeping a public long-term girlfriend. He also, confusingly, said it would be for his pleasure. I was so young and would have done anything to 'progress', but when he initiated the physical activities and then asked me flat out one night if I wanted sex, I said, "No," as what I had in mind was nothing so mundane, and the everyday term put me off. I thought it was a test of sorts.*

264

'There was also definitely an 'inner circle' involving attractive young women and some of the men with activities going on that others weren't privy to.

'A few years later something happened which resulted in physical harm to me, and then due to failures within the sangha to prevent or acknowledge this harm and with Rinpoche himself not wanting to know, I distanced myself from him and the sangha. It then became apparent that all his promises to be my protector, to never leave me proved hollow. When I tried to meet with him recently, several years later, to see if things could be mended, after hooking me back in and luring me interstate, he then avoided the meeting, turned his back on me and lied to me.

'Now I know that as a young neophyte I was groomed and later cruelly dismissed and betrayed .... It's so difficult to process that amongst the amazing stuff, so much harm was also done. He seems to have really lost his way—if he ever really was sincere.

'After so many years of devotion and commitment, I am now exhausted, sceptical and although I have faith in the essence of the teachings, I have a complete aversion toward Tibetan Buddhism and many lamas. After giving absolutely everything and undergoing much hardship and trials along the way for so many years, I have no energy left for that path.

'How could someone who appeared so passionate about the dharma, who publicly advocates good communication as imperative to guru disciple relationships and for healing, just totally shut down and abandon his student whom he

265

kept so close for so many years? It is nothing less than criminal.'

Added to this, I discovered that abuse was widespread in Tibetan Buddhist monasteries. The young Kalu Rinpoche on YouTube talks about being gang raped in a video titled *Confessions of Kalu Rinpoche*. I saw a video of a monk beating a young monk—badly—and a friend told me of nuns she had spoken to in India who were regularly raped by the local monks, monastics who apparently have no concern over breaking their vows.

How, I wondered, could a religion allow this kind of behaviour? But, of course, there is no central authority in Tibetan Buddhism, no accountability at all. Each lama is the ruler of their own kingdom, and lamas do not comment on each other's methods unless they have something positive to say. A teacher in a Western school would also generally refrain from criticising another teacher—except in cases where there were serious ethical violations. And this is where the lamas seem unable to make an exception to their cultural predisposition to not speak badly of a dharma teacher.

I read in *The Life and Times of Jamyang Khyentse Chokyi Lodro* what Sogyal's revered master did when he turned up at the Katok monastery:

'The people of Katok experienced Khyentse Chokyi Lodro's arrival as something of a tsunami. They said he was like an "invading force" (they used the same Tibetan word to describe the advance of the Communist Chinese) because his sovereignty over them was absolute and indisputable. Monks were punished ten at a time. When a flogging was called for, Rinpoche insisted in

266

four or five hundred lashes, never a mere hundred, and he always watched from the window of his residence as the punishment was meted out.'

That shocked me, not only the flogging but also that he watched. How is this the action of a compassionate man? It's more akin to the callous action of a feudal overlord. In *The Tibetan Book of Living and Dying*, Sogyal spoke about this man as if he were a saint, and I revered him on the basis of Sogyal's description. After reading this passage, I felt as if I'd just discovered that my grandfather had abused my family. It seemed that Sogyal came from a lineage of abuse. Is it any wonder he didn't see anything wrong with his behaviour?

Given his upbringing as a tulku with this man as his role model and students who don't question his behaviour, is it any wonder that Sogyal is ethically challenged? Seeing all these causes and conditions helped me to see him with compassion. Yes, he is ultimately responsible for the harm, but these many contributing factors fostered his tendencies.

For him to assume the role of 'Vajrayana master', however, he must have undertaken some conscious man-ipulation of student's and prospective student's perceptions. I didn't realise this until I discovered he hadn't done the required Buddhist studies for the role. When his contemporaries were studying Tibetan Buddhism, Sogyal was in a Catholic high school in India. The legitimacy of his claim to be an incarnation of the great master Terton Sogyal has also been questioned.

On realising the extent of the abuse throughout the religion, I decided I didn't want to be a Tibetan Buddhist anymore, or even a Buddhist—though I'm not adverse to reading or listening to dharma. I don't want anything to do with any religion. Leaving the religion behind was incredibly liberating and threw me right back to the guts of the practice, turning my mind inwards at every moment to recognise my true nature. That has nothing to do with religion—except that a religion taught me how to do it!

29
THE CODE OF CONDUCT

Rigpa finally released their code of conduct, and though on the surface it looked like the kind of code that would make sure the emotional, physical and sexual abuses in Rigpa could never happen again, since Rigpa had still not acknowledged that any harm had been done and no real apologies had been made, it seemed like hollow words—a document designed to make students and the public feel the right thing has been done, but with no change of heart as its basis.

If management and devoted students of Sogyal Rinpoche do not recognise abuse as abuse, if they are still confused about the real meaning of words such as 'kindness', 'abuse', 'inappropriate behaviour', 'benefit' and 'harm' when used in relation to a master/guru/lama then their use of these words in their code of conduct is meaningless.

For example, the Rigpa press statement that came out in 2012 in response to the Canadian video *In the Name of Enlightenment*, which exposed Mimi's abuse, said, 'We have only ever seen him [Sogyal] act for the benefit of other people, and with their best interests at heart.' And yet the people in management at the time experienced and witnessed abuse.

That press release also said, 'Nevertheless, any allegations of inappropriate behaviour are taken very seriously by the organization.' Not seriously enough to act when people complained, though. One can only assume they were either lying or they have no idea what inappropriate behaviour looks like.

I also discovered in the supporting document, 'Shared Values and Guidelines for the Rigpa Community,' a special section for tantric gurus in the 'specific' category of Vajrayana and Dzogchen. Although a representative from Rigpa assured me the actual code did cover all levels of engagement in Rigpa, the section appeared to do nothing other than enshrine in code the beliefs that had long enabled the abuse. It spoke of 'ethics and commitments specific to Vajrayana and Dzogchen.' And said that anyone wanting to follow the Vajrayana path had to make 'a formal request for this level of spiritual guidance' and that such formal requests 'constitute consent to this level of spiritual guidance.'

Consent?

Later we are told 'each connection between a student and a teacher is unique and based on mutual consent.'

There's that consent word again.

Isn't it reasonable to ask what it is about this 'level of spiritual guidance' that requires consent? What is to stop this 'consent' assumed on formal application for Vajrayana teachings being used to escape the requirements for behaviour laid out in the code of conduct?

The document explains that before undertaking such an application, students should 'discuss with experienced instructors about the nature of the teachings and what it means to receive this level of spiritual guidance.' What it used to mean to receive 'this level of spiritual guidance' was that Sogyal could abuse you and you had to see the abusive behaviour as beneficial, even if it wasn't. And we have seen no indication that the beliefs enabling the abuse have changed. So what will those experienced instructors be teaching? What it will mean if you give such formal 'consent' is that you will not be able to sue any lama who abuses you because according to the code of conduct, you've given your consent.

Unfortunately, students' desire for the teachings and for enlightenment is so strong that they *will* make a formal request and give their 'consent' to 'this level of spiritual guidance' and whatever that entails. But when the person requesting consent holds something of value (like special teachings and a fast track to enlightenment) back from the person from which they want consent, then any consent given is not truly consent because of the power imbalance. This is a point many people will miss, and it's a real problem, because when someone complains, they can be reminded that they 'consented'. That 'consent' will be held over them, a weapon to disempower them and keep them quiet.

Withholding something 'special' unless a student has sufficient devotion to the leader is also a common control tactic in cults.

The supporting document does say, however, that it's 'perfectly acceptable for both the student and the teacher to make their boundaries known.' But a student in a traditional Tibetan Buddhist guru-student relationship is under great pressure to have no boundaries, and those with codependent tendencies will be unable to do this.

We were so keen to get the Dzogchen teachings, we were willing to do whatever it took, which included putting our hands up for 'training'. We were perfectly willing to ignore the possible repercussions of giving our power so totally to another, and perfectly willing not to examine it too closely. This will still be the case. Lured by the promise of enlightenment, students will still willingly embrace the demands placed on them by tantric gurus. Rather than the protection one expects a code of conduct to give students, in Rigpa's case, consent to whatever the teacher considers the Vajrayana 'level of spiritual guidance' could be seen as little more than a method for protecting the teacher from legal action should he or she misbehave.

This 'code of conduct' is something Rigpa can use to show charity commissions and the public that they have dealt with the issue, even though—to date—they haven't dealt with it at the fundamental level of the beliefs that enabled the abuse. Unfortunately, the code's existence could make students think they're in good hands. Only at later stages of involvement with the organisation would students learn what is meant in the code by 'ethics and commitments specific to Vajrayana and Dzogchen'.

An article titled 'Cult Recruitment' on the *How Cults Work* website says:

> 'The main methods of cult recruitment revolve around deception and manipulation. Potential recruits are not told the true nature or intentions of the group. Instead, recruiters portray it as something mainstream, low-pressure and benign.'

30
SHUT UP AND KICKED OUT

Rigpa Facebook discussion groups and pages soon banned me from any participation, even though I didn't say anything nasty, just asked questions they didn't want asked. Most of the communication I received from Rigpa members seemed primarily designed to shut me up. A comment on one of my posts on the blog told me my focus 'should' be on the lojong practices—in which one sees those who harm us as our greatest teachers. They told me if I had any true wisdom awareness it would not set me 'on a campaign', and they seemed to see my openness in talking about the challenges I faced in light of the revelations of abuse as a sign that my spiritual progress was lacking.

I was told to 'drop the desire to share', not get caught up in 'the wildfire of social media'—apparently that was for journalists, not spiritual practitioners—and stop holding a grudge. I was told there was 'no need to make others support your decision by being part of a campaign of righteousness.'

The assumptions underlying the comment were that I was on a campaign; sharing from hatred; holding a grudge; and caught up in social media and hope and fear. This attitude encapsulated the view of many in Rigpa towards any public

273

processing, a perspective seen by many as a poorly veiled attempt to shut up any public discussion. She also suggested I leave with a 'clear heart and mind', the assumption being that I had neither, though in reality I felt clearer in both departments than I had for decades. It's easy for those who adhere rigidly to their belief in the Rigpa 'party line' to offer advice from their still-solid ivory tower. But it isn't any help at all to those, like me, who see that ivory tower for the prison it is.

Those commenting on the blog had plenty to say in response to these comments.

> *'I don't know who this person is but her post doesn't reflect an embodiment of the dharma into one's being. No empathy but a lot of preachy 'shoulds'. If you were to follow her instructions and shut the hell up, then even more spiritual seekers would be hurt by SL's behaviour, and the Rigpa cult into the future. As for telling people that social media is for journalists, not for practitioners, OMG, WTF? I'm probably the same age bracket as the writer but I find that very funny.'*

The discussion continued:

> *'I'm flabbergasted. Your response to someone's heartfelt words about their own experience and pain that they have experienced is to give a dharma lecture about how to behave. Your utter lack of empathy is astounding. And I thank you for writing what you did, because I am reminded of how, when I was active in Rigpa, I was becoming such a disconnected and uncompassionate person—being trained in how to ignore others' suffering. What an utter perversion. I hope that you wake up.'*

Another commented:

> *'The lack of empathy here is something I've recognized in many senior students and staff. I think it's an outcome of the toxic conditioning that they are subjected to. You have to learn to repress your natural reactions to things to survive, which leads to repression of all tender emotions like compassion and love.'*

When after a few months, I realised I wasn't having much effect on the organisation from outside, I decided to return to Rigpa, hoping I'd have more power to change things from within. However, not only was I not permitted to return, I was also banned from attending the 2018 Australian retreat. When I asked for a reason, I was told only that it was a group decision. I eventually discovered the reason was because they didn't trust me not to interpret whatever they did at retreat in a negative way and write negative things about it. Of course, I wouldn't have to write anything negative if they dealt with the problems in a positive away, and if they allowed me to say my piece and be heard, but they never even discussed their concerns with me, just cast me aside as if my decades of working for them had never occurred.

My offer to talk to the Australian management team and another offer to liaise between *What Now?* members and international management were both ignored.

When I tried to rejoin, I was told Rigpa was 'only for Sogyal's students'. This came at a time when Sogyal's photo seemed to be becoming scarcer on Rigpa websites, and I could get no written confirmation that Rigpa was 'only for Sogyal's students'. It doesn't surprise me that it's not a Rigpa policy— after all, such a stance would seriously limit their intake of new members, which would affect their finances. Clearly they just didn't want me in the sangha.

Lovely feeling, that …

The way I was refused entry to both a return to Rigpa and a retreat is in stark contrast with Rigpa's statement of April 2018 saying, 'It is important that Rigpa remains a home to all, open to all, and as inclusive as possible'.

When I heard Sogyal had 'apologised' in his message to the Australian retreat, I wanted to hear it. I asked my contact in Australian management, and she told me she'd see what she could do, but she never got back to me on it. I asked again through a Messenger contact and still hit a dead end. When I tried to get access to the message through others in the community, I received a phone call from someone in management asking me not to contact members of the sangha again.

I sent via email several genuine and reasonable requests, questions, or offers which remained unanswered. The one reply I did receive, to an email address set up for students to raise their concerns, told me—and most others received a similar response—to talk to one of the Australian 'care' contacts, one of whom had sent me an abusive message via Messenger.

I sent two messages to Sogyal, one a video of me talking to him, and one a letter after the sangha was given a direct email address for him. I received no reply to the first, and though I received a reply to the second, it had no name attached and only said they'd received my message and would forward it to Rinpoche. All this happened while the communications from Rigpa talked about 'deep listening', caring for each other and healing.

Care is shown by replying to emails.

Eventually, every thought of Rigpa hurt. All those wonderful times I'd had as part of the sangha were now tainted with the brush of a new perspective. Those Rigpa people I'd thought of as friends had all too easily decided I was their enemy. All my not-so-lovely Rigpa experiences came to the fore, and I was surprised at how many there were, previously all stashed away so as not to challenge my self-created perception of Rigpa as a wonderful sangha.

I didn't want anything around to remind me of Sogyal or Rigpa.

I'd redone my shrine several times since first discovering Sogyal's abuse. It became sparser with each renovation, until no deity and no lama remained except Samantabhadra, the primordial buddha and reminder of my Dzogchen teachings. The truth of them was so far beyond religion that no stain could even reach them, let alone stick to them, even though I'd received those teachings from Sogyal.

But I decided to burn my thangka of the Rigpa Tendrel Nyesel practice, symbolic now of everything wrong with the organisation, and I videoed myself doing it. I burned it in my fireplace, unperturbed, though aware of the symbolic nature of my action. I had no ill will to the practice or even to the sangha it represented, but the burning marked the end of my relationship with Ripga. I shared it in our group, and it gave heart to others to know that they didn't need to feel stuck with all their Rigpa baggage. Many of us burned materials that now had a negative association.

I kept my practice books and the first Rigpa study pack, because it's probably the best of his teachings—though I have no intention of listening to them again—and the little booklets

Rigpa produced on Sogyal's different teaching cycles because they're true gold, getting to the essence of key teachings. I burned a huge number of notes, ones I didn't need because they resided in my heart anyway, and I felt lighter for it, liberated somehow.

∋I
DHARMA PROTECTORS

By October 2017 my disillusionment with my lama and his organisation was complete, and the number of articles related to the topic of abuse that came to the attention of *What Now?* members, particularly in a cult context, was too great to put on the blog and more suited to sharing on Facebook. However, I didn't want my personal timeline to become clogged with articles in which many of my friends and family wouldn't be interested, so I created a page called *Dharma Protectors*. I was a little unsure as to the name, but it popped up during a meditation session and, though somewhat bold, given the meaning of dharma protectors in the Tibetan Buddhist religion, it felt right. A friend also encouraged me to use it, and so *Dharma Protectors* was born.

I tried to share dharma quotes, to remind people what we were trying to protect, but they weren't as popular, and when I eventually lost interest in sharing or protecting dharma, I stopped updating that page in favour of my *Living in Peace and Clarity* Facebook page. I wanted to return my focus to the spiritual path in general, not just this one damaged area of it. This coincided with renaming the *What Now? Blog* to *Beyond the Temple* and shifting it to a self-hosted site so the resources we'd gathered could be easily found as the years passed.

The page also allowed those we'd removed from the *What Now?* group to have their say without moderation. On a page, unlike in a group, only the administrators can post, and no matter how much discussion a post gets, it falls below any new posts and eventually disappears off the page unless you keep scrolling down; whereas in a group, articles with lots of comments always come to the top. This structure was better for not overwhelming people with a whole bunch of negative or aggressive comments should someone leave them. I have only ever deleted comments by and banned from the page one person, a defender of Sogyal who consistently attacked other commenters.

The reason why I felt so thoroughly disenchanted was well put in another letter sent by seven of the eight letter writers to Sogyal in response to Rigpa management's treatment of them regarding their participation in the independent investigation. I quote here the parts that particularly spoke for me and for the majority of people in the *What Now?* group:

> 'Instead of responding to our original questions, it seems that you and Rigpa are engaging in a massive public relations effort to deflect attention from your actions. First you replied to our letter by saying that you were very sorry for our having misunderstood your intentions. You did not deny your actions but deflected blame by implying it was due to our own ignorance. Rigpa has continued in this vein by promoting Orgyen Tobgyal's comments made in Lerab Ling, Rigpa Paris, and online that our attestations of your behaviour guaranteed that

we were samaya breakers and bound for the hell realms. Rigpa also released on September 23, 2017 the video of Khenpo Namdrol telling the gathering at Lerab Ling that the eight of us are agents of demonic forces, accused us of the heinous crime of causing schism in the sangha, which is morally equivalent to killing one's parents, killing an arhat, or drawing the blood of a Buddha. ...

'Three days after we received the packet of communication, Rigpa announced publicly to the greater Rigpa sangha that we would participate in the so-called investigation and speak to Rigpa's lawyers. We were neither consulted as to whether we wished to participate with Rigpa's law firm, nor did we give our consent to said participation. This suggested to us that Rigpa was not intent on truly listening, but instead, managing their public image and in fact saving themselves from scrutiny by legal authorities. Despite all of that, some of us still considered speaking to Rigpa's lawyers with a hope that it might bring about some kind of healing for sangha members. ...

'Then, on January 2, 2018 you and Rigpa announced the establishment of a Vision Board to guide Rigpa's future activity. You said that Orgyen Tobgyal guided the decision making, and that Khenpo Namdrol was named as a principal advisor. Relying upon Orgyen Tobgyal and Khenpo Namdrol, following their defamatory remarks about the eight of us, indicates what you and Rigpa think about our motivation and character and the content of the July 14th letter. ...

'We regret that neither you, nor Rigpa's leaders, have acknowledged the abuse and trauma that you have caused, so that deep healing can begin. We hope that you and Rigpa will reconsider your approach and be truthful and act in accordance with the Buddha's teachings.

'We deeply regret the necessity of our letters. We, like so many others, have seen greatness in you. We pray that you can live up to the level of integrity of which we know you are capable. Please take responsibility for your actions and begin the path to healing. Please seek the counsel of His Holiness the Dalai Lama and mend this stain on your reputation that is causing so many to lose faith in you, the lineage, and the noble dharma.'

Unsurprisingly at this stage, they never received a reply.

32
THE INDEPENDENT INVESTIGATION

When the scope of the independent investigation was announced, many months after the revelations became public, we were once again disappointed that Rigpa had fallen short in their handling of the matter. It appeared that the eight who wrote the letter were to be investigated, not the crimes of Sogyal, and the report was not only *not* to be made public, only shared with National management teams, but also not even shared with the sangha. The eight students refused to participate if the report would not be made public. Having very good reason not to trust Rigpa, they were suspicious of the whole process and felt bullied into participating.

In the next chapter, on recovering from trauma, I note how important it is for abuse survivors to be able to take control of their lives, and here Rigpa management were trying to manipulate survivors to suit their own agenda. The very people responsible for the trauma of institutional betrayal were behaving towards the survivors in exactly the same way they'd done while the eight were in Rigpa. The result was a level of re-traumatisation.

Given Rigpa's seeming deviousness in the past, we wondered just how impartial the investigator would be since she'd been employed by Rigpa. Would she skew her report to benefit the organisation who was paying her bill?

Some of the eight went into a dialogue with Karen Baxter, the lawyer doing the investigation. She assured them of her impartiality—it was an important part of her professional integrity—that anything said to her would be confidential and that no names would be used in the final report. We didn't trust that Rigpa wouldn't somehow use the results against those who spoke to Karen. Eventually, she got Rigpa to agree to make the report public and make some other concessions that allowed some of the eight to feel they could trust Karen sufficiently to speak to her.

Others in the *What Now?* group, after much debate about whether or not to speak to Karen, decided they would make sure she knew the scope of the issue beyond the experience of the eight. They contacted Karen, and she agreed to speak with them. Some gave documented information about complaints ignored by management that had been lodged in the past on behalf of a large number of students, and others gave personal testimonies. Their participation in the investigation gave Karen a wider framework through which to view the abuse. Organisations will likely always try to limit the scope of an investigation likely to find against them, but that doesn't mean that you can't widen it simply by contacting the investigator directly. I gave her a written report detailing my own experience and what others had told me and included general information about Rigpa's beliefs and how they acted as an injunction against speaking out.

We finally received the results them in August 2018, more than a year after the revelations of Sogyal's abuse.

The Lewis Silken Report detailed the 'outcome of an investigation into allegations made against Sogyal Lakar (also known as Sogyal Rinpoche) in a letter dated 14 July 2017'. I read it hungrily and breathed a sigh of relief. The report changed everything.

The executive summary stated the truth as I had come to know it:

'Whilst I have seen evidence that many people feel that they have benefitted greatly from having Sogyal Lakar as their teacher, individual experiences are very different. There are varying degrees of closeness to Sogyal Lakar, with the closest relationships regularly referred to as the "inner circle".

'The experiences of some of the members of the inner circle are very different from the experiences of many of those who are less close. Not all of the allegations against Sogyal Lakar are upheld, as explained in the body of the report below, but based on the evidence available to me, I am satisfied that, on the balance of probabilities:

a. 'some students of Sogyal Lakar (who were part of the 'inner circle', as described later in this report) have been subjected to serious physical, sexual and emotional abuse by him; and

b. 'there were senior individuals within Rigpa who were aware of at least some of these issues and failed to address them, leaving others at risk.'

The eight had been vindicated. The truth had been established according to 'the balance of probabilities'.

The full report can be downloaded from the *Beyond the Temple* website via a link at the bottom of the 'Investigations into Rigpa' page under the 'Abuse in Buddhism References' tab. I found it disturbing reading. I'd known it was this bad, but Karen had quoted students' own words, thus creating a powerful testimony of the abuse suffered by people at the hands of Sogyal Lakar/Rinpoche.

I'll provide quotes from it where something confirms my impressions or adds something new to the picture I've already painted. Here Karen notes that witnesses in Rigpa management minimised the physical abuse:

'Witness P (Rigpa management):

"He might tap someone on the head with a backscratcher; he did it half a dozen times that I saw. It was not violent … he might shake somebody … with me, he once pretended to punch me in the stomach, it was a non-event. He would kick people up the bum, very publicly".

Witness N (Rigpa management):

"He might shake you or pull your ear or tap you with a backscratcher, this was all in the context of surprise. He never hurt me or went too far. He has punched me. It was not full force and I laughed.

Witness O (Rigpa management):

"He would occasionally [use physical force], not often. He once hit me on the knuckles with his backscratcher … I

286

didn't like it … but there was a context—I had made a
mistake of some kind.

I've seen him hit [students] with a backscratcher a few
times—a handful—I can't recall who, it is not a clear
memory".

Compare these kinds of statement to those who recognised they'd been physically abused. I reproduce just one, but it's a good example of the kinds of things said by all the survivors. These were not isolated incidents but common experiences—and yet Sogyal and Dzongsar Khyentse have both referred to student's complaints as 'misunderstandings':

'He lined [three female and three male students] up,
grilling us about something in his house. He started
slapping and punching me, and kneed me in the stomach.
He then grabbed a thick practice book and slammed it
down on my head, breaking the spine of the book on my
head. I fell to the floor … he grabbed his glass and threw
its contents in my face, then grabbed a metal stupa and
went to hit me in the head with it. He stopped and backed
off. I thought if he hit me with that, I'm going down—I
thought I might never get up.

'His favourite thing to hit us with was his backscratcher
[which he would hit his male and female attendants with]
… he would hit us four or five times on the head and he
wielded it heavily—it was wooden with teeth on the end
and he would hit with the teeth end.

'At one point, the beatings were daily; it could be several
times a day. I would be left bruised and sore. He would

287

come across as utterly ferocious and would seem to have lost control. The blows were aimed at my head and were serious, real blows.

'I saw Witness J start to take the flack—Witness J received gruelling, ferocious, constant beatings ... it was like a mauling, slapping Witness J over and over until Witness J was reduced to a frightened jelly-like person.

'He would grab your ear and twist it whilst pushing your head down and dragging you along.

'He punched me out of the blue, a full punch to my jaw while I sat in the driver's seat and him in the passenger seat because I forgot a torch.

'There was a correlation between being hit and Sogyal having fallen out with his girlfriends; out of the blue we would be screamed at for nothing.

'He hit me over the head and made me bleed; there were around twelve people sitting around the table when it happened.'

On the matter of the nun punch at Lerab Ling in front of a thousand or so people that I mentioned earlier, Karen noted a witness saying:

'The next day she appeared on the stage and had to confess her own failings and agree that this had been highly beneficial and privileged event ... she had the appearance of a prisoner of war stating how well the North Koreans had treated her.'

Having to publicly confess your own failings is common in cults. The report also includes the excerpt from the nun's statement in which she said the punch was a 'soft punch' and 'neither violent nor abusive'. Of this Karen says:

> 'The language used by Student 19 is strikingly similar to that used by the current senior students who confirmed that when they had been hit by Sogyal this had been a "soft punch", not something that caused them real pain. It gives me the impression that this is the "party line" on the issue; the striking of people cannot plausibly be denied, but its significance can be minimised.'

This minimising continues with management witnesses' response to the details of sexual abuse: Karen says that they,

> 'accepted that Sogyal had girlfriends, and sometimes more than one at a time, but all considered these relationships to be consensual and denied ever seeing or having knowledge of him behaving inappropriately, or using the teachings to persuade people to have sex with him.'

Witness P when observing Sogyal asking a student to take off her clothes, and the woman bursting into tears 'was not concerned by this instruction and considered it to be an example of Sogyal Lakar having an agreement with the female student to "intervene in [her] thought pattern by saying this".'

This is the view of abuse as a teaching and therefore beneficial. Karen Baxter notes the difference between consent and submission:

'According to the UK's Crown Prosecution Service, under the UK's sexual offences legislation consent is only given when someone agrees by choice to participate in the activity and has the freedom and capacity to make that choice. The word consent should be given its ordinary meaning, but there is a difference between consent and submission.'

And then she picks up on the power imbalance:

'Sogyal's statement—"whatever I have said or done when interacting with my students has been with the aim of helping them to awaken their inner nature"—causes me concern if and to the extent that it relates to sexual relationships. He is not saying, I thought that these were "normal" consenting adult relationships. A sexual relationship which is designed to help awaken the inner nature of a student is, necessarily, a sexual relationship between a student and a teacher; it is not a relationship between equals. In that context, if such a relationship can ever be consensual (which is a controversial question in itself), I consider that the requirement for clear and unequivocal consent is paramount. That point is made even starker in a situation where the student considers that she is not permitted to speak out against her teacher and has been taught to see everything their teacher does as enlightened behaviour.'

In her summary of her investigations into sexual abuse she says:

'It is alleged that Sogyal used his position to coerce, intimidate and manipulate young women into giving

290

him sexual favours. There is a significant weight of first-hand evidence which leads me to uphold this allegation.'

And in response to a specific incident she said:

'When a significantly older man, who is responsible for a student's spiritual development, and who uses physical force against that student, tells that student to perform sexual favours for him, I cannot accept that there is any basis upon which this could be said to be a consensual act.'

Karen noted that Sogyal's comment on his 'training methods' was: 'I believe this is very much in keeping with the culture of training that we find in Tibetan Buddhism.' This is the unfortunate idea, clearly shared by those in management and many lamas, that abuse is a legitimate form of 'training' in Tibetan Buddhism. This is exactly the idea that has to be discarded if Tibetan Buddhism is to become a healthy religion.

Baxter also notes the inability of students in management roles to believe Sogyal did something wrong, their efforts to minimise the abuse, and their closed mindedness to change. This is why I don't believe that, despite their efforts, Rigpa can change sufficiently to become a trustworthy organisation:

'Witness P was not really concerned about whether these things happened, but seems to have been prepared to accept that Sogyal intended no harm, regardless of what happened.'

And on the minimising:

'Witness O said to me *"there has been a lot of rumour and innuendo, a lot of people talking on behalf of people, a lot of exaggeration and gossip—we can't act on that as an organisation. Why in the space of forty years hasn't anyone complained?"* I found this to be an extraordinary statement from someone who was aware of Janice Doe and Student 27, as well as the complaints brought to their attention by Witness B, which I do not believe can reasonably be dismissed as mere gossip or rumour.'

And on this idea that the problem is not with Sogyal's behaviour but with some 'misunderstanding' of Vajrayana, and that those who speak out are 'turning against everything' thus making Sogyal and Rigpa the victim:

'At the start of my meeting with Witness O, Witness O said [about the letter writers] *"I'm not blaming them, [Vajrayana] is subtle and complex, but what they say shows something fundamentally hasn't clicked ... there are grains of truth in [the Complaint] but they are exaggerated and distorted".* But Witness O later said to me *"we don't believe that [Sogyal] abuses people."*

And what does Sogyal say of all this? According to Karen, he said, 'It distresses me that my actions and intentions could have been misunderstood and characterized in this way.' It seems that Sogyal and his oldest students—and presumably the remaining instructors—believe the requirements of the student-teacher relationship in Vajrayana means that abusive behaviour is simply part of the deal, that a willingness to take whatever is dished out is a necessary part of the relationship and that anyone who thinks this behaviour is abuse has misunderstood this key part of Vajrayana. Will those in the upper echelons of the organisation ever change that view? Sadly, I doubt it, and for so long as those instructing students wanting to enter the Vajrayana share this view, Rigpa and other organisations which promote this kind of thinking are not safe places in which to study dharma, regardless of their 'codes of conduct'.

Is this the kind of Vajrayana we want in the West? Since some teachers do not support the idea that students must submit to their guru no matter what he does—and have well-thought-out teachings to support their view—it seems we have a choice about to what to adopt and what to abandon here.

Rigpa's response to the report of 5th September 2018 continued their familiar vague and misleading language. The release of the report made no change to their methods. They 'acknowledge[d] the gravity of the independent report'. They did not, however, accept the findings of the report or say anything else that would indicate they understand that Sogyal Rinpoche and those who Karen said 'were aware of at least some of these issues and failed to address them, leaving others at risk' had done anything wrong. There was no admission of causing harm and no taking any responsibility for it.

I could dismantle their response in detail, but at this stage I find criticising their communications tedious because it seems to be just more of the same, the same vague language making the same kinds of promises that they invariably fail to live up to.

The new Vision Board did finally reach out to the eight, on the recommendation of the independent report. They said, 'We would like to enter into a dialogue with you, and understand what is important to you at this point, eighteen months after your initial letter. This is an open invitation in a spirit of mutual respect, healing and reconciliation, with no other wish than simply listening and hearing, in full confidentiality.'

One of the eight's reply to the Vision Board email points out that for so long as Rigpa continues:

> 'its subtle victim-blaming refrain of compassion for our "feeling hurt" as if this is simply a matter of faulty perception rather than the direct result of physical, sexual and emotional abuse by Sogyal, any attempts at true healing and reconciliation by definition are unworkable and unobtainable'.

> 'Rigpa also needs to recognise the additional layer of harm done to survivors by the response to our letter. This took the form of subtle and not so subtle victim-blaming, hostile ostracisation, character assassination by being labelled malevolent demon-possessed samaya-breakers and so on.

> 'The people harmed by SL must be deeply listened to; full responsibility must be taken by Sogyal for the harm he caused; authentic remorse and regret for his actions must be communicated in the form of an apology to the harmed; a promise personally and institutionally to refrain from this behaviour in the future and a request and delivery to the harmed of what they need in the form of restitution must be made for authentic healing to occur. These are not just my opinions but supported by both The Olive Branch protocols and the recommendations of the LS Investigation. This is the only way forward that supports my integrity and healing and, maybe just as importantly, that of SL.'

33
RECOVERING FROM TRAUMA

Since I found myself interacting with abuse survivors with complex post-traumatic-stress syndrome, I needed to find out about the process of recovering from trauma, and as previously mentioned, Judith Herman's book *Trauma and Recovery: The Aftermath of Violence-From Domestic Abuse to Political Terror* was an excellent resource. The quotes used in this chapter are reprinted by permission of Basic Books.

According to Judith Herman, the stages of recovery from trauma are 'establishing safety, reconstructing the trauma story, and restoring the connection between survivors and their community.' First, we have to get out of the situation and establish ourselves in a safe place. Then we need the help of others in rebuilding a positive view of ourselves. Those sincerely wishing to help trauma survivors need to be willing 'to recognize that a traumatic event has occurred, to suspend their preconceived judgments, and simply to bear witness'.

Anyone who thinks Sogyal did no wrong in terms of Vajrayana and that the abused students simply 'misunderstood', can't possibly recognise the psychological harm caused by their guru. Views that diminish the severity of the traumatic situation and dictate that unrealistic responses—seeing the abuse as kindness—are the appropriate ones hinder the recovery process.

Because victims remained in the abusive situation for considerable periods of time, they suffered from prolonged repeated trauma in which 'the perpetrator becomes the most powerful person in the life of the victim, and the psychology of the victim is shaped by the actions and beliefs of the perpetrator.' People subjected to this kind of trauma develop a complex form of post-traumatic stress disorder that invades and erodes the personality.

It's important for recovery that survivors of guru abuse name their array of symptoms as complex post-traumatic stress disorder. This gives them a measure of the recognition they deserve, assists them in viewing their experience in accurate psychological terms, and is respectful of their moral needs.

> 'Recovery is based on the empowerment of the survivor and the creation of new connections. ... The therapist must affirm a position of solidarity with the victim,' and understand 'the fundamental injustice of the traumatic experience and the need for a resolution that restores some sense of justice.'

Unfortunately, according to reports, in Rigpa the therapist/patient relationship was grossly misused, thus creating further trauma. Instead of showing solidarity with the victim, the 'Rigpa therapists', to whom abuse victims were sent, tried to 'correct' the survivor's perception of their abuser such that he was seen as the 'saviour' who allowed them to process past trauma. Therapists are supposed to protect and educate patients as to the nature of their symptoms, however Rigpa therapists apparently failed to do either.

Recovery is not a linear, uninterrupted sequence, and though trauma survivors may want to prematurely put it all behind them, 'at some point the memory of the trauma is bound to return, demanding attention.' However, while 'avoiding the traumatic memories leads to stagnation in the recovery process,' approaching them too soon 'leads to a fruitless and damaging reliving of the trauma.' So those of us supporting survivors' recovery, had to allow the survivor to lead the way. They had to have the power in deciding when they were ready to share. The *What Now?* group played the role of witness and ally.

The second stage involves telling the story of the trauma in depth and detail in a way that transforms the traumatic memory so it can be integrated into the survivor's life story and present world view. Viewing one's experience through the framework of the psychological literature on abuse assists enormously in this process.

To revisit your experience takes incredible courage, something those who subscribed to abuse-enabling beliefs didn't respect or honour—which is why they have no place in a survivors support group—and listening to someone's horrific story also takes a degree of courage because one's empathy means you invariably feel, to some degree, what the traumatised person feels. This was obvious in the reactions of group members when trauma survivors opened up.

Watching the *What Now?* members honour survivors' courage and validate their perception was a heart-warming experience. It contrasted starkly with the apparent inability of Rigpa as an organisation and those committed to promoting the

'Rigpa party-line' to show compassion for the survivors. But then, how could Rigpa management show compassion when they thought the victims hadn't actually been hurt, that they had only, through some fault of their own, perceived their experience as hurtful?

In order to develop a full understanding of the trauma, the survivor needs to examine the moral questions of guilt and responsibility and reconstruct a system of belief that makes sense of her undeserved suffering. And this can't be done only by thinking about it. The remedy for injustice also requires action.

The action of telling a story in the 'safety of a protected relationship' can produce a change in the abnormal processing of the traumatic memory and relieve many of the symptoms of post-traumatic stress disorder. This shows how vital it is for survivors of guru abuse to be heard without judgement, *and believed*. However, telling the trauma story 'inevitably plunges the survivor into profound grief.'

Though the grief is greater for those directly abused, we all had to face our grief over the situation. Anyone who left Rigpa after many years experienced a loss of friends, a guru, and a spiritual support and belief system we'd trusted.

I met only one survivor who seemed motivated by a desire for revenge, and yet I don't doubt many of us secretly had moments—if only fleeting—when we hoped karma—if not a court of law—would make Sogyal pay for his crimes. A desire for revenge is a natural human reaction to a situation where someone has wrought harm on another, but I suspect Buddhists are likely to quash such urges and instead try to forgive.

It's a common folk-wisdom assumption that in cases of abuse forgiveness is both possible and necessary for healing, but

Herman says, 'it is not possible to exorcise the trauma, through either hatred [desire for revenge] or love.' Trying to forgive is an attempt to transcend the rage and erase the impact of the trauma 'through a willed, defiant act of love.' However, as Herman says:

'Like revenge, the fantasy of forgiveness often becomes a cruel torture, because it remains out of reach for most ordinary human beings. True forgiveness cannot be granted until the perpetrator has sought and earned it through confession, repentance, and restitution,' but 'genuine contrition in a perpetrator is a rare miracle'.

It did me a great deal of good to realise that it was okay if I didn't feel I could forgive Sogyal for his heinous acts. It's not a mark of a lack of spiritual realisation; it's a mark of being human. Forgiveness is possible and desirable for the victim in many situations, but here we're talking about abuse that has created trauma, not just bad parenting or a difficult co-worker or family member. Not granting forgiveness in such a situation does not mean someone has an inability to forgive, or that they're somehow stuck in a grievance, the point is that in instances where someone's behaviour has caused trauma, without a genuine apology, the perpetrator simply doesn't deserve forgiveness. And some things are so reprehensible that they should never be forgiven. Should we forgive Hitler for what he did to the Jews? No way. Forgiveness is not a blanket solution to all ills. And contrary to what many believe, forgiving the perpetrator is not necessary for either recovery or happiness.

Herman continues:

'Her healing depends on the discovery of restorative love in her own life; it does not require that this love be extended to the perpetrator. Once the survivor has mourned the traumatic event, she may be surprised to discover how uninteresting the perpetrator has become to her and how little concern she feels for his fate. She may even feel sorrow and compassion for him, but this disengaged feeling is not the same as forgiveness.'

Feelings of compassion for the perpetrator arise from understanding why the perpetrator is the way he or she is and from imagining how horrible it would be to live in a mind so twisted. But compassion is neither love nor forgiveness, and it does not release a person from being responsible for their actions.

Pressure to forgive is misguided and unhelpful, as Dr David Bedrick says:

'If your understanding of the process of forgiveness doesn't include the expression of anger, even vengeance, and the fierce holding of others accountable, then advising others who were harmed will less likely be helpful, and more likely be injurious.'

Nancy Steinbeck co-author of *The Other Side of Eden: Life With John Steinbeck*, wrote about this in a survivors support group:

'I am so sick of therapists who push people toward forgiveness and demand they bypass feelings of anger, resentment and thoughts of revenge. Healing from abuse is a process, similar to the grief cycle. I prefer the term "acceptance" instead of forgiveness. Acceptance means I can keep my distance. Forgiveness feels like I still have attachment to the perpetrator. I may entertain fleeting thoughts of compassion if I think about how their childhood twisted them, like I do

about my sexually abusive father, Chogyam Trungpa and Osel Mukpo. But I always come back to "accept the things I cannot change" and run like hell from criminal behaviour. I think all this emphasis on forgiveness is a form of gaslighting.'

The quest for fair compensation is another natural and quite legitimate response in an abuse survivor, and is often an important part of recovery. However:

> 'Prolonged, fruitless struggles to wrest compensation from the perpetrator or from others may represent a defence against facing the full reality of what was lost. Mourning is the only way to give due honour to loss; there is no adequate compensation.'

As you can see, recovery is a complex business, and those who tell survivors to 'get over it' or 'just drop it' or 'let it go' presumably have no idea just how unhelpful their comments are or how erroneous their expectations that 'letting it go' is always a healthy response. Nevertheless it is an often-heard refrain in Buddhist circles. We discussed this in the group. One person said:

> *'When people have told me to 'let it go', it has been a terribly hurtful thing. It shows no understanding of the healing process. Listening is respect. Listening is love. We in What Now? are all doing that. However long it takes. Some wounds go deeper than we understand, in ourselves and in others. Spiritual wounds are difficult to define. Some losses are so great that you will never be the same, but we will change and adapt in time, in each our own manner. We don't need further wounding; we need listening.'*

The process of telling the abuse story and grieving for what was lost is painful and cannot be hurried. A member experienced in grief counselling said:

> *'No one else can determine what a survivor/grieving person needs, how much time or what direction. Particularly with any kind of trauma, the experience is a lot about disempowerment—so the survivor needs to be empowered, given back their agency, over and over, as long as it takes. Often it takes a lifetime.'*

The final stage of recovery is building a new life within a radically different culture from the one they have left behind, which is why it is not a good idea for survivors of guru abuse to 'return to the fold' or to take another guru—at least not immediately and not under the same terms. They need to come back to themselves and find a new place in the world. The survivors I know will probably never take on another guru-student relationship, and I have reason now to believe such relationships as traditionally presented are unhealthy—for reasons I'll explain later.

The following words of Herman's resonated with me and many others in the group: 'Emerging from an environment of total control, they feel simultaneously the wonder and uncertainty of freedom. They speak of losing and regaining the world.' Even those of us not directly abused felt incredible freedom from giving up our guru and the constraints placed on us by Rigpa. On one hand we felt liberating joy and on the other hand we felt terrible grief.

Herman's description of the third stage of recovery applied to *everyone* in the group regardless of their level of involvement in Rigpa:

'The traumatized person recognizes that she has been a victim and understands the effects of her victimization. Now she is ready to incorporate the lessons of her traumatic experience into her life. She is ready to take concrete steps to increase her sense of power and control, to protect herself against future danger, and to deepen her alliances with those whom she has learned to trust.'

Gradually many members commented and posted less and less in the group. We were left with a core group of people who had become very close, and many of us kept discussing developments and sharing further information because we recognised the larger issues highlighted by Sogyal's abuse.

Herman says that:

A small percentage of survivors 'discover that they can transform the meaning of their personal tragedy by making it the basis for social action. While there is no way to compensate for an atrocity, there is a way to transcend it, by making it a gift to others. The trauma is redeemed only when it becomes the source of a survivor mission.'

People don't ever fully recover from trauma. It continues to impact survivors throughout their life. 'Issues that were sufficiently resolved at one stage of recovery may be reawakened as the survivor reaches new milestones in her development.' However, the physiological symptoms of post-traumatic stress disorder can be brought within manageable limits; survivors will come to be able to 'bear the feelings associated with traumatic memories' and gain some control over their memories—able to either remember or put the memory aside. Survivors self-esteem can be restored and their important relationships re-established, and they can 'reconstructed a coherent system of meaning and belief that encompasses the story of the trauma'.

34
DID SOGYAL APOLOGISE?

We made many calls on the *What Now?* blog for an apology from both Sogyal and Rigpa. The thinking behind our calls were that healing for Sogyal and Rigpa could not begin until after they had accepted responsibility for their actions and apologised for the hurt they'd caused, and that such an apology would assist in recovery for the victims.

To date no public apology that accepts that Sogyal and Rigpa management has harmed people has been forthcoming. Even though he hadn't made a true apology, we began to hear devotees referring to 'Sogyal's apology', and eventually links to these pseudo-apologies appeared on Rigpa's main website— titled 'Sogyal Rinpoche's Apology' and 'Rigpa's Apology.' But these 'apologies' show no admission of wrong doing or acceptance of responsibility for the harm they caused. All they show is that Rigpa wants people to believe they and Sogyal have done the right thing, and unfortunately many accept Rigpa's version of reality without question.

The commonly recognised attributes of a true apology are:

1. Acknowledge what you did was wrong;
2. Accept responsibility for your action;

3. Make attempts to atone for the wrong you committed;
4. Give assurances that the transgression will not happen again.

Despite these four attributes being contained within the four powers of confession in Tibetan Buddhism, neither Sogyal nor Rigpa's 'apologies' include any of these four elements.

Some people might tell you Sogyal gave an 'apology' in a message to the Australian retreat. However, Rigpa management wouldn't allow me to listen to it, and neither did they send it to the eight letter writers. This reticence to share an 'apology' didn't make sense until I received a transcript of it from someone who'd played it several times to get the exact words. I suspect they didn't share it because they knew I'd notice it wasn't a real apology.

Here are the words: 'I know that some of you in the sangha still feel very hurt and upset, perhaps even at me. I really want to acknowledge your feelings of hurt and once again offer you my deepest apologies for anything you feel I may have done to cause you really pain.'

Note that he only acknowledges *feelings of hurt*, not harm he has caused, and he doesn't apologise for what he did, only for anything people *feel* he might have done. In his letter to the eight letter writers in response to their initial letter, he asks for forgiveness, but when you look carefully, you see that he's only distressed that his actions had been perceived wrongly, not that he did any harm, so that didn't constitute an apology, either.

The website also shares Sogyal's message to Karen Baxter, the lawyer conducting the independent investigation, which they say 'includes a written apology.' This 'apology' states (italics and comment in parenthesis are my additions):

> 'It is clear that a number of people *feel* that they have been hurt, and hold me responsible. This *(their feelings, not his actions)* is something I have to acknowledge and face up to. I am truly sorry *if* anything I have said or done has caused anyone offence or harm, and I ask in all humility for their forgiveness. What I wish now with all my heart is that whatever pain and hurt *has been experienced*, be healed and we all find space for mutual understanding and forgiveness. ...I sincerely and unreservedly apologize for any responsibility I have in the pain, *misunderstanding* and hurt *that have arisen* and I am willing, in whatever way I can, to reach out and bring resolution.' Sogyal Rinpoche.

I asked in the *What Now?* group whether or not people thought this constituted an apology and no one out of seventeen respondents thought it did. (Comments below published with permission.)

One person said they could see how it sounds like an apology if you don't give it too much thought, and they could see why the Rigpa organization insists Sogyal has apologized and may feel frustrated that others don't agree, but they still didn't think it constituted a real apology because it was too vague.

One person pointed out that he apologises for the 'pain' not for his actions, and then '*dishonestly minimises a transgression down to a "misunderstanding" thus shifting the burden of conscience from himself back onto the subjects of his actions. Also it is delivered with such vagueness as that no one would ever know*

307

what he was "sorry" for … the idea of apologising for anything ever is just absurd.'

More comments picked up on using the word, 'misunderstanding'. I particularly liked this plain-speaking comment from someone directly abused as it expresses how frustrating it is to see the manipulation in the words:

> *'How deft and fucked up is this "pain, misunderstanding and hurt"? He puts misunderstanding in the middle of pain and hurt, like a reverse shit sandwich with creamy "it's your fault for misunderstanding" in the middle of his pain and hurt.'*

How, we must ask, is knocking someone unconscious, punching people in the stomach, asking for blow jobs and so on a misunderstanding? What is there to be misunderstood here?

Another commenter pointed out that the 'if' in '*if* I have said or done anything' throws it all into doubt, suggesting that he might not have done these things, as if he's a victim. And they picked up on the passive voice sentence construction in 'misunderstanding and hurt *that have arisen*' which makes it sound as if the hurt arose all by itself, not due to his actions. Once again this places the responsibility for the hurt on the victims who 'misunderstood'.

Another commenter pointed out that if this really was an apology, Sogyal should have made sure he sent to the people he abused. He used to have no problems reaching any of the eight letter writers and countless others he was close to and has since left injured in one way or another. He has their phone numbers—a point which makes his statement that he's willing to reach out sound rather hollow.

One commenter called it '*a non-apology apology*', then pointed out:

> '*For it to be a real apology, Sogyal Rinpoche would have to say what it is that he has done wrong, categorically apologise for that, say what he is going to do to make amends, and promise that he will never do such things again.*'

Perhaps something like this?

'It is clear that I have hurt a number of people. I acknowledge that I behaved wrongly and that I am responsible for the harm I have caused. I sincerely and unreservedly apologize for the pain and harm that I've caused. I vow never to behave in these ways again, and will do whatever I can to atone for the wrongs I have committed. I am truly sorry for my behaviour and ask in all humility for the forgiveness of those I hurt.'

That would suffice as a genuine apology. What a shame our teacher couldn't hear the wisdom in his own teachings on confession. Of course, someone with narcissistic personally disorder is incapable of seeing they've done anything wrong, let alone apologise, so if this is the case for Sogyal, we have no hope of ever hearing a true apology.

And Rigpa? What of their 'apology'?

What they refer to as their apology is one line on their statement on the Lewis Silken Report. They say: 'We feel deeply sorry and apologise for the hurt *experienced* by past and present members of the Rigpa community.'

They apologise only for the hurt 'experienced' not 'the hurt we caused' or better still 'the harm we caused', which would give some indication of an acceptance of responsibility. Instead they use a passive voice construction that makes it appear that this 'experienced' hurt is not caused by anything—certainly not by Rigpa management. And there is no sign of the other elements required for a true apology.

Here's what a genuine apology from Rigpa might look like:

'We, the Rigpa management and community, feel deeply sorry and apologise for the harm we have caused past and present members of the Rigpa community. We accept that in addition to our cover up, we are responsible for the psychological abuse of gaslighting, institutional betrayal, reprisals against whistle-blowers, spiritual abuse, and failure to protect people from Sogyal's abusive behaviour. We acknowledge our wrong doing and invite anyone we have harmed to contact us to let us know how we can best make amends.'

A true apology would form a real basis on which to begin re-establishing trust and restoring some degree of integrity.

35
THE PROCESS OF CULT RECOVERY

Discovery of the wealth of literature and YouTube talks on cults, how to spot them, and how to recover from your time in them was a great boon for members of our group. It helped guide us through the stages of cult recovery. For many it was Rigpa's behaviour and discovering how helpful the cult recovery literature was that finally convinced them they had indeed been in a cult.

The stages of cult recovery are:

Re-evaluation—This is the information stage in which you research cults and abuse, such that you get a new framework with which you view experience. We learned about how cults control and manipulate people, which helped us understand how we were changed and our integrity compromised, and why we stayed. We learned that being manipulated in this way was not some fault in ourselves. Intelligent people get caught up in cults. Part of this stage was evaluating the beliefs we held in Rigpa and seeing how they contributed to the manipulation and control exerted over members.

Reconciliation—This focused on how we felt now about our past experiences. Here we faced our feelings of grief, guilt and shame, and the symptoms of complex post-traumatic-stress-disorder experienced by those directly abused. We looked at who we were before our time in Rigpa and who we are now that we're free of Rigpa's constraints. People went back to hobbies they had given up or found new directions for their lives due to reclaiming what was important to them before their Rigpa time. Here we decided whether or not we wanted to keep subscribing to the beliefs we held in Rigpa or not, and everyone acknowledged the importance of trusting their own wisdom and looking to the guru within. We also reaffirmed our view of the importance of ethics, love and compassion.

Reintegration—here we integrated our cult experience into who we are now. We recognised what we'd learned from our time in Rigpa—both good and bad—re-evaluated what was important to us spiritually, and took steps to move forward with our spiritual life. This stage is a focus on the future. Our focus on our past experiences, now we've processed them, naturally falls away.

At this stage, people started to fall away from the *What Now?* group. Some didn't need the group anymore for various reasons, and some had simply had enough of all the talk of abuse and cults. I set up the *Beyond the Temple* Facebook group so our sangha of mostly ex-Rigpa people would still be able to keep in touch without relating through our shared experience of abuse.

The focus of the new group was supporting each other in our ongoing spiritual path no matter what direction that took us. We shared interesting teachings from various traditions, Buddhist and non-Buddhist alike. We watched talks and read articles by scientists, psychologists, Christians from the Desert Father's tradition, and various gurus—now through the lens of healthy scepticism. We also shared what we knew about these teachers, and several people had shocks when they discovered that teachers they'd thought were ethical had beaten their wives or done some other unacceptable thing.

These stages are not necessarily progressed through in a linear fashion, and certainly not all of us went through these stages at the same time. We flipped back and forward amongst the stages and gave each other room to process in our own way and at our own pace.

Knowing the stages helped me as moderator to be able to set up and guide discussions in a way that respected these different stages. By the time I discovered the information on cult recovery, we were well into the processing, but I gained concepts and language I could use to help me understand what I was seeing.

I remember feeling completely out of my depth when we opened *Beyond the Temple* up to refugees from other abusive gurus. In my attempt to 'keep the discussion positive' and with a focus on moving forward, I used the Buddhist framework of the eight worldly concerns to answer someone's question on why Rigpa and Shambala management seemed more interested in 'saving' their organisations than rooting the abuse out of their organisation. I thought it a useful framework for seeing how people get caught up in hopes and fear, in this case, mostly fear of losing their livelihood, but my use of this Buddhist terminology triggered re-traumatisation in an abuse victim.

Other members of the group chastised me for my insensitivity, and I felt my ignorance and lack of counselling skills keenly. I hadn't realised that Buddhist terminology might be such a trigger. At that stage I wished I'd trained as a therapist or at least had more knowledge of the effects of trauma. Since that wasn't possible, I read as widely as I could and sought to learn, adapt, and use criticism such as this to evaluate my actions.

36
EVALUATING SOGYAL'S TEACHINGS

Part of the cult recovery process was asking ourselves whether or not Sogyal's teachings had value, and during our discussions, someone pointed out that the amount of actual teachings Sogyal gave during a retreat was quite small. In his daily two-to-three hour session, the first half to one hour would be grumbling about things done wrong, bawling out workers, or giving them instructions, telephoning or texting someone on the other side of the world, talking about a student, asking where someone was and telling someone else to go and get them.

Then we would hear the accolades from students, which Sogyal called 'feedbacks', which were read out while we all sat and listened—during one session in Australia, I clocked the 'feedbacks' at two hours. After that he would get someone to read some written material collated for him by his assistants, and he would make some comments on them, usually a story or comment that rarely added anything not in the text. Sometimes that was it for the actual teaching, and he might follow it with another thirty minutes of giving instructions on running the retreat—I always wondered why that couldn't be dealt with in private sessions rather than having everyone sit there in the heat with our stomachs' rumbling. Perhaps some saw it as a training

315

in forbearance. But anyone who'd been to more than a few retreats knew not to complain about any of this. We knew 'negative feedback' would be met with a lecture on the Rigpa 'party line'.

Other times he would give 'direct teachings' which consisted of him sitting in the nature of mind and punctuating the silence with a few words. His Dzogchen instructions were vague and not at all systematic or specific, unlike the Mahamudra teachings I studied after I left Rigpa—but perhaps that's the nature of Dzogchen. Sometimes he actively did an introduction to the nature of mind, snapping his fingers, turning his hand, telling us to look in and so on. It was during these sessions that his devotion to his own masters shone through, and he appeared able to 'channel' from them a genuinely transformative power for the student's benefit—something from which I and many others benefitted. Whatever the reason, we felt great power in those Dzogchen teachings. Even with all I know now about trance states and group hypnosis, and even after deep analysis of my own experience, it still seems as if his presence did, in association with other factors, facilitate a genuine introduction to the nature of my mind.

I discovered that since he hadn't done the prerequisite study and practice, Sogyal wasn't officially qualified to teach Vajrayana, which is presumably why he brought in other teachers. However, that didn't stop him teaching Dzogchen. For general teachings, his words while teaching formally did appear faithful to the dharma, but he certainly didn't embody the teachings, so we can't trust his personal interpretations or anything he said while *not* in a formal teaching role.

Sogyal actually took great care to teach authentically—at least as he understood it—and those who assume we were badly taught don't know the true situation. We were not as ill prepared as some like to think. The problem in Rigpa did not come because we didn't know Vajrayana, or that we 'misunderstood' what was required of us; the problem was that Sogyal abused the power given to him by his students, and we made the mistaken assumption that his actions were genuine crazy wisdom.

We diligently studied core texts of Vajrayana such as *The Words of my Perfect Teacher* by Patrul Rinpoche, a widely respected text on the Vajrayana preliminaries. As you'll see in the next section, the problem came not because we didn't study the teachings, but rather because we took those teachings too literally. It is very convenient, after all, for lamas wanting a comfortable place as a feudal lord to take teachings that cement that position at face value and have their students do the same.

Madhyamika—a classic Buddhist philosophy that provides the ground for genuine Vajrayana and Dzogchen practice—was not taught other than in the Stream Three course which Rigpa abandoned in the early 2000s, and even then the study was not done systematically or deeply. Australia did for a short time have a brief course on Buddhist philosophy, but it wasn't used in other countries. If you wanted to learn Madhyamika, you went to the Rigpa Shedra or read books and listened to recordings of the shedra—we weren't supposed to go to other teachers. Few students went to the Rigpa Shedra, and classic Buddhist philosophy was not part of the general curriculum. This is a major problem because without a correct understanding of Madhyamika it's very easy for people to fall into nihilism.

Also omitted was the analytical meditation of Vipassana which provides a preliminary to recognising the nature of our minds. Our examination of the nature of our minds was very limited and very vague.

Hardly mentioned were the qualities of teachers you *shouldn't* follow. Nor was more than lip service given to the idea of fully examining a teacher. It was given in a form something like, 'Well, of course, you should examine a teacher well before you take them as your teacher, but if you've already had an introduction to the nature of mind, then you already have samaya with Sogyal anyway.' Meaning that he was your teacher whether you recognised it or not.

Even at the early stages, Sogyal emphasised teachings and interpretations of teachings that facilitated our acceptance of his abuse, and ethics were never mentioned after the one or two classes given to the topic in a foundation course. Sogyal did often mention that the basis of the Buddha's teaching was to do no harm, but it seems he didn't pay anything other than lip service to that idea.

Though we received a sound general introduction to Buddhism, we missed out on teachings that fostered discernment and logic, and had an excessive number of teachings on devotion and how to serve a teacher. The faults were those of omission and emphasis. Given his agenda to have his every whim attended to, some part of what he taught and we practiced, likely came from his own need to benefit sexually and financially from his followers. Certainly, as you'll see in the next section, some aspects of his teachings were used to serve the silence required by his abuse. Even our basic meditation instructions taught us to 'drop' our thoughts and emotions without giving any credence to the reason for their existence—like recognising that his behaviour was abuse not kindness.

Mingyur Rinpoche said in his Lion's Roar article:

'The most basic way to measure our practice, is the degree to which we are moving closer to the simple ideals of kindness, humility, honesty, and wisdom. If—as individuals or as communities—we find ourselves moving in the other direction, something is off track.'

And both Sogyal and Rigpa certainly moved in the wrong direction, so something is indeed off track somewhere. What in what he taught was genuine Buddhism, or genuine wisdom, and what did he teach primarily to further his personal agenda? And how pure is the lineage he was supposed to represent when other teachers like him would've also emphasised what suited their agendas? Though Sogyal undoubtably imparted some wise words, anyone can read a book and parrot its wisdom, and to assume that the spiritual teachings of someone who abuses others have lasting value is naïve. Yes, we gained benefit from them at the time we heard them, but on some level they must be flawed because he used them to create a culture that normalised abuse.

For the future, I feel it's best to simply discard all his teachings and try a different teacher. To get a clear sense of where the distortions and lacks in our education were, we need to do further study with a reliable teacher—if we can still stomach any Buddhism at all.

Those of us who'd been Dzogchen practitioners wondered if a student could gain some measure of genuine realisation through relying on an unqualified teacher. And Jetsun Tenzin Palmo answered this in an email to me. She said:

> 'It is possible to gain genuine realisation even when the teacher later proves to be unqualified. If the student has a direct realisation of the nature of the mind, then that is so, whatever the status of the lama who gave the pointing out instruction or facilitated this insight. Some teachers have the ability to open the minds of the students even when in other ways the conduct and wisdom of the teacher may be questionable. This is one reason for the confusion nowadays with lamas who have helped so many students yet have been shown to be unworthy of their role. Still these students were helped.'

Some might take comfort in the words of Mipham Rinpoche in *The Sword of Wisdom* where he said:

> 'Therefore do not rely on individuals, but rely upon the dharma. Freedom comes from the genuine path that is taught, not the one who teaches it. When the teachings are well presented, it does not matter what the speaker is like.'

However, though I didn't want to admit it for a long time, in this case, given the results, I realise now we can't guarantee that we *were* taught genuine dharma in terms of its general meaning as a path of true wisdom. Certainly what Sogyal taught was based on a genuine tradition—that of Tibetan Buddhism—but where is the wisdom and compassion of genuine dharma in a path where a teacher can abuse his students with impunity?

37
FINDING CLOSURE

Everyone will find their own way to closure of this period of their lives. That doesn't mean we'll forget or we'll never revisit or speak of it again, just that we'll come to some kind of equanimity about the events and our role in them. As an author, writing is a logical form of closure for me, and this book is an excellent way for me to lay out the issues as I see them and recognise what I can and can't do something about. Certainly, there is nothing I can do about the religion, and it is a great relief to see that and leave it to the lamas and their students.

I processed my feelings through writing, and so did Sangye and others. We found it very helpful for acknowledging our feelings, recalling helpful insights, and ordering our ideas when examining the issues. Writing is an often-used tool in therapy, and a journal can take the place of someone to talk to with similar benefits for healing. Some kept their writing private or limited to the *What Now?* secret Facebook group, while others found encouragement for sharing more widely on Facebook or the blog.

A big part of finding closure for me was stepping back from my experience and looking at it again from outside the belief system to which I'd previously subscribed. I asked myself what my twenty years of Vajrayana practice had done for me. Some have told me they felt they wasted their time accumulating mantras, but that's not my experience. Vajrayana works with the practitioner's Buddha nature, and though I did fall into spiritual bypassing in some areas, after all that practice, I do have a strong sense of my own and others' Buddha nature, and the world does look different to me now—no longer solid, fixed or separate; it's insubstantial, fluid, and interconnected. And that's why, despite the terrible things he's done, I will always be grateful to Sogyal for introducing me to Vajrayana practice and teaching me Dzogchen.

So the benefits of following the Tibetan Buddhist path can be enormous for those who resonate with its approach—even with a teacher who turns out to be someone unworthy of their station. Perhaps that's because I always took the following words of the Buddha to heart:

'Rely on the message rather than the messenger. In the message, rely on the meaning rather than just the words. In the meaning, rely on that which is really true rather than seemingly true. And rely on the wisdom mind, not on the ordinary mind.'

It is my sincere wish that those affected by abuse in Tibetan Buddhism can find closure for themselves, whether through writing or other forms of self-expression; connecting with others who've been similarly affected; psychotherapy; other Buddhist, religious or spiritual groups; or a combination thereof. If you're a survivor of spiritual abuse at any level, I hope this book helps you on your journey to closure. Remember that you're not alone.

PART TWO:
AN EXAMINATION OF
ABUSE-ENABLING BELIEFS

'As more disclosures come to light, it may be time to go beyond the scandal cycle, which makes it all too easy to scapegoat a specific teacher and feel the problem is fixed if they step down from their role. This approach obviates the need for further inquiry into deep-rooted and systemic issues having to do with power and its potential for abuse.' Holly Gayley. *Revisiting the 'Secret Consort' (gsang yum) in Tibetan Buddhism,* MDPI, Religions, 2018

38
A Misuse of Buddhist Beliefs

After reading the cult-recovery literature, the group began evaluating in a more systematic fashion the beliefs and instructions we'd held that had enabled Soyal's abuse—the Rigpa 'party line'. We found and shared teachings that clarified these beliefs and instructions in a way that didn't enable abuse. And it was a great relief to discover that not all teachers viewed these teachings in an unhealthy way.

For Rigpa and other sanghas in the same situation to truly become communities where abuse cannot occur in the future, they cannot rely on teachers who support abuse-enabling interpretations of Vajrayana beliefs. Only a reformed understanding will result in the removal of *the causes* that facilitated the abuse. I share these examinations here to aid students and teachers in recognising the difference between a healthy and an unhealthy approach.

It's important that Buddhist teachers understand how these kinds of beliefs can be, and are, misunderstood and misused so they can teach in a balanced way that will avoid this outcome. Differences between Eastern and Western cultures are a factor here due to fundamental differences in outlook from the Judeo/Christian 'original sin' as being at the core of our identity, and the Buddhist concept of all people having Buddha nature—something inherently good—as the core of our beings. I feel this is one of the reasons why Westerners do fall easily into self-hatred and self-blame, and so will read such things into teachings when they are not intended. Also language taken from Christianity, such as the word 'devotion' carries overtones that may not be helpful in Buddhism.

The misuse of these beliefs and instructions, I believe, comes primarily from using them to judge and blame others and oneself, instead of using them as a lens through which to examine *oneself* and one's *own* experience. We used teachings meant to empower us to blame ourselves and others for failing to realise them.

For instance, the Buddhist view is that although external circumstances do have some effect, ultimately our happiness and suffering depend on our mind. Even if we're poor, for instance, we can still be happy if we have inner peace and contentment. And even if we're rich, we can still be unhappy if we're not content with what we have. So Buddhist thought turns us inward towards developing an inner peace and contentment that isn't diminished by external circumstances. We can't control what happens to us externally, but we can control our mind state, so this is an empowering teaching which tells us how to maximise our happiness regardless of external circumstances.

Sogyal used to say that happiness and suffering are in the mind, and if you take this too literally, you might think a person's suffering is *completely* their responsibility because it all depends on the state of their mind. If you give no credence to the role of external events in one's happiness or suffering—a stance that doesn't stand up to scrutiny—then you may blame yourself for your suffering and blame others for theirs. Add to that the idea that Sogyal's behaviour is a teaching and the onus is on the student to see it that way and deal with it in a positive way, and you've put more pressure on the victim and increased the likelihood of assigning blame to the victim for 'experiencing' the abuse as harmful.

By extension, if someone thinks the fault for experiencing abuse as harmful lies with the victim because their mental state is not one in which they can be unperturbed by the abuse, then they assign no responsibility for the harm on the perpetrator, especially if they also believe the perpetrator is a crazy wisdom master and therefore everything he does is ultimately beneficial. Adherents of this way of thinking lay the 'blame' for 'feeling' hurt squarely and unjustly on the victim.

The perception in Rigpa became something like: if you feel hurt because the lama hit you or yelled at you or asked you for a sexual favour, it's your problem. If you were more realised, it wouldn't bother you. The lama is giving you an opportunity to give up grasping at self, and if you react, then it shows how little spiritual realisation you have. It shows you're still protecting yourself, still subscribing to the idea of a self to protect. You should be changing yourself, not trying to change something outside of yourself.

Rather than holding abusive gurus responsible for the harm they cause, this way of thinking blames the victim for his or her 'feeling' that they've been abused. The self-esteem of an abuse victim in a culture that assigns, for any reason, responsibility for harm onto the victim will be even more diminished by abuse than in a culture that doesn't subscribe to such beliefs. Feelings of shame and self-blame normal in any abuse victim will be exacerbated, making the trauma far greater than that caused in any situation without these additional beliefs in play.

We need to be clear that this is not a correct understanding of dharma. It completely ignores that every individual is responsible for his or her actions. The abused are not responsible for their abuse; the abuser is. The teachings that direct us to look at our own mental state in relation to our happiness and suffering are not meant to imply that somehow a victim is to blame for the suffering they experience. If someone harms another person, they accumulate negative karma, regardless of how the victim responds—and I will examine how this applies to a supposedly-enlightened being later.

The teachings are telling us that the perpetrator doesn't have *complete* power over the abused in this situation—he or she can't control your thinking. So the point of these teachings is to empower us to do what we can to help ourselves, not to blame us for our feelings and perceptions, and certainly not to absolve another of their responsibility for their actions. We can't control what happens to us, but how we respond and deal with them is in our hands. That's the truth here; the blame-game is the distortion.

The codependent tendency many Westerners have to blame ourselves can easily be fostered by the Buddhist teachings' focus on looking to ourselves, at how we think about our experience, as the key to our happiness. The warning here for Buddhist teachers is to be aware of this tendency and make sure that in their teachings, they make it clear that seeing our own patterns and choices does not mean we are to blame or somehow responsible for what happens to us.

39
UNHEALTHY GURU-STUDENT RELATIONSHIPS

When a student follows the traditional teachings on how to follow a teacher, as outlined in *The Words of My Perfect Teacher,* they can become trapped in a submissive/dominant and codependent relationship. The belief system is basically:

- You examine the teacher, and if you decide they have the necessary qualifications, including having some realisation of the teachings, you take them as your teacher;

- On the other hand, you're told you can't question a teacher's realisation (even one that isn't your own) because ordinary beings can't tell who is and who isn't a bodhisattva, and it's bad karma to criticise or see faults in a bodhisattva;

- Once you've taken the lama as your teacher and received empowerment from them you have a samaya with that lama, which means you have to try to see them as a Buddha and their every action as enlightened action;

- Devotion to your lama is key to recognising the nature of mind, so if you don't feel devotion naturally, you must 'fake it until you make it' by recalling and focusing on all the good qualities of the lama and all the good he or she does for you. You ignore anything bad;

- The practice of devotion includes obeying your teacher and serving them with your body, speech and mind, 'following his instructions to the letter', and seeing *everything* they do as a teaching for you. You must aim to please the teacher;

- If you 'do your own thing' or don't obey, it means your devotion is lacking and you're not worthy of the highest teachings.

- If you criticise your teacher it means you're not seeing them purely, therefore it's a break of samaya which, unless that breakage is purified through Vajrasattva practice—which includes having regret for your criticism and promising not to do it again—will result in your falling into the hell realm;

- If you leave your teacher you're breaking samaya;

- One should not have anything to do with samaya breakers.

A student-teacher relationship based on this belief system is one that fosters codependency, rewards silence and obedience, and promises dire consequences for students leaving the relationship. In such a relationship the student is completely submissive to the dominant teacher. This can lead to a certain sense of selflessness in the student, as in dominant/submissive sexual relationships.

A good, if disturbing, analogy of the Rigpa view of Vajrayana is that it's like an exclusive sadomasochistic club with its own rules that you abide by once you enter. As long as members have agreed with the behavioural parameters and haven't been coerced into signing up, club membership and activities are no else's business because it's presumably between consenting adults. But the club's activities are easily 'misunderstood' by those not in the club. If members complain that they've been abused, other members would see the problem not as the behaviour inside the club, but that those who complained didn't understand the rules or what they'd 'signed up for'.

Sound familiar?

The analogy falls down on one important point, though: in sadomasochistic relationships and clubs, participants have a 'safe' word they can use when they've had enough 'punishment'. They say the word and their partner or partners stop their activity. Sogyal and other lamas who think as he does, however, provide no 'safe' word, no way for students in such a relationship to opt out. The provision of a 'safe' word allows those in a sadomasochistic relationship to retain some control, but Vajrayana students are given no such control over their situation. They are completely at the mercy of their abusers and unable to escape due to limiting beliefs, and so trauma occurs.

The Story of O by Pauline Réage indicates that a sado-masochistic relationship can give the submissive partner a certain freedom from self which can be experienced as 'spiritual' in flavour. For those inclined to the submissive role, giving up their will and sense of self in order to serve another brings some relief from their problems; the weight of having responsibility for ones' life is removed by giving the dominant partner complete control over them.

This kind of submission does not remove ego, however. It creates another ego, that of a servile, meek and devoted person. A basic sense of self or healthy ego—the self-esteem and self-awareness that allow us to function in a healthy way in relation to life and others—is the psychological foundation we need for true spiritual realisation. But a submissive/dominant and codependent relationship undermines this basic sense of self, especially where the submissive has no way of calling a halt to their treatment at the hands of the dominant partner.

Dzongsar Khyentse on page 19 of his book *The Guru Drinks Bourbon?* in a section headed 'Liberation Through Imprisonment' admits that in the student teacher relationship as traditionally laid out in Tibetan Buddhism, 'The potential for abuse of power exists.' Then, in the very next sentence, he speaks of a fully submissive relationship in which if the student wants to be enlightened, they can't even *call* abuse abuse. He says:

> 'However, once you have completely and soberly sur-
> rendered, you may not interpret certain manifestations
> and activities of the guru as the abuse of power. If you
> want to be fully enlightened, you can't worry about
> abuse.'

This leaves the student of an abusive teacher no way out.

No wonder the most devoted students in these sanghas of abusive lamas refuse to admit that the behaviour was abuse or that harm was done. They see complete submission as their path. And this is not just Dzongsar Khyentse's view; he is just stating the traditional view of his lineage, and he is doing a great service by being honest and open about it. Now we know what he and others like him expect, we can choose to avoid them entirely, or refuse to accept a relationship on these terms, or trust that the lama really does have sufficient realisation and skill to make this kind of relationship something other than one leading to codependency and slavery. The sheer degree of abuse in the religion, however, indicates to me that the last option is more than naïve, it's dangerous. Students who, once they understand what is being asked of them, choose to accept this feudal-style relationship are like sheep going willingly to slaughter.

To make this situation worse, the instructions on how to follow a teacher in Tibetan Buddhism seem to be in contradiction with the Buddha's teachings—for instance the teaching that we are supposed to examine and test everything is in contradiction with the instruction that we are supposed to obey the lama without question.

One student not only expresses well the contradictions we faced but also indicates how damaging this kind of Tibetan Buddhism can be:

'The notion of "basic goodness" was a tremendously helpful teaching to hear, having suffered from severe self-doubt, even self-condemnation, my whole life. The teachings told me I could simply trust in my clearest and sharpest intelligence and understanding, and in my heart. This was the best news I'd ever heard in fact. But then the teachers undermined this, over and over. (I should add that I wasn't even a Vajrayana practitioner, had not taken samaya vows with any teacher.)

'I came to a retreat centre and was treated with a lot of unkindness, right off the bat. It was entirely bewildering, because I'd thought that if anything Buddhists ought to be a bit kinder than the norm, not the reverse. But then, over

time, I realized that "unkindness" didn't do justice to what I was seeing and experiencing. The effects were very harmful to me, but when I tried to communicate this to the relevant people, I was ignored and ignored. Until I got angry, then I was treated like a criminal for getting angry. Then I was ignored again… Or, in trying to express why the treatment I was receiving was harmful, I was told to "drop the story line."

'Later I was told that my issues with a teacher's unkindness were a result of my having a disturbed mind, that Buddhism was not for anyone who sought healing in any way but was instead (this a direct implication) for more advanced beings. In the end there were multiple humiliations, and there was scapegoating, and ostracism.

'A double bind was created. Which was correct, the teachings or the teachers? The problem was, I was also taught that the teachers were representatives of the lama, who in turn embodied the entire lineage, thus standing in for all the buddhas and bodhisattvas. Nor would anyone else in the community ever contradict a teacher — most had taken loyalty oaths to the hierarchy as a whole. I would discover that this made for a toxic environment of groupthink.

'Even though, again, I was not a Vajrayana student, there did not seem to be any distinction made between the different levels of Buddhist practice. So when a senior student one day hinted that the early accidental death of a sangha renegade, a man who'd published a critique of the *community in 1994, perhaps ought to be taken as an object lesson, I began to wonder if maybe this was, in fact, a cult after all. It certainly felt like a warning to me.*

'All of this was going on at a terribly vulnerable point in my life, and it resulted in my becoming totally lost, certain I was condemned, in fact doomed, cursed. (The monsters in the shrine room thangkas drinking blood from human skulls and trampling on skeletons didn't help, of course.) But no one is condemned — that is what the teachings say. Yet, in fact, I was condemned. I reached out a number of times, from the depths of my heart even, to those who had pronounced judgment upon me, and was continually ignored. I'd been effectively disposed of. But no one is condemned ... and yet ... But no one ... and yet ...

'Tibetan Buddhism had introduced me to the notion of basic goodness — and then stomped all over it. Cognitive dissonances multiplied. Eventually they short-circuited my everyday functioning, resulting in paralysis, and periodic all-consuming fear lasting weeks at a time.

This examination is likely to make many readers shy away from Tibetan Buddhism entirely, but the other option is to forge a new kind of relationship with teachers, one that if we can't redefine it completely, we, at the very least, ask for a safe word—an out, so if we're exhausted or asked to do something we don't want to do, we say the word and walk away without any consequences. Better, however, is if we search for teachers who don't subscribe to this unhealthy submissive/dominant dynamic, or if that's not possible, we don't buy into it, we don't play the submissive role—be a renegade when necessary!

40
ABSOLUTE AND CONVENTIONAL TRUTH

The Buddhist teachings talk about two truths. Conventional or relative truth involves our everyday experience and understanding of the way the phenomenal world appears and functions. It includes valid cognition which is the ability to distinguish conventional truth from conventional falsehood— such as recognising when something is harmful rather than helpful. However ultimate truth recognises that these conventional phenomena we experience are neither self-created nor self-enduring; they have no nature or essence of their own and arise only in dependence upon causes and conditions. Ultimate truth is simply expressed as 'the direct, non-conceptual perception of the emptiness of phenomena.' (Susan Kahn. 'The Two Truths of Buddhism and the Emptiness of Emptiness'.)

That doesn't mean things don't exist; it just means they don't exist the way we think they do. There is no emptiness apart from conventional phenomena—no independently existing state of emptiness. So 'emptiness' itself is empty of inherent existence as well as everything else. It does not exist independently of what it is referring to as 'empty'.

This might seem unnecessarily philosophical, but it relates here to one's perception of right and wrong and hence how one acts when faced with ethical questions. Rigpa sent an article titled 'No right, No Wrong,' to Rigpa students in which Pema Chodron states, 'As far as I'm concerned, if you're going to make things right and wrong you can never even talk about fulfilling your bodhisattva vows.' (Your vow to attain enlightenment for the sake of all beings.) She refers to 'don't know mind'. 'Don't know right. Don't know wrong' and uses this idea to suggest that that's how students can view dodgy behaviour in their guru. In this day and age, a statement like this is highly misleading, if not outright damaging, and is really just a way of avoiding making a decision as to whether or not the abusive behaviour of your guru is right or wrong.

It's also a misuse/misunderstanding of the teachings on emptiness. People will no doubt say of me, 'Who is she to question Pema Chodron?' But that's the point here, isn't it? We all have to question teachers when something doesn't seem right, no matter who they are.

From the perspective of absolute truth, you *could* say right and wrong don't exist, but such a statement isn't strictly true as it doesn't convey the full meaning here. The concepts of right and wrong only don't exist from the perspective of absolute truth, which means they don't exist in an independent, permanent and singular fashion. They do, however, exist in a conventional sense, the truth regarding how the conventional world functions.

The thinking gets muddied by the fact that even in conventional truth, right and wrong are not set concepts—what I think is right, someone else might think is wrong. Where we draw the line between one side and the other is dependent on many other factors. However, we can still in any specific circumstance make a valid cognition as to whether or not a behaviour is harmful (wrong) or helpful (right). In fact we must make such cognitions in order to engage with life in a healthy fashion.

Saying 'there is no right and wrong' without qualifying it by talking about absolute and conventional truth easily gives the impression there is no right and wrong on a conventional level, and that's a misunderstanding called nihilism—thinking nothing actually exists—and that is not what the Buddha taught. If you think this way, you've forgotten, as Pema seems to have, that the only reason we can say that in ultimate truth there is no right or wrong is because on the conventional level there *is* right and wrong.

We distinguish right from wrong in reference to the coherence of interdependent conventional existence, not because right and wrong have their own independent or self-existent nature. This is the teaching of dependent arising, the teaching of the Middle Way.

This point that ultimate truth does not exist independently from conventional truth is also very important for the correct understanding of pure perception. As the Buddha said in the Prajnaparimita sutra, 'Form is emptiness. Emptiness is Form. Form is no other than emptiness. Emptiness is no other than form.'

A traditional story that shows the danger of having a nihilistic view is that of the yogi and the mouse. When a big mouse jumped on his table, the yogi, who hated mice, grabbed his shoe and thought, 'I am emptiness; the shoe is emptiness, and the mouse is emptiness!' Bam! And he killed the mouse, thinking he had nothing to worry about because he also thought bad karma was emptiness.

Any view that denies the existence of conventional reality is nihilism, and that's considered a wrong view in Buddhism.

In the 5th Video on the Western Dharma Teachers Conference in 1993, HH the Dalai Lama says:

> '[For] someone who properly meditates on shunyata [emptiness] the result *must* be more compassion and discipline. If there is not a positive result then something must be wrong.'

The 'view' in Dzogchen is this view of emptiness, of seeing the absolute reality of everything, and even Sogyal told us in *The Tibetan Book of Living and Dying*:

> 'A teaching as high and powerful as Dzogchen entails an extreme risk. Deluding yourself that you are liberating thoughts and emotions, when in fact you are nowhere near being able to do so, and thinking that you are acting with the spontaneity of a true Dzogchen yogin, all you are doing is simply accumulating vast amounts of negative karma.'

Tulku Urgyen Rinpoche on page 81 of *As It Is, Vol II*, expresses this same thing:

> 'Padmasambhava said: "Though the view should be as vast as the sky, keep your conduct as fine as barley flour." Don't confuse one with the other. When training in the view, you can be as unbiased, as impartial, as vast, immense, and unlimited as the sky. Your behaviour, on the other hand, should be as careful as possible in discriminating what is beneficial or harmful, what is

good or evil. One can combine the view and conduct, but don't mix them or lose one in the other. That is very important.

'"View like the sky" means that nothing is held onto in any way whatsoever. You are not stuck anywhere at all. In other words, there is no discrimination as to what to accept and what to reject; no line is drawn separating one thing from another. "Conduct as fine as barley flour" means that there is good and evil, and one needs to differentiate between the two. Give up negative deeds; practice the dharma. In your behaviour, in your conduct, it is necessary to accept and reject.'

And this quote from the book *Crystal Clear* by Khenchen Thrangu Rinpoche, p 109 makes the same point:

'What takes place in this unfolding of experience is not the ultimate truth; it only seemingly occurs. We call it relative or superficial reality because once you look into it, you see that no real thing can be identified or pinpointed. Just because mind, in its nature, is non-arising and empty, we cannot pretend that nothing exists, that there is no good and evil, no pleasure and pain, etc.

'As I explained earlier, each thing is dependent upon another and this also goes for good and evil—they do have consequences. Our actions do result in benefit or harm, happiness or suffering; this is undeniable. In fact, the more the experience of our true nature deepens, the more we realise that we should be ever more careful in our behaviour, attitudes and motivation. We will then develop even more compassion and be kinder to others and more diligent.'

Conventional and absolute reality are discerned in mutual dependence upon each other. There is no absolute truth without conventional truth, no emptiness without form and vice versa. Emptiness or absolute truth is always a description of something conventionally existent.

41
SEEING THE GURU AS A BUDDHA

The problem with the teachings on pure perception which instruct a student to see their teacher as a buddha and all their actions as 'pure' is that some students mistakenly think their teacher truly *is* a buddha and everything he or she does really *is* the enlightened action of a buddha. There is a difference between seeing him or her as a buddha and thinking they actually *are* a buddha.

In trying to find teachings that help us understand this correctly, I found Alexander Berzin's book, *Wise Teacher, Wise Student: Tibetan Approaches to a Healthy Relationship* incredibly helpful. Berzin says:

> 'Since impure and pure appearances have several meanings, an appearance may be pure in one sense of the word, and impure in another. Many texts, however, use the two terms without specifying the precise meaning intended. Their lack of specificity often serves as a further source of confusion or misunderstanding.'

> 'For example, highest tantra texts instruct disciples to see their tantric masters in pure forms. Any faults perceived in the master are figments of the imagination.

343

Without differentiating the various meanings of *pure*, disciples may easily mistake the statement to mean that even if mentors sexually abuse students, their actions are the perfect conduct of enlightened beings. ...

'The intended meaning of the statement, however, is quite different. The impure appearance of a tantric master's abusive behaviour *as independently existent* is a fabrication of a confused mind. [Because] the abusive behaviour *has arisen dependently* on many causes and circumstances. Although the deceptive appearance of how the behaviour exists is false, the fact that the behaviour is abusive is true.'

Where some get confused is thinking that because the teacher's actions are empty of independent existence (pure), they either don't really exist—and so can't cause harm—or since many Nyingma and Kagyu texts discuss a tantric master's behaviour as beyond good or bad, the behaviour isn't really bad, it only appears that way. As you can see by Berzin's following words, this is an incorrect view:

'Beyond good or bad means beyond the dualistic categories of independently good or bad. It is not a denial of behavioural cause and effect. ... Pure actions still produce effects. Otherwise, a Buddha's enlightening actions could not benefit anyone.'

What further complicates this view that we can't evaluate a tantric teacher's actions as good or bad is students thinking the teacher is enlightened, and since enlightened beings are 'beyond' karma and everything they do is beneficial, they believe that somewhere in the future the student will experience benefit from Sogyal's actions, and therefore the action was not actually harmful in the long term, it just appears so in the short term.

According to Buddhism, a truly enlightened person no longer creates karma for themselves nor are they driven by it. But such a person is so thoroughly grounded in compassion that their acting out of self-interest or confusion would be, by definition, impossible. Those who believe Sogyal is genuinely enlightened use this idea to convince themselves that his actions must be beneficial even though they may not appear that way. Sogyal saying he 'never, ever, acted towards anyone with a motive of selfish gain or harmful intent' supports their view especially in light of his teaching that the intention behind an action is what makes it good or bad, not its result. Given the clearly harmful results of Sogyal's behaviour, however, this is a questionable idea.

Even if Sogyal was fully realised, as Berzin says:

'Tantric masters may view their own abusive behaviour from a resultant level of a fully realized clear-light mind and thereby experience no suffering from the action, although their reputations may fall. The victims, however, validly view and experience the abuse from a basis level of an unrealized Buddha-nature and consequently suffer greatly. Therefore, out of compassion, properly qualified tantric masters always refrain from abusive behaviour.'

Not to mention that if he genuinely had the wisdom of a buddha, he would surely notice he was causing harm!

When it comes to the instruction to 'see the teacher as a Buddha' one needs to distinguish between the teacher in his absolute/pure aspect, which we relate to in our practice as a buddha, and the teacher in his or her conventional/impure aspect. No matter whether you see their pure/empty/absolute aspect or not, the actions of their conventional self function as a cause for harm or benefit. The impure and the pure exist at the same time. You can see the empty luminous nature of an action while recognising that it's conventionally harmful.

And we don't have to understand philosophy to get the main point, as HH Dalai Lama says in his book *The Path to Enlightenment*:

> 'The problem with the practice of seeing everything the
> guru does as perfect is that it very easily turns to poison
> for both the guru and the disciple. Therefore, whenever
> I teach this practice, I always advocate that the tradition
> of "every action be seen as perfect" not be stressed.
> Should the guru manifest un-dharmic qualities or give
> teachings contradicting dharma, the instruction on
> seeing the spiritual master as perfect must give way to
> reason and dharma wisdom. I could think to myself,
> "They all see me as a Buddha, and therefore will accept
> anything I tell them." Too much faith and imputed
> purity of perception can quite easily turn things rotten.'

As we know!

But from where does the Rigpa emphasis on seeing everything the guru does as perfect come? Rigpa students chant the following in their daily Longchen Nyingtik Ngondro practice:

346

'Towards the lifestyle and activity of the lama,
May wrong view not arise for even an instant, and
May I see whatever he does as a teaching for me.
Through such devotion, may his blessing inspire and fill
my mind!'

This shows the kinds of aspirations students of the Longchen Nyingtik lineage are supposed to develop. Wrong view here refers to seeing the teacher impurely, and I have already shown how easy it is to misunderstand the subtleties of the teachings on pure perception, so if you think this means whatever your guru does is okay, that's what you're telling yourself daily—it's a kind of self-hypnosis or brainwashing.

So what is a student to do when they are told to revere such texts? To get out of this bind they need to understand that seeing purely is merely seeing that the absolute nature of the actions—be they abusive or not—is empty of inherent existence; it's not thinking that the actions are good or right or morally 'pure'.

This idea that you have to see anything your guru does as okay is not helped by one commentary on this text used by Rigpa which adds another phrase to the last verse: 'and may I see whatever he does, *whether it seems to be in accordance with the dharma or not*, as a teaching for me.' *A Guide to The Words of My Perfect Teacher,* another commentary on this Ngondro, expands this idea on page 261 by saying:

'His [the teacher's] charisma may attract men and women alike, but even if he were to seduce a hundred girls daily, see it as the activity of bringing under control. And when he causes trouble, stirring up disputes and so on, even if he slaughters hundreds of animals every day, regard this as the activity of fierce subduing.'

That's an incredibly dangerous thing to teach. But here is the 'scriptural authority' that guides Rigpa students in the matter of their guru's behaviour. When I read this during my studies, I never thought a lama would actually do such things. I assumed the aim of the words was simply to encourage students to give themselves fully to their teachers, not to suggest it was okay for the lamas to behave in such a manner.

In an age when teachers can't be trusted to behave ethically or in accordance with the Buddha's teachings, however, we need to re-evaluate the relevancy of such texts. I suggest students avoid teachers who teach the Longchen Nyingtik Ngondro, particularly those who use *A Guide to The Words of My Perfect Teacher* as a commentary. Alternatively, they should at least question them deeply on their interpretation of such passages and be prepared to walk away if the teacher can't provide an interpretation that *does not* enable abuse.

42
SAMAYA AND NOT CRITICISING

Samaya can be a very complex subject if you're trying to memorise all the actions that constitute a breakage of samaya, such as criticising your teacher. Unless you repair the breakage by confessing, regretting the action and vowing not to do it again, the result is said to be that you'll go to hell. Such a belief could possibly be seen as nothing more than a handy way to keep people quiet and submissive—a spiritual gag—but assuming there is some validity to it beyond that, is the teaching on samaya really saying you mustn't criticise your teacher or bad things will happen to you?

In *Dzogchen Essentials: The Path That Clarifies Confusion* on page 55, Chokyi Nyima Rinpoche says:

> 'The foremost samaya is when you compose yourself in a state in which you, in actuality, experience the fact that all sights, sound and awareness are visible emptiness, audible emptiness and aware emptiness. To have that certainty is called keeping all the hundreds of thousands of samayas.'

So in this sense, samaya is quite simple. You can say what you like about your teacher, so long as you recognise his true nature and the true nature of everything else as well—i.e. see everything purely all the time. That's not easy to do, of course.

The essence of samaya in Vajrayana and how it relates to pure perception is explained in his usual concise and clear way by Mingyur Rinpoche in his *Lion's Roar* article. He says:

> 'Many people misunderstand samaya and think it refers only to seeing the teacher as a buddha, a fully awakened being. That is part of samaya, but it misses the key point. Samaya is about seeing everyone and everything through the lens of pure perception. The sole purpose of viewing the teacher as a buddha is so we can see these same awakened qualities in ourselves, in others, and in the world around us. It is a tool that helps us to gain confidence in the purity of our true nature.'

However, Dzongsar Khyentse in his Facebook essay on the matter of Sogyal's behaviour wrote:

> 'Frankly, for a student of Sogyal Rinpoche who has consciously received abhisheka [tantric empowerment or introduction to the nature of mind] and therefore entered or stepped onto the Vajrayana path, to think of labelling Sogyal Rinpoche's actions as "abusive", or to criticize a Vajrayana master even privately, let alone publicly and in print, or simply to reveal that such methods exist, is a breakage of samaya.'

Clearly, different teachers and lineages have different views; I suggest choosing a teacher who doesn't send you to hell for speaking the truth.

But let's look a bit more at this idea that we shouldn't criticise our teacher. Is there any basis for it other than keeping a feudal lord on his throne?

This instruction is probably designed to help us examine our projections and assumptions in order to help us avoid fixating on a teacher's petty behaviour, so we are more easily able to focus on his absolute or 'pure' nature. If we constantly grumble about little things we 'don't like' about a teacher, that will not be good for progress on a path that relies on the student seeing the teacher's enlightened or 'pure' nature. Alexander Berzin explains:

'We may not appreciate the kindness of our "less-than-perfect mentors" due to faults in mental labelling. If we have fixed ideas of what kindness is, then we grasp at *kindness* to refer to only one specific form of kindness. Our fixed ideas make us unable to include other forms of considerate behaviour in our concepts of kindness. Thus, we are unable to recognize and label those forms of behaviour as kind and, consequently, we do not appreciate them.'

This idea has merit, but it was hijacked in Rigpa so it became a way to make us doubt our perception of what constituted harm. Seeing Sogyal's abusive behaviour as unkind was not a fault of mental labelling, as we were taught, it was a valid cognition. So in Rigpa this concept was wrongly used to justify Sogyal's behaviour.

How could criticising be seen as something that could send us to hell? Berzin says:

Hell in a Buddhist context 'is a tortured, tormented mental state, with a physical counterpart, that lacks any joy and in which one feels trapped and unable to escape. Although the classical texts contain vivid descriptions, the important point is the mental state and accompanying physical feeling they describe.'

He also points out:

'The description of hells in Buddhist texts is not intended to make people feel guilty or to scare people with low self-esteem into obedience. The description is intended to educate people about the consequences of self-destructive behaviour.'

So is there something self-destructive about criticising a teacher? That depends on how we approach it. Berzin says:

'Following a misleading teacher can bring the disasters of unsound practice or spiritual abuse that can ruin enthusiasm for the spiritual path. It can turn open-minded seekers into bitter cynics, completely closed to further steps toward liberation and enlightenment. The joyless, disillusioned mental state of such people is difficult to break. It is a living hell.'

This is why Tibetan Buddhist teachers stress speaking out with a good motivation, keeping some appreciation for the benefit you gained from your time with a teacher and not viewing them with hatred. If we remember their good qualities, we can leave the teacher or the religion without self-destructive repercussions, but if we find ourselves in a state of bitterness or all-consuming anger, such that we lose all joy in life and close ourselves off to any further spiritual development, that is a hellish state. We don't avoid this because it is a breakage of samaya, we avoid it because it's a very unpleasant mind state in which to live and it does us no good.

His Holiness the Dalai Lama used this angle in the conference for Western Buddhist teachers in 1993:

> 'Speaking out against the action does not mean that we hate the person. ... Thus, we may criticize a teacher's abusive actions or negative qualities while we respect them as a person at the same time. There are still some beneficial aspects of the guru. A mistaken action doesn't destroy their good qualities. If you criticize in this way, there is no danger of hellish rebirth as a result. ... Motivation is the key: speaking out of hatred or desire for revenge is wrong. However, if we know that by not speaking out, their bad behaviour will continue and will harm the Buddhadharma, and we still remain silent, that is wrong.'

So, according to His Holiness, if we don't speak from hatred and still value any benefit we gained from our time with them, then if we criticise them, even publicly, we have not broken samaya. All that really means is that we are walking away with a balanced view—after all, few people are *all* good or *all* bad.

Realistically, however, some negative emotions towards someone who abuses you are to be expected. So, though this view supports people speaking out against teachers who abuse them, it doesn't address the psychological needs of an abuse survivor to process negative emotions as part of their healing. It could even contribute to an unhealthy suppression of those emotions. We could simply see it as a suggestion to help us not dwell on the negative aspects of our experience once we are sufficiently healed to look back on our experience in a balanced way, and that is a healthy thing to do. But His Holiness's view also doesn't recognise the fact that some students truly don't gain any benefit from their time with an abusive lama. In such a case, I suggest the student either consider that the teacher broke samaya, not the student, or give up the belief system entirely, which is likely the most healthy move for the sake of such a survivor's mental health.

Such gratitude or appreciation does not make up for or justify unethical behaviour, of course, nor does it mean one doesn't also have considerable disgust for a teacher's abusive behaviour; both can be held at the same time.

And even within these general guidelines, Berzin says that 'according to the Buddhist teachings, only specific, extremely negative thoughts and actions toward a mentor result in a hellish state of mind,' and these do not include 'accurately seeing as mistakes actual faults in their mentors, such as misjudgement, abusive conduct, or involvement in spiritual power politics'. He also points out that 'regardless of how terrible, no hellish state lasts forever. Through regret, open admission of their mistakes, and so forth, disciples may avoid or recover from tortured spiritual devastation.'

So if on reflection we find we have become trapped in a bitter, negative state, we can get out of it. And that doesn't mean we have to regret speaking out, just regret allowing bitterness to take us over to an unhealthy degree. Looking for something good from our time with the guru, and appreciating even something small will begin the process of bringing us out of any self-destructive mental state.

You can criticise a teacher and still retain a heart connection—Sogyal's definition of samaya. For me it's something akin to the kind of relationship you'd have with a member of your family who went off the rails—you don't agree with what they did; you don't even like them, but they're still your relative. Sogyal was an important figure in my life for twenty years, and because of him I studied and practiced dharma and gained much benefit. Despite my disgust at his behaviour, I retain some gratitude towards him for the benefit I gained due to his influence.

However, I wasn't directly abused, so perhaps this kind of 'middle way' of recognising both the good and the bad equally is a luxury only someone like I can afford. Had I, like some, gained absolutely no benefit from my time as his student, then there would be no reason to be grateful or to see any good in him at all, but I could still look for something—just in case. And I like to think I could still avoid developing an all-consuming hatred towards him by understanding the pressures on him from his childhood. If we can't manage compassion, pity would be preferable to hatred.

Presently I mostly feel sadness for Sogyal. What a terrible tragedy it is if he thinks he's enlightened and acting spont-aneously for the sake of beings, when he may just have a bad case of narcissistic personality disorder and be creating a terrible amount of bad karma for himself.

43
'CRAZY WISDOM' OR JUST CRAZY

'When there is contradiction between someone's apparently high realization and their ethical conduct, that realization may not be as high as it seemed.' HH Dalai Lama. Conference with Western dharma teachers, Dharamsala, March 1993.

Crazy wisdom is the idea that a realised master can see when an action normally considered harmful, when undertaken at just the right time and to just the right person, could shift a negative pattern in that person and so be beneficial for their spiritual development. For this reason what the Tibetans call 'unconventional' behaviour by a master is seen as enlightened action and so permissible behaviour.

Shocking behaviour waking us up to something of which we might not otherwise be aware isn't a completely unacceptable proposition. Like all these ideas, there's an element of truth to it—that's why we accepted it. The problem is that people are not aware of the parameters. It's the same idea as when a mother shouts at their child not to run on the road, or grabs them and forcibly yanks them off the road, rather than quietly saying, 'Darling, please don't run on the road.' The shouting or grabbing of clothing and yanking the child back will likely be more effective in facilitating the child's learning not to run on the road than its softer option, which may not even be heard over the traffic. However, if that mother constantly shouts at or beats the child, then her behaviour is no longer a valid wake-up call, it becomes abuse.

There is a huge difference between a single and rare unconventional action done to a student who the teacher is certain is able to use it as a stimulus for awakening and daily beatings for all the students working closely around a lama.

It appears, however, that Sogyal used corporal punishment regularly and indiscriminately, and anyone not indoctrinated with the Rigpa 'party line' could see the abusive nature of his behaviour. The idea of crazy wisdom was used to excuse and justify the abuse, something that, as Dr Nida Chenagtsang, in his book *The Yoga of Bliss* points out, is all too common:

'Unfortunately the term "Crazy Wisdom" has now become so popularised that people will use it to explain any kind of bad behaviour by gurus, as if "Crazy Wisdom" is some special Tibetan cultural practice which allows a Vajrayana guru to ignore all laws and vows, all of the Buddha's teachings on ethical behaviour, and any consequences for their actions!'

The following 'activity teaching' by Sogyal, recorded in a student's notes as it was streamed from Rigpa House in Bluey's Beach (date unknown), shows how he taught his students to accept his behaviour:

'So *whatsoever* the lama does, calling you names, hitting you, teasing you, changing your jobs, is to purify your karma, is to help you. When you make difficulty, when you resist, you lose!'

But as Dr Chenagtsang says, 'The time for the misuse of "Crazy Wisdom" is over. "Crazy Wisdom" is not an excuse for breaking vows or for bad behaviour.' In light of this misuse of the concept, what is needed today is for teachers to make a commitment not to use such 'methods' at all. And students need to recognise how extremely unlikely it is in the modern world that any guru or student has sufficient realisation for genuine crazy wisdom to occur. After seeing the web of delusion Sogyal wove around his students, I consider that any lama referred to as a crazy wisdom master is one best avoided.

His Holiness the Dalai Lama agrees that crazy wisdom is no longer appropriate:

> 'Historically, although some Buddhist saints have acted with strange modes of ethical conduct, they were fully realized beings and knew what was of long-term benefit to others. But nowadays, such conduct is harmful to the dharma and must be stopped. Even though one's realizations may be equal to those of divine beings, one's behaviour must conform to convention. If someone says that since everyone has Buddha mind, any kind of conduct is acceptable, or that teachers do not need to follow ethical precepts, it indicates that they do not correctly understand emptiness or cause and effect.'

359

44
OBEDIENCE WITHOUT QUESTION

One part of the Longchen Nyingtik Ngondro, which I chanted daily for twelve years, says:

'May I rely upon my vajra lama meaningfully,
as though he were my very eyes,
Following his instructions to the letter,
and taking to heart the profound practices he gives ...'

The Words of My Perfect Teacher and a commentary on it, *A Guide to The Words of My Perfect Teacher,* are texts Rigpa uses to study the Vajrayana preliminaries or ngondro—the entrance into the Vajrayana path—and both books make it very clear that once you've taken a teacher as your tantric master, you have to do what he or she says, see them as a Buddha, see *everything* they do as enlightened activity, and never criticise. The trouble with following these books comes, as it did in Rigpa, when these aspects are stressed over the sections that moderate them, such as the section outlaying what kinds of people we should take as a teacher and what kinds we should avoid (p 138 – 143).

Had we paid attention to the following, which is just one aspect of Patrul Rinpoche's list of requirements of a genuine teacher, we would have realised Sogyal was not someone worthy of being taken as our teacher: 'Not having many disturbing negative emotions and thoughts, he should be calm and disciplined.' Sogyal's lack in this area wasn't hidden. No wonder Sogyal never stressed this part of the book.

The point missed in Rigpa was that the instructions on following a teacher in *The Words of My Perfect Teacher* ONLY apply to a student of someone who meets the requirements for a qualified teacher. Since Sogyal didn't meet those qualifications, the rest of the book isn't applicable to him or his students. I don't think this text is appropriate in an age where, in the words of the book in question, 'All the qualities complete according to purest dharma are hard to find in these decadent times,' and where, even if such a teacher were found, the kind of student-teacher relationship suggested fosters codependency and submission rather than a healthy balanced relationship.

As we've seen in Rigpa, the result of applying these teachings to a flawed teacher can be an abusive cult, and the number of lamas accused of similar behaviour makes it quite clear we cannot blindly trust that any of them have our best interests at heart. We do not have to take everything in Tibetan Buddhism on board or at face value. We can choose what to accept and what to reject. We must never give up our right to say, 'No,' our right to criticise, and our discernment as to what is harmful or helpful. Any teacher who asks you to give these up is one to avoid. But be warned, some teachers will say one thing in public and expect something else in private.

The Cloud of Jewels Sutra says:

> 'With respect to virtue act in accord with the gurus'
> words, but do not act in accord with the gurus' words

with respect to non-virtue. Therefore, you must not listen to non-virtuous instructions. ... Rather, excuse yourself politely, and do not engage in what you were instructed to do.'

And HH Dalai Lama said:

'If a teacher tells you to do a non-Dharmic action, you should reject that advice. ... According to Vajrayana (or tantrayana), if a guru gives an instruction that is not in accord with the dharma, the student should not follow it and should go to the teacher to clarify and explain why they cannot. ... The purity of the teacher's motivation is not enough: the instruction must be appropriate for the situation and the culture of the place.'

45
DEVOTION WITHOUT DISCERNMENT

'The danger with indiscriminate idealised devotion to the guru is that we are trusting that the guru will really hold a place of complete integrity and that he will have no personal agendas.' Rob Preece.

Dzogchen is a path of devotion, and Dzogchen is what Sogyal was best known for. In Dzogchen, according to Sogyal, devotion is seen as the fastest way to realise the nature of your mind. It works like this: You already have the pristine awareness of the true nature of your mind, so the guru doesn't give you anything you don't already have. Our problem is that we don't recognise this level of our being, this true nature of our mind; however, someone who has recognised the nature of their own mind can show you the nature of your mind so you can go, 'Ah ha, that's it. Now I see it.' It's like holding up a mirror so you can see your face.

Once you've recognised the nature of your mind and become confident that you really have got it, you can go away and practice maintaining that awareness. And the devotional practice of guru yoga will help you to reawaken that recognition using the guru as inspiration. 'Tuning in' to the human guru's presence as he or she rests in the nature of their mind is the method used to awaken the student to the presence of their inner guru, which is the true/empty/ultimate nature of our minds.

In order to 'get' the introduction, we need a qualified teacher with an authentic method and we need to be totally open to the person giving the introduction. Devotion is this total openness to the guru. In *The Tibetan Book of Living and Dying*, Sogyal says devotion is 'not mindless adoration; it is not abdication of your responsibility to yourself, nor undiscriminating following of another's personality or whim. Real devotion is an unbroken receptivity to the truth. Real devotion is rooted in an awed and reverent gratitude, but one that is lucid, grounded and intelligent.'

This sounds perfectly fine, doesn't it? I would never have gone for a devotion that meant mindless adoration or undiscriminating following of someone, and yet, despite Sogyal's words on the matter, adoration is what he demanded and what most students gave.

But I can testify to the power of devotion. It does open you up to being able to sense the nature of mind in the guru and so evoke it in yourself so that you have a taste of that level of awareness. So it's not something to avoid at all costs; it's a relationship that has to be tempered with discernment, that's all. At the moment of introduction, you can open yourself up to that absolute/Buddha nature/pure view of a teacher while still recognising that he's just a human with faults. As Dr Berzin says, a guru 'is both an ordinary human and a buddha from different valid points of view.'

We all have buddha nature, even the very worst of us, and someone who has some recognition of the nature of their mind can still be quite deluded when not resting in that state of awareness—as Sogyal has shown us. It's a lot less confusing, however, to have devotion for someone who also has good qualities as a human being, so it's important to evaluate a teacher carefully before becoming their student and particularly before taking any kind of empowerment with them.

Rob Preece in an excellent article titled 'Devotion with Discernment – A question of Personal Responsibility' on the *Tibetan Buddhism in the West* website says:

> 'In our devotion to a teacher we can have a strong sense of respect, appreciation and indeed love, but not in a way that blinds us to their human fallibility. We need to retain our sense of discernment that recognizes and faces when things are not acceptable or not beneficial. If this means a level of disillusionment, then so be it. At least we will end up with a more realistic and real relationship. Again as HH Dalai lama once said, "too much deference actually spoils the guru."'

So what constitutes 'too much deference'? As well as demanding devotion from his students, in the last few years, Sogyal and Rigpa teachers and instructors encouraged us to see him as the deity Guru Rinpoche as if he were the man in flesh. This is the reason it is so difficult for many former students to do any practice with Guru Rinpoche as the focus: Sogyal is too closely associated with the deity in their minds.

We were told we had to 'fake' devotion until it became real, to focus on his good qualities and his kindness. Focusing on the teacher's kindness and good qualities in order to develop devotion is a genuine teaching, not something Sogyal made up, but it took on an unhealthy cast in a situation where there were so many bad qualities that we were expected to ignore. Respect must be earned, and devotion should be allowed to develop as a natural result of a student's deepening relationship with a teacher. As they see that the teacher is worthy of their devotion, it will flower. A teacher who demands your devotion is best avoided.

I can't believe now that I didn't see this was all just a little twisted, but there were so many little things, places where expectations and interpretations were just a little off, and one thing by itself wasn't enough to wake me up to how much of Rigpa was there entirely to serve Sogyal's base desires. It took the revelations by those eight courageous students for me to start to put together a picture of how all these little slightly off elements added up to an unhealthy whole.

Dr Alexander Berzin in chapter nine of *Wise Teacher, Wise Student: Tibetan Approaches to a Healthy Relationship* says:

'A healthy relationship with a spiritual mentor does not include an abrogation of responsibility for one's life. It does not engender psychological dependency, nor does it entail following a mentor's advice unquestioningly like a soldier obeying a command. Buddhism never calls for submissive obedience, even of a monk to his abbot or a nun to her abbess. After all, one of the major qualifications of a disciple that Aryadeva specified is common sense. This means having both the ability to discriminate and freedom of choice.'

Wise Teacher, Wise Student: Tibetan Approaches to a Healthy Relationship should be mandatory reading for all students of Tibetan Buddhism because it goes into all these tricky areas in the guru-student relationship, examining them from a scholarly perspective that finds the correct understanding of the teachings that we need if we are to avert the Rigpa type disaster in future. It can be read for free on Berzin's website, *Study Buddhism by Berzin Archives.*

46
KARMA

Karma means actions and their results. Action now, not just the result of past actions. It may be someone's karma to be in a certain situation, but that doesn't mean I leave them to their fate or do nothing about their situation. It is always our responsibility to assist those in need, and it creates bad karma for us if we do nothing to assist when we have the ability to do so. Whereas anytime we help others, we build merit/good karma for ourselves and assist them in changing their karma.

A misunderstanding of karma is that it is a kind of punishment for something or that a victim is somehow 'responsible' for the misfortune caused by someone else. This is a gross distortion, however, because we are responsible only for our own actions, not for those of another.

Of course, we have a role in any relationship. We turned up. But that doesn't make the abuse our fault. We likely had some codependent tendencies as well, but these are dynamics that affect the situation, they are not causes for it. The behaviour of the abuser is the cause, and the toxic culture in Rigpa was a condition that facilitated the abuse. We all contributed to that culture, but we did not raise the stick or land the punch. We are not responsible for that any more than a rape victim is responsible for her rape.

If we believe the Buddhist teachings on karma, then our being in a place and time when someone or something harms us will, if we haven't done something sufficiently negative in this life, be seen as the ripening of negative karma from one or more lifetimes ago. However, even if this is so, the person we are now can hardly be held 'responsible' for something we've done in a life we don't even remember, so even if there is some causality functioning, that doesn't make us, as we are in this life, responsible in terms of it being 'our fault'. If this idea is a true reflection of reality, then it just means there's a causal link. All that connects us to those other people is the karmic imprints they left in our storehouse consciousness. No matter how many lives we may have, we are only this conventional self once. Besides all that, whatever our karma, it does not excuse or justify the harmful actions of others towards us.

As for the idea that abusive behaviour by a teacher purifies a student's karma and so fast-tracks them to enlightenment; this is clearly a very dangerous idea. Difficult circumstances may be seen as a purification of our own karma, but that doesn't mean anyone should take it upon themselves to be difficult or harm others using the excuse that the harm they cause is somehow karmically of benefit to their victim. This is twisted thinking—even by a so-called realised master.

Did the Buddha want his teachings on karma used to blame victims for trauma they received at the hands of another, and to absolve the perpetrator of a crime from responsibility for the harm? Pretty sure he didn't.

47
A COMMON-SENSE VIEW

A friend emailed Tenzin Palmo on my behalf and asked her to talk about these beliefs in light of the abuse. The reply from her was a breath of fresh air, a relief. At last, someone was saying something sensible, something that rang true. Here's what she said:

> 'Samaya goes both ways: the student has samaya to the teacher but the teacher also has samaya to the student. The student's samaya is to cultivate devotion, trust and openness in order to receive the mind blessings of the guru. The teacher's samaya is, through their knowledge and compassion, to develop the spiritual potential of the student. Therefore we must ask, do the actions and words of the guru lead to the students' well-being, advancement on the path and general feeling of enrichment—or not?
>
> 'Spiritual teachers cannot use the dharma as an excuse for licentious or abusive behaviour. Tantra isn't about coercing vulnerable women into having sex. Where is the compassion in exerting your position of power and

373

authority to betray the very people who trust and obey you? Where are basic ethics and kindness?

'If the students (usually—but not always—female) as a result of a sexual relationship with the guru, do feel enhanced, empowered and confident, then that was skilful means on the part of the teacher. But if the result is humiliation, confusion and disillusionment, then where is the wisdom and compassion in that? Where have they been helped?

'Clearly the manipulative nature of these encounters causes so much distress. It all seems so egocentric and devoid of empathy. How can these teachers justify such behaviour to themselves? Although it is a mixture of power, loneliness, emotional immaturity and so on, still this does not excuse the kind of behaviour that would be condemned by anyone anywhere. That these teachers do have problems is one thing, but that they cannot use their own training to deal with these issues (or even acknowledge them) is really a problem! Actually, it is pathetic. Gurus need to observe the same ethical standards as doctors, psychologists, teachers and so on in order to be trusted and respected and not to drag down the reputation of Buddhism.

'As Mingyur Rinpoche pointed out, we cultivate pure perception towards everyone, not just the guru. Nonetheless, present day lamas are not Guru Rinpoche or Tilopa, any more than the student is Yeshe Tsogyal or

Naropa. Is the student benefitted? Good. Is the student psychologically harmed? Not good. It is so simple.

'Tibetan Buddhism is based on a feudal system of total authority (however corrupt) and abject obedience. We do not need to go backwards to outdated social attitudes in order to be good practitioners. One troubling aspect is the effort to 'cover up and defend' by lamas who really should know better. Part of the 'Old Boys Club' syndrome. To try to defend indefensible behaviour by quoting tantric texts and accuse the victims is to equate Tantra with violence, over-indulgence and sexual predatory activity, which hardly speaks well of that method as a valid path to Enlightenment.

'When students are instructed to never question the teacher and to do everything to please them, then of course it leaves the doors wide open to exploitation. This feudal thinking has to be tempered with common sense and common caution. If it feels wrong, don't do it, no matter who asks you. It is not breaking Samaya to say No.

'As someone said: '… the happiness of the privileged is based on never starting the process towards becoming accountable … the revelation of truth is tremendously dangerous to supremacy.'

'So be grateful for what teachings the Lama has given and appreciate everything that has been helpful. But do not feel guilty about seeing and acknowledging where the boundaries have been overstepped by the teacher. The fault is with limitations and wrong conduct of the guru.'

Compare this voice of reason from within the tradition with something I later read in Jeff Brown's book *Grounded Spirituality*. His perspective, coming from outside the religion, summed up the feelings and perceptions shared by many of those who had been spiritually abused:

'A form of spiritual fascism has developed, one that benefits only a small few. If you call out the lying guru, you are met with the 'no gossip' mantra and, for those who are intoxicated by them and subjugated to their teachings, the irrational fear that they will sic their Shakti-powers on you. If you feel triggered by their teachings or violated in any way, you are reminded that spirituality should not include anger or negativity. You are handed back the burden of blame—that it is just your own 'issues and resistances'. I had always imagined spirituality a quest for truth, but that is not the all-pervasive consensus.

'There is widespread investment within the spiritual community in having particular opinions protected. Even common sense judgements, acts of conscious discernment, evidence of wrong doing firmly grounded in reality, have been conveniently mischaracterized as anti-spiritual, a philosophy that plays right into the hands of ill-intentioned gurus. If we can be persuaded that it is unspiritual to judge the teacher, if we can be conditioned to believe that our judgements about their integrity are merely a reflection of our own issues, then anything goes.

'We can easily understand why gurus and spiritual leaders would want to put a protective veil around themselves. It preserves their market share egoically and financially. It grants them permission to sell their teachings as impenetrable gospel. Yet they aren't. Not even close. They are as worthy of debate as any other concept or notion. Better we speak our truths and let the karmic chips fall where they may. Every voice and perspective matters.'

PART THREE: LESSONS FOR THE FUTURE

'Blind faith in authorities is the enemy of truth!' Albert Einstein

48
CHOOSING A TEACHER

The perception I might have left you with is that Tibetan Buddhism is a terrible religion but we must remember that abusive lamas and their cults are Tibetan Buddhism *gone wrong*. Many people assure me that there are genuinely kind and caring lamas, and you can see from the quotes I've used in the last section that not all lamas think the same way. Hence, the importance of examining teachers thoroughly before 'joining their club.'

If you're really interested in how your mind works and how you can best work with your mind, then Tibetan Buddhism is a great thing to study and practice—so long as you don't use the practice to bypass your emotional issues by seeking a pleasant spiritual 'high'. The teachings on Dzogchen and Mahamudra are particularly deep and inspiring, and have changed me for the better, but you do need a teacher.

So if you haven't yet studied and practiced these teachings very much, don't cut yourself off from the benefit for fear of the bad. However, if you've genuinely studied and practiced for decades such that you know the teachings well and can recognise your true nature, then rather than always looking out for more teachings and more time with your teacher, or any teacher, you might be better off just practicing what you've learned. It's too easy for following another to become a way of avoiding the main point, which is examining your mind and reality—something no one else can do for you.

If we want Tibetan Buddhist teachings, our task is to find reliable teachers, expose those who do abuse their power, and forge healthy relationships with our chosen teachers, even if that means ignoring some of their directions.

In an attempt to encourage some more native Tibetan lamas to state their position on abuse, some of us got the letter by the eight translated from English into Tibetan and sent it, along with the Lewis Silken report and over 100 signatures to thirty-eight lamas, with a question. We asked: Do you think the behaviour of Sogyal Lakar/Rinpoche as described in the 2017 letter by eight close students and confirmed by the Lewis Silkin Report is ever an acceptable way for Tibetan Buddhist teachers to behave towards their students?

We received only two replies. It seems that few Tibetan lamas are prepared to say that abuse is not an acceptable behaviour in a lama. We explained how important it was that they respond, how their silence is seen as complicit, and still they didn't respond. I understand there are cultural reasons that make speaking out difficult for them, but to not do so after we made it clear in our email just how important it was shows a lack of concern for students.

In light of lamas' lack of willingness to engage with the guru abuse issue, it's clear that it's up to those students who still want something to do with this religion to draw the boundaries and simply not accept abusive behaviour. No matter what some teachers and students suggest, we do not have to accept the idea that abuse is a legitimate part of the Tibetan Buddhist religion. It isn't—or at least, it ought not to be. Unfortunately, Tibetan culture appears to give the reincarnated lamas (tulkus) an 'anything-goes' pass which allows them to do what they want with impunity.

We have to choose our teachers wisely and cautiously, not put our money anywhere there is a whiff of scandal or bad behaviour, and walk away with our wallets at the first indication that a teacher or sangha is not behaving as they should. Loss of income will hit them more powerfully than any words.

The Words of My Perfect Teacher by Patrul Rinpoche is not all bad in its advice. A long section speaks of the qualities of a genuine teacher—ethical, properly educated, kind, compassionate, with a motivation to benefit all beings and help bring them to enlightenment, and with extensive practice experience, genuine realisation and a lifestyle that is in accord with the dharma. The author also talks about the kind of teachers to avoid and makes it clear that nowadays it's difficult to find a teacher with all the qualities required. So let's stop assuming we've found a truly enlightened teacher. Our desire for that causes us to project qualities onto lamas that are just not there. They are first and foremost human beings, and we should never forget that. As Martine Batchelor pointed out when speaking about Tibetan Buddhist teachers on a YouTube video:

> 'What is dangerous is the fact that the student needs their teacher to be amazing. They think the teacher is totally, completely awakened. And then, after that everything the teacher does they read as awakened. But it's not. They are just human beings. They may have read a bit. They may have done some things. They may have

been born. They may have been discovered. The idea of the Rinpoche: This is the total luck of the draw! Some turn out good, like the Dalai Lama, some don't turn out good, like Sogyal Rinpoche. But they all have the same title: they are Rinpoche. As soon as you hear the name 'Rinpoche', you think that person must be great. But it is just an accident, the fact that they think this person must be the reincarnation of that person. But you have no idea: They are two or three years old, how are they going to turn out?'

Rob Preece in an article called 'Devotion with Discernment' adds to this tendency for us to project:

'In the case of someone who becomes our guru we project an image of our "higher Self" onto a person who can act as a carrier of that unconscious quality. When this begins to happen it is as though we become enthralled or beguiled by this projection. In the case of the projection of the Self onto a guru we give away something very powerful in our nature and will then often surrender our own volition to be guided. ... So if you are someone who yearns for the perfect guru, watch out that your desire for such doesn't lead you to create a perfect guru in your mind that has little or no basis in reality.'

I'm pretty sure that's what I did, got caught up in the romance of the idea.

I suggest students choose teachers who have made a *clear* public statement against abuse, who honour the importance of students' discernment, who show respect for students, and who have otherwise shown they are worthy of their role as a spiritual teacher. We have to check their behaviour and not be fooled by fancy hats and titles, prestigious lineages and charisma, or by the number of devoted students—blind and emotional devotion is a cult warning sign; intelligent appreciation is not. The high level Tibetan lamas are the aristocrats of Tibetan culture, the most entitled, with the kind of power held by a feudal lord. They're brought up with the expectation that they will live just as the masters before them lived, and so they are the very ones of whom we need to be most suspicious.

We also need to check anything a lama says about politics or society and see whether he or she is indicating an attitude that is in accord with the dharma. Are they showing love and compassion for all, or are they seeing with an us-against-them attitude? Arrogance is a huge red flag—it's the opposite of humble. And if a lama's disciples are not seeing when a lama is not speaking in accord with the dharma, then stay far away from that sangha, because if they're not using their discernment, it's a cult, not a healthy spiritual community.

Watch carefully how they treat their students during a teaching, and be wary of any hint of unkindness, arrogance or sexual harassment or innuendo. As students it's important we only give our money to teachers who teach, practice and embody a healthy interpretation of the teachings.

On finding a good teacher Dr Alexander Berzin advises: 'A misleading teacher is someone who is ruled by disturbing emotions, such as greed, attachment, anger, or naivety; who pretends to have qualities that he or she lacks; or who hides his or her actual shortcomings. Moreover, such a person has a weak sense of ethics, teaches only for personal gain, or gives incorrect information and instruction. Naive spiritual seekers may incorrectly consider some of the person's faults as assets or ascribe good qualities to the person that he or she lacks. Consequently, they build distorted relationships that are based on deception and lies.'

The big problem in researching a teacher is that it's very hard to find out what goes on behind the scenes. We've seen how students minimise the bad things and are not supposed to say anything critical about their lamas. This catch-22 of having to examine a teacher and not being able to because no one will say anything bad about them cannot be overcome, so it's up to us to maintain a certain reserve and not throw ourselves blindly into any relationship with a lama.

Check the potential candidate against the list of attributes of a narcissist. The guru role is perfect for narcissists to have their needs met, and Sogyal is not the only Tibetan lama who exhibits these attributes. As I suggested previously, aspects of a tulku's upbringing could encourage narcissism, and in some lineages we may have a case of narcissists breeding more narcissists. For this reason I suggest you find out as much as you can about a potential teacher's upbringing. Particularly important is checking the person most important in their upbringing for narcissistic tendencies.

Upbringings vary within the tulku framework, as can the child's reaction to such an upbringing. Elinor Greenberg, Ph.D. says in her article in *Psychology Today* on 'How Do Children Become Narcissists?' that, 'Occasionally, these children resist their role as "The Golden Child," do not become narcissistic, and are embarrassed by the excessive praise that they receive. They feel burdened by the role they are asked to play in the family.' So it would be unwise to assume all tulkus are narcissists.

However, also do not assume that because a child has been 'recognised' as a great lama's reincarnation that they genuinely are such an incarnation. For financial and political reasons, a child from a poor or politically insignificant family is much less likely to have been 'recognised' as an incarnation—another reason to look at their family background.

Don't be sucked in by the mystery, the magic, and even the sexiness of some of these lamas. Don't take *everything* they say as wisdom just because *some* of what they say rings true. Like all human beings, they have faults.

Be a spiritual warrior and pull them up whenever you hear misogyny, gender inequality, prejudice, arrogance and cultural disrespect. Stand up and ask questions whenever you hear something that doesn't sound right; don't allow them to have power over you. If you don't feel you can do this, then a guru-student relationship is probably not healthy for you. Let them earn your respect. And if they don't respect you enough to answer your questions without putting you down, get a new teacher.

We must forge a new way of relating to our spiritual teachers, a way that allows us to talk to them and give them real honest feedback. They need it if they are to be effective teachers, for despite their knowledge of their religion, most Tibetan lamas know little about their students or Western culture, and some are clearly immature in the area of emotional development and excellent at spiritual bypassing. If they can't hear you when you have reasonable concerns, then walking away is your best option.

Such a relationship, however, can only be achieved by someone who does not have codependent tendencies, someone who has clear boundaries and good self-esteem, but those who seek gurus may be weak in these areas. If you don't think you can manage not to fall into a submissive, codependent relationship with a guru, I suggest you do some solid work with a psychotherapist before seeking a guru.

And finally in this chapter, it saddens me to have to say it, but given the religion's beliefs around sex being beneficial for both the lamas and the women they lure into their bed, and the tradition of lamas having sex with students and seeing nothing wrong with it, I don't think we can trust any of them to abide by the Buddha's injunction against sexual misconduct or Western ideas on what constitutes sexual harassment. And considering the prevalence of sexual abuse in Tibetan Buddhist monasteries, I include monks in that. And abusive childhoods aside, it's naive to assume that Buddhist monks are any better at keeping their dicks in their pants than Catholic priests.

The only way out of this mess, I think, is for students to vow to never compromise their personal integrity, to take responsibility for their own spiritual path rather than handing control over to another, and to keep their critical thinking faculties engaged at all levels of the path rather than blindly accepting every pronouncement by a lama as wisdom. To give any of that up in the name of devotion is neither wise nor in line with what the Buddha taught.

49
CULT WARNING SIGNS

The Lerab Ling community raised the question of whether or not Rigpa was a cult by suing the French lawyer who shared some of the results of his investigation into Rigpa in a French newspaper. This set off my research into cults. Had I done this before I joined Rigpa, I would have recognised the warning signs. Anyone thinking of taking a guru of any kind should research what constitutes a cult. It could save a lot of trauma. No one wants to join a cult, but plenty of intelligent people do simply because they don't know the warning signs.

I've pointed out some of the ways in which Rigpa operated like a destructive cult, and you can see how the beliefs I discussed in the previous section can easily be misunderstood and misused so that Tibetan Buddhist lamas can step over the line and assume the role of a cult leader and thus turn their community into a cult. It's vital that students recognise when that has occurred because a cult environment, even without guru abuse and with the wisest-sounding teachings and most-inspiring practices, is not conducive to true personal and spiritual development. We may feel safe in our weekly course with our lovely instructor, but if the organisation is saying one

389

thing and doing another, then they're manipulating you. Cults always look benign on the surface.

Can a cult stop being a cult? Not unless they admit the ways in which they have been operating as a cult, give a full apology to their members, and vow not to continue in that manner. Even then, I doubt it's possible, certainly as long as those in control still subscribe to the same beliefs that made the manipulation and control acceptable to them in the first place.

When I first looked at one of the what-makes-a-cult checklists, I didn't want to accept that perhaps I'd been in a cult, and if you haven't evaluated your group in this way, you'll likely feel the same, so when you evaluate, try to put aside your desire not to be in a cult.

Margaret Thaler Singer, Ph.D., a clinical psychologist and emeritus adjunct professor at the University of California, Berkeley, who has counselled and interviewed more than 3,000 current and former cult members, relatives and friends says in a talk published on YouTube that 'the difference between cults and religions is that in religions the devotion goes to an abstract principle whereas in a cult the devotion is to an individual.' And, 'The follower turns over their decision-making and gives complete obedience in return for having secrets revealed to them.'

Being required to give unquestioning devotion and obedience to a teacher in order to get secret or special teachings is the mark of a cult, and because of the central role devotion to the guru plays in Vajrayana, it's very easy for Tibetan Buddhist communities to become cults. Therefore students of Tibetan Buddhism need a strong cult-alert radar. However, I believe the elements that make a community a cult are *not* inherent to a

Tibetan Buddhist community. The previous section lays out interpretations of the teachings that should not lead to a cult environment.

The problem with a community that fulfils even one of the characteristics of a destructive cult, or several aspects to a moderate degree, is that there is danger of abuse within that organisation, and not only emotional, physical, and sexual abuse but also the general spiritual abuse of being manipulated by a teacher and organisation that cares more about filling its coffers than truly being of benefit to their members. Wherever those at the top get perks such as a lavish lifestyle, sexual favours, and/or a bevy of attendants focused on fulfilling their every need, it's likely the leader and organisation are not as altruistic as they make out.

What follows is a list of the main characteristics of a destructive cult in a religious context, and under Sogyal, it seems to me that Rigpa met every one of them. If people in Rigpa behave the same way with new teachers as they did with Sogyal, then that's an indication they still have a cult mentality. A healthy Tibetan Buddhist community will not have cult characteristics.

1. The leader has absolute power & demands personal devotion.

If a leader has complete power and authority without the dynamics of open accountability, and if members aren't allowed to question or challenge decisions made by leaders, but instead members loyally submit without any right to dissent, we have a cult with a high risk of abuse.

391

The distinction between devotion that goes to an abstract principle and where it goes to an individual is particularly useful in determining what constitutes 'excessive' devotion in a Tibetan Buddhist context. In Vajrayana, the role of the guru in practice is an abstract principle, that of the 'cosmic' guru principle, which is ultimately the true nature of our own mind. The physical guru is only one aspect of this guru principle, which also includes the teachings themselves and the teacher aspect of our own experience. So any teacher who directs students' devotion away from themselves towards the ultimate guru principle in the student is not in danger of becoming a cult leader. They can do this by insisting you *not* visualise them in Guru Yoga practice but use Guru Rinpoche, for instance, and by not allowing prostrations to them or any special fanfare on their arrival.

A cult warning sign is a lama who permits or suggests that a student visualise them in their Guru Yoga practice rather than the lineage founder, and any who demands devotion to *themselves,* be it covertly or overtly. Devotion arises naturally as a result of the guru showing the student he or she is worthy of such devotion; it should not be demanded and certainly not used as a requirement to get higher teachings.

Watch out for students who tell you their teacher is a Buddha or is enlightened, especially if you hear it in a group teaching or practice session. If someone is standing in front of your group saying their teacher is enlightened, ask yourself why they're doing that in a group? If it's done a lot, it's a red flag. Any outpourings of excessive devotion are a warning sign. The more gushy and wide-eyed students are when they talk about their guru, the more likely it is that they have fallen into an emotional and, likely, blind devotion. And where devotion is blind, it's dangerous.

Another red flag is student's reading out or otherwise sharing *only* positive feedback, and you never hear a single negative word. This is simply feeding a narcissist's need for adoration and adulation. And of course signs of narcissism in the leader should have you walking straight out the door. Narcissists use and abuse people. You cannot have a healthy relationship with a narcissist.

Beware of any lama who insists on obedience and no criticism, especially if they have two categories, one for general students and one for those who have taken tantric initiations. If you want the 'higher' teachings, you'll eventually end up in the tantric group where you're required to subscribe to these two major abuse-enabling beliefs. You must always retain the right to use your critical thinking faculties and raise issues should you need to.

2. The leader manipulates and controls his or her students.

Another mark of a cult is when fear, guilt or threats are routinely used to produce unquestioning obedience and group conformity, and these may include stringent tests of loyalty. The leader-disciple relationship may become one in which the leader's decisions control and usurp the disciple's right or capacity to make choices.

If you see a lama directing students' personal lives or making demands on them, step away. They should not be advising on who to have sex with or marry, what to eat and wear, what job to take and so on. Nor should they be acting like kings ordering slaves around. They should be treating students as equals. If there is no equality, there is no respect from the teacher to the student, and that's a red flag.

Watch for fear. Do the students leap up and rush around to fill the teacher's needs rather than doing so in a relaxed way? Do they look stressed or at ease, especially when they engage with him directly? Do they never question, even just to clarify something? Are questions even allowed? In Rigpa we couldn't ask questions live, they had to be written down. Then they would be edited into something that didn't necessarily even look like your question anymore and then he'd answer the written question—if you were lucky. Instructors selected which ones would be answered.

Does the lama demand to be served, his every need attended to? Students should look after their teachers, of course, but if a guru demands that others serve him or her, that's a red flag. There is a difference between asking for a cup of tea and demanding one.

Can you ever approach the guru, speak with him or her directly, or are they always surrounded by members of their 'inner circle' such that they create a bubble around the guru so he or she can never speak to ordinary students? These are warning signs of groups and lamas to be avoided.

Look for signs of gaslighting, trance induction, overloading of information, schedules that leave students running on less than eight hours sleep and indications that the guru is fostering codependency in his or her students.

3. The group is elitist and 'above' the law.

Cults depict themselves as unique and as offering something special students can't get elsewhere. They assign the status of the chosen, the wise, the good, and so on to those inside the group and see those who have left as enemies or criticise them publicly. Members are discouraged from associating with those outside the group. They also tend to be separate from other bodies and institutions, and are not subject to any outside authority.

No Tibetan Buddhist teacher is subject to any outside authority, so that's a problem—though they ought to have other lamas they consider their teachers or advisors. If their advisors are heads of cults, however, they're only a bad influence.

Sogyal instilled in us the idea that no other group teaches dharma as well as Rigpa, and the only way we could realise Dzogchen was through devotion to him.

A major marker of a destructive cult is when members believe they and/or their leader is above the law. Sogyal apparently showed no concern that his behaviour was against the law, and since the organisation has not denounced his behaviour, we have to assume that at least those running it still don't believe he did anything wrong. Rigpa advisor Dzongsar Khyentse even stated in one of his talks in a Rigpa centre that Vajrayana law was 'above' worldly law. A dangerous view, as we've seen.

If you hear a teacher suggesting that he or she or their teaching is the *only* way you can progress, or hear them denouncing other groups, methods, or teachers without good reason or hear them promoting themselves as having something the others don't have, or insisting that you have only one teacher—them—then mark these things on your cult warning signs checklist.

4. Conformity to the group's beliefs are required in order to 'progress'.

Cults foster rigidity in behaviour and require conformity to the group's beliefs and ideals in order to progress through the hierarchy.

The Rigpa 'party line' was constantly reinforced and subscription to it was required in order to get the 'highest' teachings. To get into the Dzogchen Mandala you had to write something indicating your undying devotion to Sogyal. Shambhala leaders have to sign something indicating their commitment to their leader before they can take leadership roles.

One student told me:

'In Rigpa you have to do what the group does and it is particularly that way in Lerab Ling. You have to show up for practices and are pressured if you fail to. Your view is moulded to fit the ideals. You might live off-site, but there are all these devotees and they report on dissent. When I left I was threatened, guilt tripped, and they tried to bribe me to stay.'

In Rigpa this rigidity wasn't apparent unless you found yourself in a situation where you came up against it. For instance there were rules about who could and who couldn't have certain practice books, and I got into trouble when I made an exception to the rule for a student who couldn't attend practices at the centre. The exception was not only reasonable but also necessary and not contrary to the reason for the rule's existence, but other instructors were not willing to make any exceptions to the rules at all. Rigpa members' rigid adherence to rules was a frustrating part of life in Rigpa, particularly for someone who, since I never fitted the normal boxes, always seemed to be bumping against them.

Students being required to stand up and confess their faults or 'wrong' views, or explain away an apparent fault in the lama is a cult warning sign. We saw this when students who had been verbally abused later publicly explained how the abuse had 'helped' them to solve some personal failing.

Also look for catch phrases used over and over again. When used to deflect questions, concerns, or difficulties, or indicate a lack of depth in general students' understanding, they are cult warning signs. Ones I heard often in Rigpa were, 'It's all perception anyway;' 'Don't make stories;' 'It's just risings;' 'Let it go;' 'Visualise don't conceptualise;' and so on. Though slogans can be helpful in certain situations, they can also be used to silence and manipulate people.

During instructor training sessions we were told not to 'use our own words.' The reason for this was so we wouldn't compromise the 'purity' of the teachings with our ignorance, and that's certainly important for preserving the genuine teachings for the future, but like all these ideas, they can be taken to extremes, such that an instructor supresses their personality. So check if instructors are allowed to share their personal experiences and perspectives, and whether or not they sound like they are merely parroting the teacher. If they all sound the same, there's a problem. If they can't answer questions directly and without parroting the lama, there's a problem. If they lack individuality or appear dull or lethargic, there's a problem. An inability to show any personality or respond in any way that does not conform to the 'party line', whatever it is, can also be seen in ordinary students.

5. Dissent is suppressed and transgressions disciplined.

Cults tend to suppress any kind of internal challenge to decisions made by leaders.

In Rigpa, students raising concerns found it hard to get a meeting with anyone in authority. They were re-directed countless times—passed from one person to another—and it was virtually impossible for the ordinary student to meet with Sogyal privately. If we did get to talk to someone, the usual response was a reiteration of the 'party line'.

We were allowed to give 'feedback' but any criticisms or suggestions for improvements were ignored even if they were quite reasonable, easy to make happen, and would improve things for a large number of people. Reasons given were that 'This is what Rinpoche told us to do,' or 'This is how they did it in Ventura so we have to do it the same here.' You should be able to take suggestions to the top if necessary, and if they're rejected, it should be for good reasons, not just the whim of the lama.

After Sogyal left, Rigpa still shut down criticism in the form of removing social media comments, blocking participation, preventing 'troublemakers' from attending meetings, limiting face to face discussions with a rigid adherence to session forms or a declaration that time has run out, and not replying to emails or giving dismissive or stock replies.

Fear of hell is a powerful form of discipline for those who believe in it, and fear can keep people from speaking up about anything negative. The best teachers will tell you to let them know if you have a problem with anything they do and will remind you to use your common sense.

One student told me, *'Once you decided to make your own decisions then you were pretty massively shunned if they found out.'* You won't see this on first encountering a group, but you could ask pertinent questions of long-term members.

Information control is also a way cults keep their members thinking the 'right' way. After the letter by the eight in July 2017, Rigpa only sent out information that supported their 'party line'.

Check out the guru and community's Facebook pages and groups to see how differences of opinions, questions and criticism are dealt with. Are all the comments kind of the same? Do they use the same catch-phrases? Red flag if they are. Is there nothing negative? No questioning or difference of opinion? Red flag. It either means someone is suppressing dissent by removing comments, or students don't even think to share any difference of opinion. How do students of this guru respond to criticism of their guru? Are they highly defensive? Why?

50
SUPPORT TRUTH TELLERS

Few Tibetan Buddhist lamas have said students should speak out publicly about serious ethical violations. The traditional advice is to leave quietly, but all that does is allow others to fall into unhealthy situations at the least and abuse at the worst. When something is wrong in the lama or community, we must discourage silence and support truth-tellers without hesitation—honour their courage and truly hear their pain.

Silence is not golden where it hides abuse. Speaking out about our experiences with lamas—good and bad—are vital if we are to help each other choose our teachers wisely.

The more we expose those who abuse their students, and the more we proclaim that abusive behaviour is not acceptable, and the more we asks questions, don't take teachers' or texts' words at face value, and educate ourselves on what constitutes a cult, the more likely it is that the lamas will come to understand that if they want Western students, if they want the money we provide, then they'll have to behave ethically.

And we must never forget. Try to understand what it's like to have been abused by your spiritual teacher, and don't ever demand that truth-tellers 'get over it' or 'drop it already' or assume they and their supporters are angry and bitter. In the book *Be Angry*, HH Dalia Lama is quoted as saying:

'If one is treated unfairly and if the situation is left unaddressed, it may have extremely negative consequences for the perpetrator of the crime. Such a situation calls for a strong counteraction. Under such circumstances, it is possible that one can, out of compassion for the perpetrator of the crime—and without generating anger and hatred—actually take a strong stand and strong countermeasures. In fact, one of the precepts of the bodhisattva vows is to take strong countermeasures when the situation calls for it. If a bodhisattva doesn't take strong countermeasures when the situation requires, then that constitutes an infraction of one of the vows.'

On the topic of compassionate anger, His Holiness says, 'Anger toward social injustice will remain until the goal is achieved. It has to remain.' And what is my social justice goal here? It's to protect people from joining harmful cults and to remove abuse and the potential for abuse from Tibetan Buddhism. So please remember the red flags that warn you of a cult, and don't ignore them as I did.

And remember the price of silence. Abusers keep abusing. And students are led astray. It's too great a price to pay. And though hearing the truth is painful, everyone in the *What Now?* group is grateful to the truth-tellers for snapping them out of a lie.

Someone calling themselves an ex-monk and ex-Buddhist left this comment on the dharma Protector's Facebook page:

> *'Thank you for addressing the issue of abuse in Buddhism. It's long overdue and extremely necessary. Abuse by spiritual teachers causes profound psychological damage, impairs soteriological endeavours, and damages or destroys people's faith in the dharma. A tradition ostensibly predicated on principles of compassion and wisdom should never tolerate abuse. Teachers who attempt to cloak their perversity and cruelty as "enlightened activity" should be exposed and we need to comfort their victims, not denigrate them.'*

The reality for victims recovering from spiritual abuse is, as one student told me:

> *'The profound betrayal is very difficult to get over. A spiritual path I have dedicated the larger portion of the past twenty-nine years of my life to. An organization, a lama, friends, that I never once even thought of leaving. To assess oneself and the chasm of ignorance. Not really seeing what we were supporting. Hints, signs, ignored, tuned out. Until the weight of what has really happened shocks you awake from a dream. Waking up is hard to do. But I don't want to be dreaming, not about this. Just awake.'*

Sangye gives us this advice:

> *'Watch out for words that perpetuate the myths around abuse and Vajrayana, those that suggests it's all up to the victims to frame it [as not abuse] and take it on their path. I'll tell you how to take abuse on the path; you learn from it. You have to.*

- *Remember ethics; don't let them get away with it;*

- *Get the hell away from abusers and the false path;*

- *Figure out the correct, true path and find honest, kind companions and not exploitation-based institutions.*

'Never forget the abused! We are survivors and we were victims—you can say all the "don't play the victim" guilt crap you like. Who came up with that? Abusers did. It's not "playing the victim" when you really have been harmed. You have to know truth, and heal, not be told you are bad for accepting the truth of what happened to you. Letting people be violent, yell, scream, beat, wound, denigrate, steal your time, steal your life-force while they lied about who they were up in their luxury palace, grooming young women as sex slaves for their orgies of food, drugs and suppression. They had to have a lick of everyone's ice-cream, these backwards, selfish infants. Some things they say suggest they are wise and you are wise to follow them, but you are anything but wise if you had the opportunity to know what really happened but just moved on, trying to not care.'

51
An Unfinished Story

This story is not finished. Tibetan Buddhism will survive in one form or another, perhaps with a more defined split between those who cling to abuse-enabling views and those who value ethics as the foundation of all forms of Buddhism. And between those who mock, and even demonise, Western values and those who recognise that, even though Western governments regularly fail to live up to their own ideals, the great ideas of the West—rationalism, self-criticism, the search for truth, the separation of church and state, the rule of law, equality before the law, freedom of conscience and expression, human rights, and liberal democracy—are in accord with those taught by the Buddha. They are a means for all people, no matter what race or creed, to live in freedom and reach their full potential. Such values do not destroy dharma; they support it.

Western values do destroy feudalism, however. But feudalism, in which ordinary people have no rights and must give homage and service to the all-powerful nobility, is not dharma, not Buddhism, and neither is it Vajrayana—it's a social system. Feudalism is the baggage which must be dropped from Tibetan Buddhism if it is to overcome this tendency for lamas to act like the leaders of destructive cults.

The Dalai Lama agrees. At the Central Institute of Buddhist Studies in Leh, Ladakh, India on 1st August 2017, he said, 'I feel some of these lama institutions have some sort of influence of the feudal system. That is outdated and must end— that feudal influence.'

Note that he says, '*Some* of these lama institutions ...' It's up to each lama how he or she relates to their students, and how much emphasis they put on the problematic instructions discussed previously. Since not all lamas think as Sogyal and Rigpa's advisors do, Tibetan Buddhism is clearly flexible enough for individual lamas to take a less feudalistic approach to their relationship with their students.

One lama on Facebook said:

I can only speak for myself when I say to those who have taken refuge with me or to those who hold me in their high regard, if you see me cause injury to others, mental or physical, it becomes your sacred duty to protect yourself and your vajra brothers and sisters. Don't let anyone suppress your free will to reason. Don't be afraid to question me if you feel my actions and speech are not in accord with the dharma.'

So if you choose your teacher well, this may simply not be an issue. However, lamas who feel that non-criticism, servitude and obedience—all elements of feudalism and of destructive cults—are essential parts of Tibetan Buddhism will likely feel threatened by suggestions that feudalistic influences be done away with. And I understand why they might feel that way. They are estranged from their country and trying to keep their culture alive, but this is not an attack on Tibetan culture; the suggestion that feudal structures be done away with is advice aimed at helping the religion adapt to the modern world and lessen the likelihood of further abuse. Of course, any lama who doesn't think Sogyal did anything wrong—be it in terms of Vajrayana or not—will not care about preventing such behaviour in the future, only on making sure students don't tell anyone about it. But lamas who do care and who don't want their communities to become destructive cults should give this book due attention.

Lamas who reject the removal of cultish aspects of Tibetan Buddhism as some kind of 'Cinderella', 'soft' or neutered form of Buddhism, are likely coming from a defensive and ill-informed position. The damage done to the religion by abusive gurus who act like feudal overlords and cult leaders is simply too great to be overcome without changes to how lamas treat their students.

Removing the feudalistic influences would not remove any of the power of the Vajrayana as the student's trust and devotion would develop naturally for any lama who warrants it. And the core teachings remain untouched. The problematic areas would simply, as His Holiness suggests, not be stressed, and when taught, would be taught carefully so they're not misunderstood or used only to cement the lama's power. Cults require a leader with total power, so we need to avoid any kind of organisational or devotional structure that gives a single person that kind of power.

They say it takes at least one-hundred years for Buddhism to adapt to a new culture, and we're at nearly sixty years now if you consider the sixties as the start of Buddhism coming to the West. It's imperative we stop accepting abuse and unhealthy relationships as part of the deal.

If managements of Buddhist communities do not denounce the abusive behaviour of their lamas, then any apparent change is just a smoke screen. And if those at the top level of the teaching hierarchy don't think a lama's abusive behaviour is wrong or truly harmful, then that's what they'll teach—if only on the Vajrayana level. But emotional, physical and sexual abuse are not defined by whether or not someone 'feels' hurt by the actions; abuse and its resultant trauma are clearly defined by psychologists. And complex post-traumatic stress disorder is not a symptom of someone unable to apply the Vajrayana teachings; it is the well-documented result of the kind of trauma created by abuse. Any group run by people who don't understand this is a group to avoid.

This comment from a member of the *What Now?* group is not just speaking to Rigpa, because other sanghas have reacted to the same kind of 'situation' in exactly the same way.

> *'An admission that there was wrongdoing and categorical apologies from everyone who was involved in wrongdoing is the only viable starting point for resolution. How does the Rigpa leadership expect to resolve anything with their current approach? Rigpa's continual claims that there have been apologies and that they are acting on the Lewis Silkin report recommendations cannot withstand scrutiny. Simply saying over and over that you are doing the right thing is not a sustainable strategy.'*

Unless we're in a central management role, we can't do anything about how organisations respond to revelations of abuse. They will do as they wish, and the inevitable results will follow.

In His Holiness the 14th Dalai Lama's interaction with students from the University of California at his residence in Dharamsala, on the 6 Sep 2017, he said:

'I think in many cases, religious teachers or religious spiritual leaders or institutions, frankly speaking, in some cases are rotten. ... When people really suffer due to exploitation, then people should develop courage in order to topple that institution.' And when people 'use the name of dharma for exploitation, they themselves have not properly practised the dharma, including some Tibetan Lamas.'

It's up to us to avoid rotten institutions who use Vajrayana teachings to excuse abuse, and if enough people walk away, they will topple under the weight of their unpaid bills. What use is all their 'good work' if they propagate a view—if only in secret—that countenances harm and therefore contradicts the fundamental teachings of the Buddha?

The student I quoted above continues: *'Long term, if what has occurred in Rigpa becomes identified as somehow a legitimate aspect of the Vajrayana, the harm done by Rigpa will far outweigh the good.'*

Unfortunately, some lamas clearly do believe that if a student has received a Vajrayana initiation for which they were 'properly prepared', then from the Vajrayana point of view, there is nothing wrong with the teacher's subsequent actions no matter what they are. We cannot change the minds of those who subscribe to this belief, but we can walk away.

The behaviours outlined by the eight students in their July 2017 letter to Sogyal Rinpoche *do* constitute 'serious emotional, physical and sexual abuse', as stated by Karen Baxter in her report. How one views these actions and their perpetrator does not change the fact that abuse causes harm, and he who abuses is the cause of that harm. Causing harm breaks the fundamental vow of the Buddhist path—do no harm. And any teacher teaching that it is acceptable for a guru to harm someone, regardless of how they justify it, is not teaching Buddhism.

Despite its flaws and misuse, there is great wisdom in the tradition. Personally, since Sogyal never abused me, I gained far more benefit than harm from my study and practice of Tibetan Buddhism. Under Sogyal's tutoring, I did suffer a loss of discernment and bypass my feelings in a way that compromised my integrity and negatively impacted aspects of my life, but I also learned how to live in peace and clarity and experience the world as a fluid and unified whole. For that I will always be grateful. Being able to experience the ground of our being may not be everything we need to fully evolve as human beings, but it gives us a vast, unfettered, cognisant view that frees us from mental suffering—if only while cognisant of that level of awareness.

Though the Tibetan Buddhist teachings have much to offer, some aspects are easily misunderstood and/or misused by unscrupulous gurus and their communities. Thus it's vital to, as the Buddha said, 'critically examine' the teachings and the teacher and 'only accept what passes the test by proving useful and beneficial'. Watch out for lamas who, as Sogyal did, quote the Buddha on the importance of critical examination but also refuse their students the right to criticise their words and actions once they've signed up for Vajrayana.

As Jeff Brown says in *Grounded Spirituality*:

'A conscious scrutinization bows before no lineage, unless it honestly reflects and genuinely supports our individual and collective evolutions. If we don't acknowledge dangerous spiritual teachings, the world of sacred possibility that we seek will never come to pass. The only sacred cow is truth.'

Though the abuse itself caused great harm, the fallout from the revelations of that abuse, though challenging, has for me and many others been enormously enlightening. For that I am extremely grateful to the eight students and others who honoured the truth above all. Because of them I've reclaimed responsibility for my 'spiritual' path, which at the moment means being fully immersed in, aware of, and responsive to the present in its full manifestation. Life is my path.

Follow Up

Did you find this book enjoyable, illuminating, intriguing or helpful? If so, I'd really appreciate it if you could write a review and publish it on Amazon or anywhere else you can. The book needs your review to help interested people find it and know if it's the right book for them.

And, of course, there's nothing better than talking about it, so others can find out that it exists, so please share your thoughts about it on social media. The book is available worldwide at all major bookstores.

Visit the *What Now?* blog, now called *Beyond the Temple*, at www.beyondthetemple.com, and follow the links in the sidebar to subscribe to *Living in Peace & Clarity* on YouTube and Facebook.

You can also keep in touch by following 'TahliaNewland' on Twitter and like 'Tahlia Newland, Editor, Author, Publisher & Artist' on Facebook. And you can contact me via the contact page on my website at www.tahlianewland.com

ABOUT THE AUTHOR

Metaphysical-fiction author Tahlia Newland has published seven novels—four of which have won literary awards—one book of short stories, and a non-fiction book on writing. She now works as an editor and publisher for AIA Publishing and in her spare time makes masks and steampunk accessories.

Before her love of literature turned into a profession, Tahlia spent twenty years scripting and performing in visual theatre and theatre in education. She is also a trained teacher and taught high school creative and performing arts for several years.

Tahlia devoted twenty years of her life to the study and practice of Tibetan Buddhism, twelve of those years in partial home retreat. She lives in the Australian bush with a musical husband, a filmmaker daughter, and a couple of cheeky Burmese cats.

Want to read more of Tahlia's books? How about a free one?

See all Tahlia's books at www.tahlianewland.com/bookshop, and click the **'Free Book Download'** button on the right-hand side to receive *Lethal Inheritance*, book one of the *Diamond Peak Series,* free of charge.

Adult Fiction:

Worlds Within Worlds—a Buddhist fiction thriller on cyber-bullying and the nature of creativity and identity.
The Locksmith's Secret—magical realism on the themes of belonging, emancipation, prejudice and love.

Young Adult Fiction:

The award-winning *Diamond Peak Series*—new adult contemporary fantasy/magical realism. This visionary tale is an analogy for the journey to enlightenment.
You Can't Shatter Me—an inspiring and empowering young adult magical realism novel on the topic of how to handle a bully.

Non-Fiction

The Elements of Active Prose: Writing Tips to Make Your Prose Shine—a book on self-editing for authors.
How to Meditate Easily, Effectively & Deeply was removed from publication in August 2017.

REFERENCES

Bibliography

A Guide to The Words of My Perfect Teacher, Khenpo Ngawang Pelzang, Padmakara Translation Group. Shambhala (June 22, 2004)

As It Is, Vol II. Tulku Urgyen Rinpoche, Rangjung Yeshe Publications; 2 edition (December 1, 2013)

Be Angry, Dalai Lama (Author), Noriyuki Ueda (Contributor), Hampton Roads Publishing (March 1, 2019)

Buddha Nature: The Mahayana Uttaratantra Shastra with Commentary, Arya Maitreya, Jamgon Kongtrul Lodro Thaye, Khenpo Tsultrim Gyatso Rinpoche. Snow Lion Publications, Ithaca, New York, (2000)

Cave in the Snow by Vicki MacKenzie, Bloomsbury UK (December 26, 2008)

Crystal Clear by Khenchen Thrangu Rinpoche, Rangjung Yeshe Publications (May 18, 2004)

Dzogchen Essentials: The Path That Clarifies Confusion, compiled by Marcia Binder Schmidt, Rangjung Yeshe Publications (July 16, 2004)

Grounded Spirituality, Jeff Brown. Enrealment Press (March 15, 2019)

Healing Anger – The power of patience from a Buddhist perspective, Snow Lion, USA 1997, pp 83-85, HH the Dalai Lama, Tenzin Gyatso.

Karmamudra: The Yoga of Bliss, Sexuality in Tibetan Medicine and Buddhism, Dr Nida Chenagtsang, Sky Press (April 25, 2018)

The Body Keeps the Score: Brain, Mind, and Body in the Healing of Trauma by Bessel Van der Kolk, Penguin Books; 1 edition (September 25, 2014)

The Buddha Before Buddhism: Wisdom from the Early Teachings, Gil Fronsdal. Penguin Random House Publisher Services 2017.

The Gelug/Kagyu Tradition of Mahamudra, HH Dalai Lama & Alex Berzin, Snow Lion; USA ed. edition (January 1, 1997)

The Life and Times of Jamyang Khyentse Chökyi Lodrö: The Great Biography by Dilgo Khyentse Rinpoche and Other Stories. Dilgo Khyentse and others, Shambhala (July 25, 2017)

The Mahāsiddha and His Idiot Servant. John Riley Perks, Crazy Heart Publishers, July 1, 2006.

The Path to Enlightenment, HH the Dalai Lama, Tenzin Gyatso, translated by Glenn Mullin, Snow Lion, 1982 and 1995; pp. 70-71.

The Words of My Perfect Teacher, Patrul Rinpoche. Yale University Press; Revised edition (July 12, 2010).

Travels in the Netherworld: Buddhist Popular Narratives of Death and the Afterlife in Tibet. Bryan Cuevas. Oxford University Press (2008).

Trauma and Recovery: The Aftermath of Violence - From Domestic Abuse to Political Terror by Judith Herman, copyright

1992, 1993, 1997, 2008, 2015. Quotes reprinted by permission of Basic Books, an imprint of Perseus Books, LLC, a subsidiary of Hachette Book Group, Inc.

Treasury of Precious Qualities by Rigdzin Jigme Lingpa (1729-1798), with the commentary of Kangyur Rinpoche (1898-1975), Shambhala Publications.

Wise Teacher, Wise Student: Tibetan Approaches to a Healthy Relationship by Alexander Birzin (Ithaca: Snow Lion, 2010)

Internet Articles and Websites

'A Point of View', Matthieu Ricard on July 29, 2017. https://www.matthieuricard.org/en/blog/posts/a-point-of-view--2

'DARVO - Deny, Attack, Reverse Victim and Offender,' *Restored,* Esther Sweetman, 07 November 2017. https://www.restoredrelationships.org/news/2017/11/07/darvo-deny-attack-reverse-victim-and-offender/

'Devotion with Discernment – A question of personal responsibility.' Rob Preece. *Tibetan Buddhism in the West.* https://info-buddhism.com/Devotion_with_Discernment_Rob_Preece.html

'Dodging Energy Vampires with Dr. Christiane Northrup – Are Toxic Relationships Draining Your Energy? *Energy Blueprint* Podcast, Jan 5th 2019, https://www.theenergyblueprint.com/dodging-energy-vampires

'Gaslighting 101: Signs, Symptoms, and Recovery.' Psychotherapist and relationship expert, Darlene Lancer, LMFT https://www.whatiscodependency.com/gaslighting-signs-symptoms-help/

'Guru and Student in the Vajrayana,' Dzongsar Khyentse, Facebook 15th of August 2017 https://www.facebook.com/djkhyentse/posts/2007833325908805

'How Do Children Become Narcissists?' Elinor Greenberg, Ph.D. *Psychology Today.* https://www.psychologytoday.com/au/blog/understanding-narcissism/201705/how-do-children-become-narcissists

'How to make a sincere apology,' *Psych Central,* Excerpts copyright 2019 PsychCentral.com. All rights reserved. Reprinted here with permission. https://psychcentral.com/blog/how-to-make-an-adept-sincere-apology/

'How to spot a narcissist,' Psychotherapist and relationship expert, Darlene Lancer, LMFT https://www.whatiscodependency.com/spot-narcissist-npd-symptoms-narcissism/

'Institutional Betrayal and Gaslighting: Why Whistle-Blowers Are So Traumatized,' Kathy Ahern, PhD, RN. *Continuing Education, J Perinat Neonat Nurs,* Volume 32 Number 1, 59–65 Copyright C 2018 Wolters Kluwer Health, Inc. https://nursing.ceconnection.com/ovidfiles/00005237-201801000-00014.pdf

'Is Codependency Blaming the Victim?' Sharon Martin, LCSW, *Psych Central.* 6 Jan 2018. Excerpts copyright 2019 PsychCentral.com. All rights reserved. Reprinted here with

permission.
https://blogs.psychcentral.com/imperfect/2016/04/is-codependency-blaming-the-victim/

'Lies Damn Lies and Lerab Ling,' *What Now? blog.* https://whatnow727.wordpress.com/2018/08/15/lies-damned-lies-lerab-ling-part-1/

'Meditation, Dissociation, and Spiritual Bypassing,' *The Saturday Centre for Psychology.* June 2015. http://saturdaycenter.org/meditation-dissociation-and-spiritual-bypassing

'Revisiting the "Secret Consort" (gsang yum) in Tibetan Buddhism.' Holly Gayley, Department of Religious Studies, University of Colorado, Boulder, *MDPI Website, Religions 2018 9*(6), 179; doi:10.3390/rel9060179, 1 June 2018. https://www.mdpi.com/2077-1444/9/6/179

'Missing the Connection' *What Now?* https://whatnow727.wordpress.com/2018/10/17/missing-the-connection/

'Rigpa Students in a Quandary: What to Do When Seeing Your Guru Punch a Nun in the Stomach Crosses a Line', Joanne Clark, *Buddhism Controversy Blog.* https://buddhism-controversy-blog.com/2017/06/28/rigpa-students-in-a-quandary-what-to-do-when-seeing-your-guru-punch-a-nun-in-the-stomach-crosses-a-line

'Symptoms of Codependency' Darlene Lancer, JD, MFT, Psych Central. 8 Oct 2018. Excerpts copyright 2019 PsychCentral.com. All rights reserved. Reprinted here with permission. https://psychcentral.com/lib/symptoms-of-codependency/

'The Manipulation of Spiritual Experience: Unethical Hypnosis in Destructive Cults' by Linda Dubrow-Marshall, Ph.D. and Steve K. Eichel, Ph.D., ABPP. https://www.carolgiambalvo.com/unethical-hypnosis-in-destructive-cults.html

'The truth about domestic violence and abusive relationships,' Darlene Lancer JD. MFT. https://www.whatiscodependency.com/the-truth-about-domestic-violence-and-abusive-relationships/

'The Two Truths of Buddhism and The Emptiness of Emptiness,' Susan Kahn https://emptinessteachings.com/2014/09/11/the-two-truths-of-buddhism-and-the-emptiness-of-emptiness/

'What is Codependency?' Darlene Lancer LMFT. *What is Codependency?* blog. https://www.whatiscodependency.com/codependency-symptoms-cause-treatment/

'What is Trauma Bonding?' *Psych Central*, Sharie Stines, Psy.D. Excerpts copyright 2019 PsychCentral.com. All rights reserved. Reprinted here with permission. https://pro.psychcentral.com/recovery-expert/2015/10/what-is-trauma-bonding/

'When a Buddhist Teacher Crosses the Line,' Mingyur Rinpoche, *Lion's Roar* , 9th August 2017. https://www.lionsroar.com/treat-everyone-as-the-buddha/

'Why Don't Victims of Sexual Harassment Come Forward Sooner.' Beverley Engel, *Psychology Today*. Excerpts copyright 2019 PsychCentral.com. All rights reserved. Reprinted here with permission. https://www.psychologytoday.com/au/blog/the-compassion-chronicles/201711/why-dont-victims-sexual-harassment-come-forward-sooner

Confessions of Kalu Rinpoche
https://www.youtube.com/watch?v=z5Ka3bEN1rs

Ethics in the Teacher-Student Relationship: The Responsibilities of Teachers and Students: Interview with HH the 14th Dalai Lama, Tenzin Gyatso. https://info-buddhism.com/Ethics-in-the-Teacher-Student-Relationship.html

His Holiness the 14th Dalai Lama at the Central Institute of Buddhist Studies in Leh, Ladakh, India on 1st August 2017. https://www.youtube.com/watch?v=0wP4rsM7AZQ

His Holiness the 14th Dalai Lama's interaction with students from the University of California at his residence in Dharamsala, on the 6 Sep 2017. https://www.youtube.com/watch?v=2fWZWwSSkXs&feature=youtu.be

Martine Batchelor Interview. Published by Timothy Fishleigh on 6 May 2011, https://youtu.be/S8DfH6BYZ3w

Tibetan Buddhism in the West: Problems of Adoption and Cross-cultural Confusion. www.info-buddhism.com

Videos of the Western Buddhist Teacher's Conference with HH Dalai Lama in Dharamsala 1993. The main points for this topic are noted in the document on Ethics in the Teacher-Student Relationship: The Responsibilities of Teachers and Students. http://meridian-trust.org/category/conference/?sub-categories=the-western-buddhist-teachers-conference

www.ingramcontent.com/pod-product-compliance
Lightning Source LLC
Chambersburg PA
CBHW021843020426
42334CB00013B/170